History of the University of Virginia, 1819-1919

HISTORY OF THE UNIVERSITY
OF VIRGINIA
· 1819--1919

Volume II

THE MACMILLAN COMPANY
NEW YORK   BOSTON   CHICAGO · DALLAS
ATLANTA · SAN FRANCISCO

MACMILLAN & CO , Limited
LONDON · BOMBAY · CALCUTTA
MELBOURNE

THE MACMILLAN CO OF CANADA, Ltd.
TORONTO

THE ROTUNDA
South Front

HISTORY
OF THE
UNIVERSITY OF VIRGINIA
1819–1919

The Lengthened Shadow of One Man

BY

PHILIP ALEXANDER BRUCE, LL.B., LL.D.

AUTHOR OF

"Economic, Institutional, and Social Histories of Virginia in the
Seventeenth Century;" "Plantation Negro as a Freeman,"
"Rise of the New South," "Life of General Robert E
Lee;" "Brave Deeds of Confederate Soldiers,"
"Short History of United States," etc

Centennial Edition

VOLUME II

NEW YORK
THE MACMILLAN COMPANY

CONTENTS

VOLUME II

THIRD PERIOD

PAGE

THE BUILDING OF THE UNIVERSITY (Continued) . .   I

XIX — The English Professors Arrive, XX.— The Three American Professors; XXI — The Library, XXII — Administrative Organization, XXIII — Administrative Organization, continued.

FOURTH PERIOD

FORMATIVE AND EXPERIMENTAL STAGE, 1825–1842 .   59

I — How the University Was Reached; II — Beginning and Length of the Session, III — Origin and Number of Students; IV.— Matriculation, V — School of Ancient Languages, VI — School of Modern Languages, VII — Schools of Mathematics and Philosophy, VIII — School of Law, IX — School of Medicine and Anatomy, X — Military Exercises, XI — Minor Courses of Instruction, XII — Methods of Instruction and Examination, XIII.— Degrees; XIV — Public Day, XV —Successors to the First Professors, XVI — Successors to the First Professors, continued, XVII — Successors to the First Professors, continued, XVIII — The Professors' Fees, XIX — The Library; XX — Librarians and Rules; XXI — The Dormitories and Their Regulations, XXII.— The Hotel-Keepers; XXIII.— The Hotel Fare; XXIV — Health of the University, XXV — The Uniform Law, XXVI — First Code of Discipline; XXVII — Minor Offenses Noisy Disturbances, XXVIII — Major Offenses Dissipation, XXIX — Major Offenses Tavern Haunts, XXX — Major Offenses Assaults, XXXI — Major Offenses Riots; XXXII — Major Offenses Riots, continued, XXXIII — Punishments, XXXIV — Diversions; XXXV.— Diversions, continued; XXXVI —Diversions, continued, XXXVII —Athletics; XXXVIII — Publications, XXXIX — Debating Societies, XL.— Religious Exercises, XLI — The Chaplains, XLII — Care of the Buildings; XLIII — Martin Dawson

HISTORY OF THE
UNIVERSITY OF VIRGINIA

THIRD PERIOD

THE BUILDING OF THE UNIVERSITY

XIX. *The English Professors Arrive*

When the report ran over the United States that numerous English professors were to be brought in by Jefferson to fill the different chairs in his recently finished university, it was received in some quarters with acrid and satiric comments. The *Boston Courier* had been catholic enough in sentiment and sufficiently independent in spirit to say that the whole country would be profited by the addition to its citizenship of this group of foreign scholars and scientists. Not so the *Journal*, of Connecticut. The favorable remarks of its contemporary in the neighboring State seemed to churn up all its provincial bile. "What American," it exclaimed with unrepressed bitterness, "can read the above notice without indignation? Mr. Jefferson might as well have said that his taverns and dormitories should not be built with American brick, and sent to Europe for them, as to import a group of professors. . . . Mr. Gilmer could have fully discharged his mission, with half the trouble and expense, by a short trip to New England." The *Journal*, it would seem, was not aware that definite offers of chairs had been made to Ticknor, of Boston, and Bowditch, of Salem, by the

1

Board of Visitors, at Jefferson's suggestion, and that both had declined to accept them. The *Gazette,* a newspaper published in Philadelphia, also averred that its own community had been as much slighted as New England by this patronage of Oxford and Cambridge Universities. Why did not Mr. Gilmer come to the Quaker City before going to London? Why did he not seek among its cultured people for what he put himself to such irksome and costly inconvenience to find among the Englishmen? "There could be but one explanation: as Pennsylvania was barren in stump orators and Presidents, the Virginians must have inferred that nothing of value was brought forth on its soil And yet all men must know that the first physicians, philosophers, historians, and astronomers, and printers in American annals, had been citizens of this State." The *Gazette,* in conclusion, gave further vent to its ruffled feelings by summarily asserting that the University of Virginia, in sending an agent to England to obtain professors, had been guilty of one of the " greatest insults which the American people had ever received."

As a matter of fact, the *Gazette* was running upon as false a scent as the *Journal,* for the second professor contracted with by the University was Dr. Cooper, who had resided so many years in Pennsylvania that he had become as much a congenial and loyal son of that Commonwealth as the mayor of Philadelphia himself. It is interesting, in further contravention, to point out that the man invited by the Board of Visitors, at a later date, to fill the first vacancy that occurred in the Faculty was Dr. R. M. Patterson of that city. It is as clear as noonday that political hostility tinged these unreasonably adverse comments on Jefferson's choice, with its own jaundice; but it is, however, creditable to contemporary journalism to find that the *Boston Courier* was not the only newspaper to discard party feeling. " We have heard with pleasure," reported the *New York American*, " of the arrival of Messrs. Long and Blaettermann, the professors of ancient and modern languages in the University of Virginia. They are well-known and highly esteemed in England. Their talents and acquirements will, doubtless, be highly advantageous to the cause of public instruction in the country."

Anticipating the early arrival of the English professors, Jefferson had, with characteristic consciousness of small details, been uneasy on account of the very meagre arrangements which had been made for their comfort. He was apprehensive lest they should, in the beginning, be forced to look for food and shelter to the coarse local taverns, and he, therefore, endeavored to persuade one of the persons who had rented a University hotel to move into it at once, so as to be ready to supply the strangers with their daily meals until they could hire cooks for service under their own roofs   The pavilions were now fully completed; but they were still bare of all furniture — a deficiency that would seem to demonstrate neglect on the part of the committee of superintendence itself, for how could a half dozen professors, just from Europe, be expected to acquire such indispensable articles with any approach to the necessary dispatch? Jefferson himself acknowledged that they could not, on the instant, obtain " in a place of so little resource as Charlottesville even those things that they could not a day do without, to wit, a bed, table, and chairs." Why had not such necessary furniture been purchased by the proctor several weeks before their arrival? Jefferson had more than once dwelt with complacency upon the exhilarating influence which the University's classical architecture would quickly throw over the minds of the foreigners;

but it might easily have been anticipated that the impressions of beauty and nobility which that architecture was so well calculated to produce, would be driven from their heads as they inspected the naked walls and vacant floors of their pavilions. It is even possible that, for the moment at least, they would have preferred those barns which he had deprecated so earnestly, had they but contained a few comfortable chairs, tables, and beds. While the pavilions and dormitories were in a finished state at the beginning of the winter of 1824, the Rotunda was not; and there must have been perceptible in the general aspect of Lawn and buildings, at that time, the repelling bareness of excessive newness, accentuated by the presence of so few inhabitants in such extensive and imposing precincts.

Long, who was accompanied by Blaettermann, seems to have been detained in New York, after his arrival, by the fatigue of his voyage, although it does not appear to have been exceptionally protracted or tempestuous. Having brought with him letters of introduction to persons of distinction residing in that city, he beguiled his time very pleasantly in the society of his new acquaintances. From that place, he dispatched his numerous packages of books by water to Richmond, and engaged a seat for himself in the stage for Washington. Passing through the Capital without stopping, he halted for a night in Fredericksburg, and while seated in the public room of the tavern there, was spoken to by a gentleman who resided in the town, who hospitably invited him to his house   There, Long made his first acquaintance with two products of Old Virginia which appear, by his own subsequent actions, to have left a permanent impression on his tastes,— young ladies and corn-bread. He found the indigenous corn-cake so good that,— as he wrote his

friend and pupil, Professor Tutwiler, half a century afterwards,— he continued to use it regularly until his return
to England, thus exhibiting a difference in palate from
his fellow aliens, who could never become sufficiently accustomed to its flavor to eat it.   The young ladies were
described by him as charming.   As he carried back to
his English home a Virginian wife, the quality of the
womanhood of Fredericksburg, like that of its corn-bread,
must have been found by him, in his later observations,
to be thoroughly representative

His journey southward over the rude, neglected roads
of the country. districts caused him many painful and
jarring sensations.   They were, at this season, at the
zenith of their imperfection; and the jolts which he had
to endure were recalled by him after an interval of fifty
years.   He described the inns as mean in their accommodations, and the company as congenial in quality with such
crude surroundings.   The dirt, drinking, and tobacco-
spitting that degraded so many of these roadside taverns,
during that period, naturally enough were revolting to
the tastes of a refined and sensitive foreigner like the
scholarly Long.

On his arrival at the University, he drew pavilion v by
lot; and having no family, was soon able to adjust himself
to the numerous inconveniences of the place, which, at
that time, as he said, " was without inhabitants, and
looked like a deserted city."   He described himself as a
man " who had a capacity to make himself happy " in any
situation,— a Virginian tavern obviously excepted,— and
it was now again searchingly tested, for he was the only
professor who was present continuously within the precincts during the months of December, 1824, and January, 1825, and a part of the following February.   With
justifiable complacency, not devoid of humor, he mentions

the fact that, when his English colleagues arrived, they found him " eating corn-bread, and a Virginian in tastes and habits." The subtlest proof of the truth of this complacent assertion was that, within a few months, he had come to be known about the University as " The Colonel." His dependence for daily companionship seems to have been confined at first to the families of Mr. Brockenbrough, the proctor, and Mr. Gray, who had rented one of the hotels. Among the members of the latter circle was Harriet, the sister of Mrs. Brockenbrough, and the widow of Judge Selden, of Arkansas, who had been shot in one of the bloody duels then so common in the social life of the South. Mrs. Selden was a comely woman of many charming qualities, and as Long breakfasted, dined, and supped under the Grays' roof, he was early brought under the spell of her fascinations, fell in love with her, and ultimately married her. The interest which the two felt for each other was well known to the students in attendance during the first session. Long was light in weight and short in stature, and this gave additional point to the couplet which the youthful wags filched from Goldsmith to repeat in the hearing of the embarrassed couple:

> Harriet wants but little here below
> But wants that little Long.[1]

[1] A young lady who attended the wedding of Long and Mrs. Selden wrote of it as follows· " When we got there, we found Harriet, not at a mirror arraying herself with the pride of dress, not weeping through excessive sensibility, not covered with the confusion and blushes of extreme modesty like modern fair ones; but sitting alone and perusing, with apparent composure, Plutarch's *Lives!* When she descended, she was more beautiful than you could conceive She was dressed with simplicity, and admirable taste, and behaved, during the ceremony, and throughout the evening, with the most becoming dignity The Colonel (Long) was matchless in beauty, and grace, and engaging conversation. I am not surprised that Harriet was willing to follow him to the World's End The cheer was excellent. The wine flowed, the company, and even the preacher himself, was facetious and entertaining" As to Mrs.

In the beginning, pavilion v, where Long found shelter, must have offered a very slim prospect of accommodating more than one. So extravagantly high, according to his own description, did he discover the prices of Charlottesville to be, that he refused to diminish the amount of his already slender purse by purchasing many articles of furniture there. Fortunately, he was able to procure beds, dressing tables, and screens, by an order which he sent to Richmond to be filled under the supervision of Colonel Peyton. When winter had fully set in, there came on a heavy fall of snow, which, during several weeks, cut him off from all associations, except with his " black friend," his faithful servant Jacob, and the family of the Grays at his hotel. So soon as his books arrived, they gave him occupation in the way of study and recreation alike, during the repeated intervals of his detention within doors by the rigorous weather. He had been hoping that Gilmer, who was then residing in Richmond, would be able to spend the holidays in Albemarle. The two young men, so congenial in their natural and cultivated tastes, seemed to have been frequently exchanging letters. " Coming into a new country," Long wrote in January, " and being, in some measure, unacquainted with the customs of the place, I experienced at first some difficulties, which you will be glad to hear are now removed. I have been busily employed in arranging my pavilion and making preparations for my professional duties. I am sorry that the effects of your illness have prevented you from coming amongst us this Christmas. Your company would have been a valuable addition to our limited society."

Long's composure, which was supposed to be proven by her being found reading Plutarch's *Lives*,— about which she was teased afterwards,— she asserted laughingly "When they said the ——s were coming, I seized Plutarch's *Lives*, and buried myself in it, but it was upside down!"

Long had not been settled at the University many days before he visited Monticello to make Jefferson's acquaintance in person. Shown into the drawing-room by one of the servants of the household,— no doubt with all the elaborate politeness that distinguished the highly trained negro butler of those times,— he had only a few minutes to himself to examine the interesting portraits and furniture in the apartment, before a " tall, dignified old gentleman " entered, who, pausing an instant, looked at the small and youthful Englishman with unconcealed surprise. " Are you," he said, " the new professor of ancient languages?" " I am, sir," was the reply. " You are very young." " I shall grow older, sir." This quiet answer caused Jefferson to say with a smile, " That is true." They at once fell into a brisk talk on a variety of topics, and Long was cordially invited to dinner. Throughout the visit, Jefferson did not relax from his habitual gravity, not to say coldness of manner, but he treated his guest with the most friendly politeness. " I was pleased with his simple Virginia dress,"· says Long, " and with his conversation free from affectation." This first call was several times repeated, and in the end, as Long himself has recorded with pleasant brevity, " he became, I thought, better satisfied with his boy professor." And this impression was correct, for, within a few weeks, Jefferson wrote of him to Cabell, " He appears to be a most amiable man, of fine understanding, well qualified for his department, and acquiring esteem as fast as he is known."

There is no reference in Long's written recollections of these early months to the presence of Professor Blaettermann at the University. He seems, however, to have been within its precincts during January,— for a few days, perhaps; but no association between him and the young

Englishman has been traced. This may have been due
to the prejudice against Continental foreigners, or, more
probable still, to those personal qualities of this instructor, which, throughout his sojourn in Virginia, deprived
him of even a moderate degree of influence and popularity.

As the winter of 1824–5 drew towards February without information of the whereabouts of Key, Dunglison,
and Bonnycastle, who had sailed from London on October 26, a sharp alarm began to be felt in Virginia for
their safety. Long alone failed to share this sense of
uneasiness, although he regretted, on account of the University and his own comfort alike, that they should have
consented to set out on their voyage in what he contemptuously described as an " old log." This old log was the
ship *Competitor*. He complained that the people of
Charlottesville, " having nothing better to concern themselves with, invented stories on this unfortunate subject."
The delay in the arrival of the *Competitor* was really due
to the headwinds and gales which had prevented her from
dropping from the English coast and sailing straight out
into the ocean. As late as December 5, forty days after
she had swung loose from the wharf in London, she was
still tied up in the harbour of Plymouth. This information found its way into a newspaper published in Norfolk,
and was brought to Jefferson's attention by Cabell, who
had happened to read the item. " That they (the professors) are safe," he replied, " raises me from the dead."
He was not only solicitous for the personal well-being of
the voyagers, but he was chafing with disappointment over
the prospect of serious delay in the inauguration of the
lectures. The enemies of the institution had already begun to whisper in public places that this dilatoriness would
be certain to damage its hope of permanent success; and

Jefferson himself feared the same result. "We apprehend," he wrote Cabell in January (1825), "that the idea of our opening on February 1 prevails so much abroad,— although we have always mentioned it doubtfully,— that students will assemble on that day without the further notice promised. To send them back will be discouraging, and to open the University without mathematics and natural philosophy would bring on us ridicule and disgrace."

Eight weeks had passed since December 5, the date on which the presence of the *Competitor* in Plymouth harbour was reported, and unless the voyage had been disastrous, the ship should soon arrive in American waters. Jefferson, aware of this, was, in consequence, kept in a state of daily suspense. During the protracted interval of silence, the vessel had really gone through many perils of the seas. After it left the mouth of the Thames, a cyclone had blown its sails to ribbons, and had they not been rotten from long exposure to wind and water, the terrific impact would have turned the ship over, and no human hands could have prevented it from sinking, with every person on board. The captain, Godby by name, seems to have been worthy of so untrustworthy a vessel. "Let every soul of you come on deck instantly," he called down to the wretched passengers, "we are all going to the bottom." A feud soon arose between this man and the professors. "It is a lucky thing for you," remarked Key to him, "that you are not in the Royal Navy. You would have been shot long ago." Mrs. Key, being desperately seasick, begged Godby to send the doctor to her at once. "He can't come," was the false reply. "He is setting Mr. Key's leg, which he has broken by a fall"

Key and Bonnycastle, who were both deeply versed in

every branch of mathematics, were dubious about the captain's capacity as a seaman, and in an interval of quiet sailing, amused themselves with a trick that demonstrated his ignorance as well as their own idleness. One day, they asked the mate to let them know the degrees of latitude and longitude which the ship had reached. " The captain has ordered me not to tell you," was the reply, " but I have not been forbidden to chalk them up." Having thus obtained the information wanted, the two practical jokers took a long syringe, which they had picked up in the ship, and held it up mysteriously towards the sun, aware all the time that the captain was intently observing them from a distance. Lowering the syringe after a few minutes of apparent observation, they went to the cabin and on a table that stood directly under the skylight, they spread out a large sheet of paper, which they began at once to cover with columns of meaningless figures. They noted on the sheet, as the result of their pretended calculations, that the vessel, on that date, had arrived at such and such latitude and longitude, a mere repetition of what the mate had told them; and they followed this up with the memorandum that the conclusions were reached " in accord with Dr. Barlow's new method." While this solemn farce was in progress, the two conspirators were conscious that Godby had been looking down on them suspiciously through the skylight The paper was left on the table, and a short time afterwards, the captain was seen examining the figures with the closest scrutiny. When Key and Bonnycastle inspected the log for that day they found, to their merriment, that the longitude and latitude of the ship's location was entered as the mate had stated them, but with the addendum, " calculated by me by Dr. Barlow's new method."

Beguiling the tedium of the protracted voyage with

such boyish pranks as these, which would probably have
jarred upon Jefferson's conception of professorial dignity as much as Long's youthful appearance had done,
the three young men finally arrived at Norfolk on Thursday, February 10 (1825), three months and a half after
the " old log " in which they sailed had dropped down the
Thames. Dunglison and Key were accompanied by their
brides; and both couples must have passed through very
tumultuous honeymoons in so rough and perilous a voyage
as the one which had just closed   The packet for Richmond left Norfolk the next day, but the travellers, perhaps in consequence of their recent tossings on the sea,
were unable to continue the journey so soon; and it was
not until the ensuing Tuesday that they were ready to
depart.   They were met at the wharf in Richmond by
Thomas Mann Randolph, and his son, Thomas J. Randolph, the son-in-law and grandson of Jefferson, and by
them were carried off to the home of Chapman Johnson,
a member of the Board of Visitors.

Before the party left for the University, a large number of the principal citizens of the town were invited to
meet them at a formal reception   Though Richmond, at
that time, was a small community, it possessed, as the
capital of the State, a society of unusual culture and refinement, which embraced the families of the most distinguished public officials, lawyers, physicians, and merchants in the Commonwealth.   There were persons present who had not attended such an occasion in the memory
of the younger generation.   " The grave," remarked
Maria Randolph, in her lively description of the packed
assemblage, " seemed to have given up the dead, for
there came ladies whom I have never heard of being
out before for years to see the English people."   Having met Long and Blaettermann, she said that they were

inferior in attractiveness to Key, Bonnycastle and Dunglison.   Her astonishment, not to say disgust, was without
bounds when Mrs. Key and Mrs. Dunglison,— whom she
found " genteel, sensible, and quite pretty,"— confessed
that they had never heard of Byron or Scott, a statement
so incredible that it may have been intended as a gentle
British snub to the Virginian girl's enthusiasm for those
two writers of universal fame.   It was a period, however,
in which the average English woman was more remarkable for her ignorance than for her knowledge.   Among
the guests at the reception was Jarvis, a painter of distinction in those times, and he appears to have furnished
the chief amusement for the company, and in a form so
characteristic of English social entertainments, that the
English couples present must have felt very much at
home.   A whisper ran through the room that Jarvis
would dance a hornpipe on the top of the piano, and the
ladies at once drew together in a crowd about the instrument.   With his brush, he had made a sailor boy
of one of his hands,— the fingers were painted to repre-
sent a pair of loose white pantaloons, and the back, the
body of the figure; and " really," says Miss Randolph,
" the most elegant hornpipe and jig I ever saw he danced.
. . . to the boisterous mirth of the whole company; and
these scientific, philosophical strangers were more amused
than any one else.   You see we are nothing more at last
than full-grown children "

Cabell visited the professors and their wives the second
day after their arrival in Richmond, and wrote to Cocke
of the pleasant impression which he had received of their
personalities.   Colonel Peyton, in a letter to the proctor,
mentioned that this favorable impression was shared by
everybody.   He promptly sent their luggage on to the
University by wagon; and as it comprised numerous boxes

as well as trunks, it is probable that they had brought over at least a part of their libraries. Bonnycastle, the only member of the party who was unmarried, consigned as many as ten boxes to his care, and the others in a smaller proportion. The reputation for good breeding and high attainments which the three men had won in Richmond was confirmed after their arrival at the University and their assumption of the duties of their several chairs. " Your professors," wrote Brockenbrough to Gilmer,— and he included Long in the compliment,— " do you much honor as well as themselves. I apprehend that those solicited by the Board of Visitors will hardly give the same *eclat.*" Jefferson, who was always cautious in expressing an opinion unless confident that he had arrived at a just conclusion, also wrote that the University had been most fortunate in enlisting the services of the foreigners. " A finer selection," he said in a letter to W. B. Giles, December 26, 1825, " could not have been made. Besides their being of a grade of science that has left little superior behind, the correctness of their moral character, their accommodating disposition, and zeal for the prosperity of the institution, leaves nothing more to ask."

xx. *The Three American Professors*

We have seen how insuperable were the obstacles which Gilmer, though assisted by English and Scotch scientists of influence, had to overcome in his endeavor to secure a professor of natural history in the British universities. On his return to the United States without success in obtaining one, he offered, at Monroe's suggestion apparently, the professorship to Torrey, of West Point Academy, afterwards the distinguished incumbent of the chair of botany and chemistry in the famous College of Physicians and Surgeons, situated in New York City.   Torrey was unwilling to accept it, but recommended Dr. John Patton Emmet, whose " talents as chemist and scholar and standing as a gentleman, were," he said, " of the first rank.   I know him well and know none before him." The interview between Gilmer and Emmet which followed led ultimately to his selection to fill the vacant professorship.

Emmet was a nephew of the famous Irish patriot of the same patronymic, and had first opened his eyes upon the world in a house in Dublin   He was too young at the time of his father's emigration to have acquired many Celtic traits by actual personal intercourse with his fellow Irishmen, but those characteristics in their finest aspects had been inherited by him with his blood [1]   He was eight years of age when, coming up from the sea, he saw the Battery at New York for the first time.   As soon as eligible, he had succeeded in obtaining an appointment to West Point Academy as a cadet, and before he left that institution, had won so much reputation by his acquirements as to be chosen an assistant instructor in mathematics.   His health had been permanently debilitated by one attack after another of smallpox, measles, and whooping cough, and in the hope of throwing off the physical infirmity that resulted, he spent a year in the mild climate of Naples; and while at leisure there, amused himself with the study of Italian, and also of music, sculpture, and painting   After his return to New York, so delicate were his lungs still, that, during the harsh months of winter, he kept closely under the roof of his own home. When it was safe to go out of doors, he attended lec-

[1] The Emmet family claimed a remote Saxon origin, but intermarriage had made it essentially Celtic.

tures in the College of Physicians and Surgeons; and grad-
uating from that institution, received the degree of a
doctor of medicine.   In the meanwhile, his inquiring and
speculative mind was very deeply interested in researches
in the science of chemistry.   Setting up a laboratory in
his father's house, he pursued, with ardor, a line of experiments that looked to the creation of highly valued
articles out of very ordinary materials,— such, for instance, as the conversion of cheap wines into costly Ma-
deira and the like.

Hoping that a warmer climate would give a lasting
good turn to his health, which was still uncertain, he
settled in Charleston, in 1822, with the intention of residing there permanently as a practitioner of medicine.
A course of lectures on the sciences which he delivered in
that city was received with popular applause; and this,
with his record at West Point Academy, led Professor
Torrey to recommend him to Gilmer for the chair of natural history, when he himself was unable to accept it.

Like Professor Long, Emmet called on Jefferson within
a few days after he reached the University.   This visit
must have been made on foot, for he records somewhat
ruefully, after his return from the laborious tramp, that
he had found that, in reality, Monticello was not the little mountain which its name suggested.   " I have dined
several times in the family since my arrival," he wrote to
his father, " and would go oftener, notwithstanding the
distance and altitude, were it not for lectures, lectures,
lectures,— an extremely pleasant old man and hospitable
as can be.   We all take the greatest delight in promoting
his views, and he has expressed himself as well pleased."

Although Emmet had spent his early life in communities which had discarded the institution of African slavery, and professed to abhor it, yet, in beginning house-

keeping in his pavilion, he was anxious to purchase a black house-servant. " I have experienced nothing but disappointment from the hired ones," he wrote Cocke, impatiently. Would Cocke assist him in buying one? Very much exasperated by the condition in which he found his apartments, he wrote the proctor a hasty and uncivil note; and he seems to have been drawn into further controversy with the same official by his desire to obtain the money required to build an addition of one room to the main structure   While still a bachelor, he exhibited that fondness for the society of animals which formed such a delightful and amusing side of the daily life of the English naturalist, Frank Buckland,— his intimate companions under his own roof were numerous snakes, that slided about at will in one of the chambers, a white owl, and a very friendly bear, which, permitted to run at large in the house and garden, had the bad habit of suddenly alarming the visitors by appearing unexpectedly.   Marriage put an end to this primaeval affiliation; Mrs Emmet is said to have taken advantage of the softness of the honeymoon to insist that the owl should be let loose in the woods, and the snakes and bear killed   It was the fate of the unhappy bear to be served up at table as a very rare dish.

Emmet's mind revealed its inventive and constructive turn from the very beginning of his University career. He had not long been associated with the institution when he suggested that a vacuum of the air might be used to generate propulsive power; and that chemistry could be made very effective in forcing the growth of vegetables He proved that the kaolin in the contiguous soil offered very good material for the manufacture of pottery and porcelain vases; and he purchased ground and planted the Chinese mulberry to carry on his experiments in the nurture of the silk-worm.   He built a house in which to

manipulate the silk itself, and manufactured his own dyes.
He also cultivated those kinds of grapes, from which, in
foreign countries, were expressed the most costly wines
and brandies, and produced the latter for his own enjoyment.[1]   He grew pyrocanthus hedges, set out rare fruit
trees, planted new species of esculents, and introduced
flowers unknown hitherto in our climate.   He was interested in domestic economy so far as to test various acids
for the best means of curing hams; and experimented at
length with steam for the generation of rotatory motion.
He could compose sonnets, fashion busts from the kaolin
dug up in his own fields, and throw off sketches, chiefly
comic, with ease   His generous disposition was swayed
by the impulsiveness of the Irish nature: it was said of
him that sudden and lively emotions prompted his likings
and distastes, and that he was keenly grateful for kindness, and unreasonably resentful of supposed injuries.
" Disease, when he was in company," remarks Professor
Tucker, " could not overcome the warmth of his feelings,
cloud the cheerfulness of his temper, or dim the corrusca-
tions of his wit." [2]

[1] In the beginning Emmet occupied pavilion I, but at the end of a
few years, influenced, no doubt, by his taste for horticultural experiments,
he removed to Morea, just outside the precincts   "Dr Emmet," we are
informed by Dr Magill, his colleague, who had been calling at this
house, which is still standing, "had designed a roof garden for Morea,
from which novelty in architecture great wonders were expected. A
heavy rain had fallen, and I found Dr Emmet on the roof up to his
knees in mud, trying to stop the leaks the while   The garden was being
rapidly transferred to the lower stories"
[2] "I remember," says B B. Minor, "two instances of his humor. One
of his medical students was named Shipp, whose dormitory had been un-
covered for a new roof, and was deluged with rain   Now all ships have
to be *calked*, and in the class of chemistry, Dr. Emmet so calked this
one that he made excuse that he had so much water in his room that he
could not prepare his lecture   Quick as a flash the professor replied
' You ought to have studied all the better, Mr Shipp, because you were
in your natural element' On one occasion, Emmet had on his counter
a row of various metallic solutions illustrating the different degrees of

In a description of the University which was printed
in the columns of the *Richmond Enquirer,* in May, 1824,
General Cocke emphasized the intention of the Board of
Visitors to confine the selection of incumbents for the
chairs of ethics and law to American citizens.   In harmony
with this pronouncement, George Tucker was invited to
accept the chair of ethics.   Both Jefferson and Madison
had formed a very exalted estimate of his abilities and
accomplishments; and as they possessed the controlling
voice in the selection of the professors, they requested
Cabell to inform him of their decision in his favor.
Tucker, who was, at this time, a member of Congress
(1825), was in Washington, and so soon as the House
adjourned, he visited Monticello to find out from Jefferson in person about the duties and emoluments of the
place; and above all, as to whether the tenure would be
temporary or permanent.   There is no room for doubt
that he was influenced in abandoning public life by the
prospect of obtaining, in the new chair, the leisure which
was necessary for the full gratification of his taste for
literary composition.   Although closely identified with
the public affairs of Virginia, he was not a native of the
State or even of the American continent.   His birthplace was on the island of Bermuda, where his family
had enjoyed a position of importance, both social and
political, during several generations.   Trained to the
profession of law in the office of that island's principal
barrister, he debated, at the age of twenty, whether he
should emigrate to England or to the United States.   He
finally determined to pursue a course of study in the College of William and Mary, to which he was perhaps

affinity by successive precipitations, when a stove pipe, which passed
over his head, fell on him. He immediately exclaimed, 'You see
plainly, gentlemen, that iron can be precipitated.' "

drawn by the fact that his cousin, St. George Tucker, now a distinguished judge, resided in Williamsburg. He was soon congenially domiciled there, and has left a sympathetic description of its pleasant social life. " Some twelve or fifteen families," he said, " all in easy circumstances, were constantly exchanging dinners and evening parties, attended by visitors from a distance, and enlivened by wit, intelligence, and abundant living."

Tucker filled up the intervals of relaxation from study with writing didactic papers and memorial poetry. A visit to Philadelphia and New York brought him into the most conspicuous society of those cities. He was introduced to Jay and Clinton; and was invited to a reception given by President Washington, whose majestic figure, dressed in black velvet, and whose imposing mien, he never afterwards forgot. After one year spent in Bermuda, Tucker returned to Virginia in 1800, with the intention of becoming a member of the Richmond bar. In that town, he at once entered the literary and political circle that gave it so much charm and distinction during that period,— was a friend of Wirt, Hay, Peyton, Randolph, and Ritchie, and with them contributed to the *Enquirer,* a famous journal of that and a later day. Other papers and periodicals served as additional mediums of publication for the numerous essays and poems which he was now composing. His professional business brought him into constant intercourse with John Marshall and John Wickham,— the one, the foremost figure on the bench; the other, at the bar. Having, in 1802, married Maria Carter, the daughter of Charles Carter, of Blenheim, and a great-niece of Washington, he found himself united by the widest family ramifications with all that was socially distinguished in his adopted State. A certain prospect of a lucrative practice opening up in Pittsylvania

county, he made his home there in 1806; represented the
county in the General Assembly; and during ten years,
stood in the front rank of its learned and gifted bar.
In spite of his active calling and distance from libraries,
while a citizen of that community, he was able to write
an elaborate series of papers, which, under the title of
Thoughts of a Hermit, was published in the Philadelphia
Portfolio.   In 1818, he removed to Lynchburg, a town
of three thousand people at this time; and the force of
his personal influence was now so dominant in the district,
that he was nominated and elected a member of Congress;
and again elected at the end of his first term.

A volume of essays which he issued during his tenure
of this office, impressed Mr. Madison so favorably that
it was the cause of his recommending him to Jefferson as
highly competent to fill the chair of ethics.   He had
reached his fiftieth milestone when called to this chair,
and it was due to his greater maturity in years, his genial
disposition and popular manners, and his knowledge of
the world acquired from his association with the best society, that he was selected as the first chairman of the
Faculty.   "My colleagues," he records in his autobi-
ography, "were all agreeable, well-informed men; they
had all travelled quite extensively in foreign countries.
We were very sociable, often dining and passing the evening together; and the life which we then led, though
seemingly monotonous and devoid of interest, has, no
doubt, appeared to all, in retrospect, as one of the happiest portions of our lives."

Not long before his acceptance of the chair of ethics,
Tucker had written a novel entitled the *Valley of the
Shenandoah.*   It was printed in the United States, but
not distributed, and a copy finding its way to London, led
to a second edition, which was afterwards translated into

German.   He was now in the possession of greater leisure for his literary ventures; these took most often the
form of transient articles for reviews and daily journals;
but there were separate volumes too, which reflected his
lighter as well as his more solid tastes: *A Voyage to the
Moon; Rents, Wages and Profits; Progress of the United
States in Population and Wealth; Theory of Money and
Banks;* the *Life of Jefferson.*   The last work was too impartial to please either the Federalists or the Republicans,
but it caused Brougham to remark that it had given him a
much juster conception of the merits of the former President than he had had before.   The volume on the different phases of political economy, which were received
with so much approbation by serious students of the subject, were the target of numerous jokes among his own
pupils.   As the accomplished professor would ride by,
they would say, " Yonder goes dear old Tucker on Money
and Banks."   It is a proof of his versatility that he could
compose a novel that would be thought worthy of translation into a foreign language, and draw up a treatise that
would cause his election to membership in the Statistical
Society of Paris.   When the *Museum* was first issued by
professors of the University, he suggested that he should
contribute a story to its pages.   Dunglison, who made no
pretension to any literary culture beyond what was needed
by the scientist, was the editor of the periodical at that
time; and he was so unreasonably resentful of the proposition, that he wrote in disgust to Cabell, " If there is
anything which has detracted more than another from the
reputation of Mr. Tucker, it is the fact of his having
written works of this character.   Wherever I travel, I
hear this objected to him, and find him underrated, for
his merits are very far beyond his reputation.   Of these
objections, he does not seem aware, although the want of

success in the production of what he has issued, ought to have warned him of it."

It is to be inferred from this impatient comment that Professor Tucker's colleagues had no admiration for his imaginative faculty; and as neither his poems nor his novels have survived in popular favor, it is quite probable that their apparently severe judgment was correct. His figure, from the literary point of view alone, seems an incongruous one in the provincial Virginia of those times, in spite of the success of the *British Spy;* there was no encouragement then in the State for a *literateur* of secondary merit, as Tucker unquestionably was; and he would have found a more congenial and profitable atmosphere in London for that side of his intellectual activities, had he settled there, as he had thought of doing in early manhood.   It reveals his moderate opinion of Virginia as a bookish community, that, when he resigned his chair in 1845, in order to give up his entire life to literary pursuits, he removed his home to Philadelphia, because he was assured there of a larger reading public and of more facilities for the gratification of his dominant literary tastes.   The intellectual energy of the man, as late as his seventy-fifth year, was exhibited in his undertaking to write, at that time of life, a voluminous history of the United States; and other works, marked by pregnancy of thought and wealth of learning, did not cease to drop from his pen until he had passed his eighty-fifth birthday. His last production was a characteristic series of verses entitled, *Pleasures Left to Old Age,*— pleasures, which so far as an industrious hand, a clear, contented, and benignant mind could create them, continued to attend his gentle decline until the end.   Like so many of the members of the distinguished family to which he belonged, he possessed the clarifying quality of humor; and as that quality is most often simply common sense in a scintillant form, it will be seen that it helped him, as chairman of the Faculty, to solve many serious problems in the government of the students, with a sympathy and moderation which were frequently lost sight of by the authorities of the University in those turbulent times. As lawyer, congressman, professor, and *literateur*, he exhibited talents and accomplishments of a very high order; and in private life, was beloved for his kind, genial, and winning traits. That he had an invincible inclination for domesticity, and was by nature hostile to race suicide, was disclosed in his three successful marriages; and, in each instance, to a woman of uncommon intelligence and charm.

Of all the professorships to which appointments had to be made at the beginning, the most difficult was the chair of law. This condition was not due to the rigid Republican standard by which Jefferson had resolved to test the political opinions of each candidate. As a matter of fact, there was no disciple of John Marshall in Virginia who would have had the temerity to offer testimonials in support of his application for the position. The promptness with which such a person would have been turned down by Jefferson and Madison, had his name been presented, would not have startled any of the colleagues of the two former Presidents on the Board of Visitors. But it was not necessary to look to the thin ranks of the Federalists in the State, for there were too many astute and learned members of its bar who were fervently in sympathy with the political principles which Jefferson had so long and so successfully advocated.

The first obstacle which had to be surmounted before the chair could be filled properly was the small inducement which its comparatively meagre salary offered to men who were moving along on the crest of a lucrative

practice.   The other chairs could be filled by calling to
them persons who had occupied similar professorships in
other colleges, where, perhaps, they had been receiving an
even lower rate of remuneration; but the number of lawyers who had abandoned the bar and become instructors
in jurisprudence was too small to ensure an easy and early
selection among them, even by offering a higher income
than they were already earning.   Of all the local colleges,
the College of William and Mary alone had employed a
regular lecturer in this department of study; and in 1824,
there were probably not more than three or four private
law schools in Virginia.   On the other hand, the number
of capable barristers in proportion to the number of inhabitants was never so great in the history of the same
community; and yet, as we shall see, the chair of law at
the University was only permanently filled after a monotonous reception of somewhat mortifying declinations
Gilmer, in a letter addressed to Cabell, mentions the
second reason which, with the first, fully explains the
unwillingness to accept this chair.   " In Virginia," he
said, " law was the foremost profession, and leads to all
preferment "   There was no man of prominence at the
bar who was not ambitious of rising ultimately to high
judicial or political office.   Political honors especially
were keenly coveted, and few with capacity to acquire
them were ready to cut themselves off from their possession by accepting a professorship in any seat of learning,
however great its importance.   Nor would it have logically followed that a very able lawyer at the bar of that
day would have been an equally able teacher of law in
the University lecture-room   The aptitudes demanded
in either calling were not then and still are not the same.
The history of the institution, during the first century of
its existence, has shown that the most competent in-

structors who have filled its professorships of law, have
been men who were drawn away from the bar in early life
before rising to eminence, and who made a profession of
teaching law, as they had, at one time, intended to make a
profession of practising it.

The first appointment to the chair took place before
Central College was converted into the University.
Among the multitudinous subjects to be taught by Dr.
Cooper were the various branches of jurisprudence, and
he was supposed to have prepared himself for it by his
career at the bar and on the bench in Pennsylvania, and
by his authorship of at least one legal treatise of value.
In 1823, there seems to have been some expectation that
Chancellor Kent could be induced to take the position
which Cooper had been forced to resign by the outcry
against his religious creed. When the Board met in
April, 1824, they offered Gilmer the option of becoming
the professor either of law or of morals. From a letter which he wrote Chapman Johnson from Edinburgh,
in the following August, it is patent that he had not
even then made up his mind to accept the chair of law,
the one which he preferred. " Long as I have delayed it,
I yet want the material for a final judgment," he remarked, " but think it proper to say, that, considering
the immense labors thrown on one, the very short vacation, and my prospects at the bar, a salary of two thousand dollars is the least I could accept. With that beginning in October, to enable me to prepare my course in
the winter, I believe I should accept it. But not knowing
that you will grant it on these terms, I think it best to
give you notice that you may look elsewhere in time. If
you would make me President or something, with the
privilege of residing anywhere within three miles of the

Rotunda, it would be a great inducement.   But to put me down in one of those pavilions is to serve me as an apothecary would a lizard or beetle in a phial of whiskey set in a window and corked tight.   I could not for fifteen hundred dollars endure this, even if I had no labor."

After Gilmer's arrival in New York from England, he seems to have abandoned whatever intention he may have had of accepting the chair of law, for we soon find him in negotiation with Professor Kent, who was now delivering at Columbia College a series of lectures which were afterwards to be expanded into his well-known *Commentaries.* So great was his fame already and so enormous would be the distinction which he would give to the Law School, should he consent to take charge of it, that Gilmer at least appears to have been ready to sink all thought of his political convictions.   As the communication between the two men was brief, and without result, it is not possible to say how far Jefferson would have approved the appointment of this political heretic, mild, and reasonable, and academic as he was.

Gilmer himself having declined the chair for himself, and having failed to secure the ripe learning of Kent, it was decided, at the instance of Cabell, it would appear, to offer the professorship to Henry St. George Tucker. Tucker was the son of St. George Tucker, of Williamsburg, who was a judge and lecturer of distinction, and also a man of unusual literary culture   Henry St. George was a half-brother of John Randolph of Roanoke and was himself a man of uncommon talents, a lawyer of extraordinary learning, and in disposition remarkable for his genial qualities, sense of humor, pure spirit, and perfect uprightness.   He was now domiciled in Winchester, where he was conducting a private law school, which en-

joyed the highest reputation among the members of the
Virginian bar.   Tucker had a large family dependent
upon him for support, and, perhaps, for this reason principally, he was unwilling to accept the law professorship,
as the salary was too small to afford him, at that time at
least, a comfortable subsistence   His family too were
attached to Winchester, where Mrs Tucker's mother was
still living at an advanced age.   An additional reason
was that he did not think himself competent to govern
so large a body of young men as would be assembled
under him at the University; and, moreover, he was distrustful of his ability to teach the sciences of politics and
political economy [1]   Such fears were not shared by the
Board of Visitors.

P. P Barbour was next invited.   Barbour was a lawyer
of equal ability, and perhaps even greater distinction, if
not at this, at a subsequent period, for among the honors
which had adorned, or were still to adorn his career,
were the Speakership of the House of Representatives,
and a seat on the bench of the Supreme Court.   Barbour
also declined the offer.   In April, 1825, several weeks
after the University had opened its doors, and when every
other chair had been filled, Madison admitted in a letter
to Cocke that he had begun to look upon the vacancy in
the law professorship with a feeling almost of despair;
and as that professorship was still unoccupied at the close
of the first session in December of the same year, this
feeling had, doubtless, only increased in intensity.   It
was fully justified, for, in addition to Gilmer, Tucker, and
Barbour, Judge Carr, a nephew of Jefferson, had refused
it, and also Judge Dade, a member of the Rockfish Gap
Commission.   In January, 1826, Jefferson's hopes, in

---

[1] By this he probably meant, " in the strictest harmony with Jefferson's
opinions on those subjects "

spite of Gilmer's low condition, seem to have turned again
to him.[1]   His health in August of the previous year was
apparently sufficiently restored by a visit to the Springs
to allow him to perform the quiet duties of the chair,
and it was thought that he would be able to do this with
the more cheerfulness because all expectation of a public
career had been abandoned as subjecting his remaining
strength to the stress of too many vicissitudes.   Before,
however, he could make any preparation for beginning a
course of lectures, his former weakness returned, and he
was precipitated again upon the downward road which
was to end so soon in his death

As late as March, 1826, when the second session was
fully underway, the vacant chair had not been filled.
Judge William H. Cabell now suggested the name of the
famous William Wirt   " If you can offer to give him
three thousand dollars, besides tuition fees," he wrote
his brother Joseph, " you might probably get him for
your professor of law.   What a splendid professor he
would make, and what numbers he would attract to the
University !   The qualifications necessary for a professor
of law enable its possessor to make so much money in
other ways, and to use such honorable professional re-
wards, that you will try in vain to get a suitable man unless you give him a greater fixed salary than you allow
to the other professors.   But you say you cannot afford

---

[1] The following pathetic note from Jefferson to Gilmer was written on
January 23, 1826, when Gilmer was rapidly sinking   " I have been
anxious to visit you, and I think I could do it, but Dr Dunglison protests
against it   I am at this time tolerably easy, but small things make great
changes at times   I can only, in this way, then ask you, how you do?
Am not requiring an answer from yourself, but from such members of the
family as are well enough   We have had a fine January, but may expect
a better February   That month often gives us genial weather, and a
little of that, I hope, will set you up again   As to the commencement of
the term, (as professor) think nothing of it   The more care you take of
yourself, the sooner you will be ready for that "

it. Then make up your mind that the University is neither to derive reputation or to confer benefits so far as that professorship is concerned. . . . Then you might make him President for the present, and give him something on that score; and then you may make his students pay a little more than the others. By these means united, I have strong hopes that you might give enough to attract even such a man as Wirt. I have not heard from him directly or indirectly on the subject. But I know the turn of his mind: that is an offer which I verily feel he would prefer to any other, provided that the emoluments could come within the amount deemed sufficient."

It is particularly significant that both Gilmer and W. H. Cabell, two lawyers who were familiar with the pecuniary side of legal practice in Virginia, suggested the association of the Presidency of the University with the professorship of law; and that both had in mind simply the most available means of increasing the salary of that chair to a point that would assure its acceptance by some man of the highest ability and learning. It was probably recognized by the Board that jealousies would be aroused in the ranks of the Faculty, should one of their number be awarded a far greater remuneration for his lectures and recitations than the rest. The value of the Presidency as an executive office does not seem to have been grasped at this time, in spite of the existence of that office in every other prominent college in the United States. The only question that interested the minds of the Visitors in connection with its creation now was its possible usefulness in aiding them to secure a competent instructor without apparently breaking the rule that fixed the salaries of all the members of the Faculty at the same definite figure. How urgent, in the contemplation of the Board, was the necessity of filling the vacant chair at once is proven by their determination to disregard Jefferson's energetic protest against the proposed innovation. It was the only instance of an important action on their part in which his wishes did not control their decision; and this shows how much perplexed the Board was after a full year of continuous effort to induce a lawyer of distinction to accept the position. Perhaps Wirt was privately informed of Jefferson's earnest opposition to the creation of the new office; but whether this was so or not, he declined the offer and remained in active practice until his death.[1]

The first suggestion of the name of Lomax, a lawyer of high standing in Fredericksburg, and a member of a respected family that had long resided in that part of Virginia, was made apparently by Geo. W. Spotswood in a letter to Cabell in January, 1826. Spotswood was one of the men, of excellent social connections, who had been put in charge of the University hotels. "Have you thought of Lomax?" he asked. "He is undoubtedly a man of talents, and I should suppose would fill the place ably. I once had some conversation with him on that subject. He observed that, if it was offered to him, he would not refuse it " The selection of Lomax seems to

---

[1] Although Jefferson had opposed the election of a President of the University, yet he seems to have waived his objection to that step in the end, and joined with his colleagues in voting in favor of William Wirt, who, at that time, (April, 1826), was Attorney-General of the United States. The letter informing Wirt that he had been chosen the President of the institution, and also professor of law, was written by Jefferson. In that letter, he refers to the gratification which Wirt's acceptance of the position would cause This correspondence will be found in Kennedy's *Life of Wirt*, Vol II 180–181 It is evident from this letter that Jefferson, finding the rest of the Board favorable to the Presidency, had considered it to be his personal and official duty to suppress the feeling of opposition which he had entertained Possibly, he could not have done this as fully as he apparently did, had not the Board restricted the Presidency to Wirt, and had he not also indulged the hope that Wirt would decline the invitation

have been made conditional upon Wirt's declination; and when this event occurred, the appointment was offered to him definitely, and was accepted. He was remarkable for his warm benevolence and sensitive probity of character. From the very start, he took a very lofty view of the moral possibilities of the professorship which he was called upon to occupy: he assured Cabell that he concurred with him in looking upon his chair as " one of the highest stations on earth." The important duties which he had now to perform were not, in his eyes, personal to himself and his students only,— he undertook them with the primary intention of contributing directly to the broadest welfare of his native State The feeling of exaltation with which he began continued throughout his incumbency. When he resigned in 1830, he declared, with transparent truthfulness, that only " apprehension on account of his family had warned him to give up a station which seldom offers itself more than once in a man's life." The salary had proved inadequate for their support; and when he was elected by the General Assembly to a judgeship, he felt under compulsion to accept it.

By the late spring of 1826, the circle of the original professors was finally and satisfactorily completed Each chair was now occupied, and omitting Dr. Blaettermann, who showed a violent spleen at times, the incumbents were remarkable, not only for their scholarly and scientific acquirements, but also, as Jefferson had said, for excellence of character and propriety of conduct. With the exception of Tucker, they were young men; so young, indeed, that, in several instances, they were just starting upon their careers as teachers.

What was their appearance? Among the persons who resided within the University precincts during the first years was Mrs Beirne, a niece of Mrs. Long, a lady of

lively talents and observant curiosity. We are indebted
to her for a brief account of her impressions of these
young men, most of whom had recently left their own
country to assist in setting the new institution in motion.
Dr. Emmet, she said, was not remarkable for good looks,
because his face was pitted with small pox, but he was
charming in his manners, and very interesting in conversation. Long, who was described by one of his biographers
as " the essence of truth and honesty, and a hater of all
sham, social or intellectual," was small in figure, blond
in coloring, but delicate in appearance. Dr. Thomas
Brockenbrough said of him that he was so young looking
that he would have passed for a " bashful boy," had it
not been for the dignity of his bearing. Nevertheless,
he told a good story and enjoyed a hearty laugh. Key
escaped Mrs Beirne's notice, but we learn from Burwell
Stark, a student during the first session, that he was nearly
six feet in height,— this tallness being accentuated by
slenderness,— and that, while his face was full of intelligence, it was not conspicuous for comeliness Bonnycastle, who, at his death, was pronounced by the Faculty
to have possessed all the domestic virtues and a delicate
sense of honor, and who had the reputation of being a
man of such universal learning that he could fill any chair
in the University with ease, was not considered by Mrs.
Beirne to be handsome, but " amiable, gentlemanlike,
and charming in his manners." Dunglison was described
as " fine looking and agreeable." But the most popular
of all the professors was Tucker, the fountains of whose
geniality never ran dry, and who never failed to delight
with his keen sense of humor, his inexhaustible fund of
anecdotes, and his racy information on every subject that
arose in conversation. Blaettermann, who was soon
plunged in quarrels with members of his class, passed

without comment on his appearance or character. Lomax was remarkable for the benevolence of his face; and as was to be expected from his lofty attitude towards the duties of his chair, he was looked upon by all, according to the same lady, as " a lovely Christian gentleman." [1]

From the day that the lectures began, it was a topic for comment that Long and Key, who were nearly of the same age, and already ripe friends through their association at college in England, showed little disposition to cultivate the society of the other professors. With at least one member of that circle, Key seems to have been on terms of irritable, if not fierce, hostility. The professor of mathematics,— so Mr. Wertenbaker has related,— " once kicked at the professor of modern languages, Blaettermann, under the faculty-table, and the latter told him that he kicked like an ass." It may be inferred from this scene that Key did not allow his new dignity to check, even in the faculty-room, any returning desire to repeat the rough horse-play with which he had dispersed the tedium of his ocean passage. Cocke, like most of his class in Virginia, was, perhaps, not fully in sympathy with the importation of foreign instructors,[2] and this probably explains the prejudiced tone of his allusion to Key and Long on the occasion of a quarrel which had detached them from their English colleague, Bonnycastle. " From what I saw of the stuff of which these two savants are

[1] Writing, May 25, 1825, to Jefferson, Cabell said, " I cannot describe the satisfaction which I felt in reflecting on the present prospects of the University Our corps of professors is full of youth, talent, and energy. Like a fine steamboat on our noble Chesapeake, cutting her way at the rate of ten knots per hour and leaving on the horizon all other vessels on the waters, the University will advance with rapid strides and throw into the rear all the other seminaries of this vast continent "

[2] " Do save us," said Cocke in a letter to Cabell, April 10, 1824, "from this inundation of foreigners, if it is possible "

composed," he wrote to Cabell, " I can well believe them capable of a cross course."

Did the foreign professors find the strange and remote community in which they were now secluded thoroughly congenial to their tastes? It would have been extraordinary had four Englishmen, of characteristic insular instincts, and accustomed to the stately English colleges, with their century-old buildings, and their traditions of scholarship running back to the mediaeval age, been satisfied, at first, in a University of red bricks too raw as yet to be covered with ivy, or to possess a single memory of achievement to spur emulation and excite the sense of pride. Moreover, the confusion that resulted from the loose regulations supposed to govern the students, was exasperating to the tempers even of Emmet, Lomax, and Tucker, who had been educated in American seats of learning. " You know," wrote Tucker to Cabell, " that of four English professors, three found the place not to their taste, and have left it; and that the fourth does not disguise the fact that he means to go as soon as he has made enough to live in England." There is no record independently of this to prove that Dunglison and Bonnycastle at least were from the start displeased with their surroundings at the University. It is true that one of the two accepted a call to another institution; but the inducement, in this instance, lay in the greater advantages of a large city, and what was perhaps even more alluring, a larger salary. Bonnycastle died at the University, and his death was deeply lamented there.[1] Long, who was married to an American woman, was, for that reason, perhaps, better satisfied than Key, and the recollections of his career in Virginia, which he committed to paper,

[1] Bonnycastle endeavored to obtain an appointment in Canada This fact was disclosed by recently discovered documents

reveal the kindly feeling with which he looked back on his sojourn in the State. There is no surviving minute of any kind to prove that Key retained a pleasant impression of his professorship. His wife was an English woman of few intellectual resources,— if her ignorance of the existence of Scott and Byron can be taken as a test,— and very probably missed the society of her own circle of kin, and the amusements she had been accustomed to in her native land. If this was the case, it was natural that she should have used her influence to diminish her husband's sense of the value of his chair in a foreign university. Key and herself returned to England before the termination of his contract; and the main reason which he seems to have given for the rupture of his relations was that the climate of Virginia, even in the salubrious Piedmont, was not congenial to his health, but as the entire State had been originally settled by English people, and his fellow English professors made no complaint of its heats in summer or rigors in winter, it is possible that this justification, however honestly put forward, was not really the principal impulse of his unexpected departure. His action was all the more open to comment because he had expressed to Gilmer an intention to become a citizen of the United States so soon as he should arrive at his destination.[1]

XXI. *The Library*

Jefferson manifested as much solicitude about the acquisition of a carefully chosen library as he did about the employment of competent professors; and he foresaw, from the start, that the books, like the men, would have to be imported from foreign countries. He spoke of the

[1] See Chapter XV, Fourth Period, for an account of the circumstances attending Key's resignation.

imposing building which occupied the centre of the northern line more often as the Library than as the Rotunda;
and certainly among all the apartments to be found in the
numerous structures of the University group, the hand-
somest and most spacious was the circular room, reaching to the spreading dome, where, in alcove after alcove,
gallery upon gallery, the large collection of volumes was
to be arranged after his death.   It was completed, in all
essential details, in time for his eyes to take in its noble
proportions; but he did not live to superintend the storage of the books in cases and on shelves, within the
round of its lofty walls

As far back as 1814, when Central College itself had
not been founded, he, in the confident expectation that a
great university would yet be built and equipped at the
expense of the State, remarked to Cooper that, when this
institution was set up, it might become a bidder for the
varied assortment of volumes belonging to Dr. Priestley,
in which Cooper was interested as Priestley's literary executor.   And this well selected store, he said, might be
further swelled in number and increased in value, by the
addition of the books at Monticello.   The library belonging to that mansion consisted of at least seven thousand volumes; and Jefferson, perhaps, was not shooting
beyond the mark in describing it as the " best chosen collection probably in America."   It was singularly rich in
works relating to American history,— such works as could
only be gathered up elsewhere after a long and expensive
search; and he exhibited characteristic liberality when he
announced that he would be satisfied for the institution,
so soon as incorporated, to acquire the entire number on
such terms as should fall well within its ability to purchase.   After the building began, Jefferson caused notices
to be inserted in the *Enquirer* and *Central Gazette,* of

Richmond, in which it was stated that the University had already received gifts of books from several munificent citizens, such as Mr. Hansford, of King George county, Bernard Moore Carter, a native of Virginia, but now a resident of London, and Mr. Coolidge, of Boston. The volumes presented by them, running up to five or six hundred titles, contained sets of the choicest stamp.   The example offered by these men of benevolent temper, he hoped, would be imitated by others, who were in a position of equal ability to confer benefit upon the recently established seat of learning.

During the winter of 1823–24, the General Assembly authorized a conditional appropriation of fifty thousand dollars for the purchase of a library and scientific apparatus.   Unfortunately, this appropriation was but another form of the claim advanced by Virginia against the Federal Government for interest on the amount borrowed for local defense during the war of 1812–15, and, therefore, could not be drawn upon until Congress had passed favorably upon that claim and ordered its payment.   How necessary was economy in the expenditures for the library was clearly brought out in Jefferson's letter to Richard Rush in April, 1824, in which he stated that the University could deposit in the hands of Gilmer, — just about to set out for England,— only a moderate sum; and that this had to be restricted to the purchase of text-books, and such apparatus as was imperatively called for at the start.   As it was, the amount was obtained only by diverting the larger part of the annuity to this purpose, and deferring, until a later period, the last touches to the internal finishing of the Rotunda. Rush recommended Lockington to Jefferson as the stationer most competent to supply the volumes needed, and in his turn, Jefferson recommended Lockington to Gilmer. Not long after his arrival in London, in June, 1824, Gilmer visited the shop occupied by Lockington's successors, and impressed upon them the importance of low prices in contracting for the books; but he finally decided to enter into no specific arrangements with them until he was assured of success in engaging professors.

It was about this time that he probably received Jefferson's letter of June 5 informing him that the University had failed to get " the contingent donation of fifty thousand dollars " made by the last Assembly, since Congress had passed by the claim, and as a consequence, there was nothing more to be anticipated during the present year for the purchase of either books or apparatus. This, however, did not touch the sum which Gilmer then had at disposal on deposit in London for that purpose. He made good use of his brief visit to Dr. Parr, at Hatton, during the following month, to obtain his assistance in arranging a catalogue of classical works.   In August, Parr offered his library, but the sale was not to be consummated until his death had occurred. The price set upon the collection was so high that Gilmer was unwilling to agree to the purchase, although the volumes were of the rarest classical stamp, and their possession would have been a badge of scholarly distinction for the infant university.

Major Cartwright, Jefferson's correspondent, a man of superior literary attainments, showed his good will by aiding Gilmer in the selection of books.   At his request, Mr. Harris, the former secretary of the Royal Institution, submitted a list of editions suitable for the proposed library and also obtained for him a catalogue of Bentham's works. Gilmer had been looking forward to the assistance of the newly chosen professors in buying the books for their respective departments, but as the hour for his sailing drew near, without his having an opportunity to make use of their special knowledge, he wrote down a list of such volumes as could not be dispensed with, and placed the order for them, as well as for the instruments also needed, in the hands of his agent in London. This agent was Bohn, who was assisted by Marx, the banker, whose firm had the keeping of the University funds.

In the purchase of the theological works, a catalogue drawn up by Madison was followed. He was not as eminent an authority on that subject as he was on all the great questions of constitutional interpretation, but his Presbyterian training had probably familiarized him with books of that general character.

Many of the volumes bought through Bohn arrived at their destination by wagon in January, 1825. There were eight large boxes, weighing nearly nine thousand pounds, delivered during this month. During the session of the General Assembly, in the winter of 1824–5, fifty thousand dollars was appropriated for the University's benefit at once; and of this sum, the proctor was, in May, instructed to deposit eighteen thousand dollars in the United States Bank in Philadelphia, subject to the order of Hilliard, of Boston, who had been appointed the University's agent in the purchase of books. Hilliard had already paid out this amount on a large number of volumes obtained directly from England, France, and Germany. The Board of Visitors, at their meeting on October 3, approved, not only this expenditure, but also the deposit of $6,300 in the hands of Rufus King, in London, for the acquisition of philosophical instruments, and $3,157.50 for the purchase of the articles required for use in the anatomical course. Five hundred dollars was also set aside for the purchase of Dr. Emmet's chemical utensils and collection of minerals.   Including an appropriation of six thousand dollars for finishing off the library room, the cost of books and apparatus purchased by Gilmer,— amounting to $7,677.81,— and also the charges for transportation, the total expenditure reached the sum of $41,980.50, which left unemployed a balance of only $8,019.50 of the fifty thousand dollars advanced by the General Assembly.   Another large sum was still required to complete the purchase of the original list of volumes.

The anticipation that this would be appropriated by the General Assembly in the winter of 1825–26, proved to be delusive.   " The vote of the House of Delegates," wrote Jefferson, in reply to a letter from Cabell, of the date of February, 1826, " was too decisive to leave any further expectation from that quarter, or doubt of the necessity of winding up our affairs, and ascertaining their ground.   I went immediately to the University and advised the proctor . .   to reserve all his funds for the book-room of the Rotunda and the anatomical theatre. . . . We have now five boxes (of volumes) on hand from Paris unopened; five more from the same place are supposed to be arrived in Richmond; seven from London are arrived at Boston; and a part of those from Germany are now in Boston.   All these and others still to arrive, must remain unopened until the room is ready, which, unfortunately, cannot be till the season will admit of plastering, and the joiners' work goes on so slowly that it is doubtful if that will be ready as soon.   The arresting of all avoidable expense is the more necessary as our application to Congress for a remission of the interest has passed the Committee of Claims by a majority of a single vote only, and has still a long gauntlet to run."

The end of that gauntlet was not reached in the life-

time of Jefferson, who died in July of the year in which
this letter was written. In the beginning, the first
pavilion erected for Central College seems to have been
used, in part at least, for the storage of the earliest
books to arrive; and it was largely Jefferson's interest in
their assortment which brought about his last visit to the
precincts. They remained under this roof until the
autumn of the same year.

XXII. *Administrative Organization*

There now remains but one aspect of the constructive
period in the University's history to be presented.
What was the nature of the administrative machinery
which was adopted, either before the lectures began, or
soon thereafter, for the direction and control of its
practical operation? The mainspring of the organization was the Board of Visitors; the subordinate one, the
Faculty; their instruments, the executive committee of the
Board, the chairman of the Faculty, the proctor, the
patron, the bursar, and the janitor. The Board drafted
all the fundamental laws and instructions; to the Faculty
was delegated a limited power of the same character;
while the executive committee, the chairman, and the
other officers, were simply the responsible agents for carrying out, within clearly and rigidly defined bounds, the
specific orders which they had received from the authority
above them, or for performing certain duties which had
been imposed upon them by the printed ordinances.[1]

There was nothing novel or original about the general
character of the Board of Visitors: it was essentially a

[1] The earliest seal of the University was a representation of " Minerva
enrobed in her peplum and characteristic habiliments as inventress and
protectress of the arts, with the words 'University of Virginia' running
around the verge, and the date, 1819, stamped at the bottom."

board of trustees, with all the functions that are usually exercised by such a public body.   A brief enumeration of these functions was given on a previous page, in the analysis of the Act of Incorporation passed by the Legislature in 1819.   A concise statement of their tenor as put in practice in 1825 will now be sufficient.   Broadly speaking, the Board was charged with the oversight and preservation of the property of the University, in whatever form it might be; was impowered to diminish or increase the number of schools; lay off the courses of instruction; determine all the fees and rents; engage the professors in the beginning; fill all subsequent vacancies in the Faculty; remove any offender in that body by a vote not to fall short of two-thirds of the Visitors; appoint the different officers, agents, and servants, and supervise them in a general way in the performance of their duties.   Finally, they were authorized to adopt such regulations as they considered judicious for the discipline and control of the students, and the general management of the University.   Severally, or all together, they were required to make a personal inspection of the actual working of each school at least once a year; and as often, a report upon the scholastic and financial condition of the institution had to be submitted by them to the General Assembly.

All vacancies in the Board, whether caused by death, or by resignation, could only be filled by the Governor's appointment.   The Visitors, however, had the right to elect one of their own number to the office of rector, and this rector and his associates formed a corporation that possessed all the powers incident to such a body in the eye of the law.   As the residences of its members would always be widely dispersed, the need of an executive committee was perceived from the hour of organization.

We have seen how useful was the share which this committee had in the building of the University; it was, in reality, during that period, indispensable; and while its importance was afterwards sensibly lessened by the chairmanship of the Faculty, it still performed a necessary part during the long intervals between the sessions of the Visitors.

" The zeal of the Board," Madison wrote in November, 1827, to Cocke, " was often tried by the difficulty of meeting at bad seasons of the year." Indeed, during such seasons, it was usually impossible to get together a quorum of the members; but there were often valid reasons for their absence, apart from the rigorous weather and the bottomless mud; thus, at the precise date of Madison's letter, every one of them was kept away by some form of infirmity or disability: Cabell and Loyall were detained by their duties in the General Assembly; Breckinridge was failing in health; and Johnson was buried in his cases before the courts. Madison himself was steadily growing so feeble that he declared that he would resign the rectorship but for his anxiety to avoid taking any step that might be maliciously interpreted as dictated by a lack of concern for the institution.[1] Monroe's interest in it had always been that of a political disciple of Jefferson, who was disposed to do whatever would be agreeable to his chief. He, too, when asked to be present on this occasion, sent back an excuse.

Jefferson, so long as he was alive, remained a member

[1] "Mr Madison was never absent except when sick," says Professor Tutwiler, "and was always accompanied by Mrs. Madison Madison was always dressed in black, wore short breeches, with knee buckles and black silk stockings His hair was carefully tied in a queue, hanging down his back, and was profusely powdered. He appeared to be below the medium height, but this perhaps was owing to the contrast which was exhibited when he and Mrs Madison walked together, as they often did " *Virginia University Magazine* for November and December, 1868.

of the executive committee, and as he was always on the ground, and Cocke, the other member, could be quickly summoned, there was no need of calling together the Board very often.   It is probable that the latter body convened as frequently as they did, because they were aware that they would enjoy the comforts of his home, and the charm of his company, while in session.   " The state of my health," he informed Cocke in September, 1825, " renders it perfectly certain that I shall not be able to attend the next meeting of the Visitors (October 3), yet I think that there is no one but myself to whom the matters to be acted on are sufficiently known for communication to them.   This adds a reason the more for inducing the members to meet at Monticello the day before, which has heretofore been found to facilitate and shorten our business.   If you could be here on Sunday to dinner, that afternoon and evening, and the morning of Monday, will suffice for all our business, and the Board will only have to ride to the University *pro forma* for attending the proceedings."

After Jefferson's death, the Visitors, whenever they assembled at the University, were compelled to find temporary lodgings in a pavilion,— a rather naked substitute for the ease and charm of Monticello.   In 1828, two of the pavilions happened to be unoccupied, and at Madison's suggestion, both were reserved by the proctor for the accommodation of a very full Board.   A few years later (1833), all the rooms on the upper floor of pavilion VII, the present Colonnade Club, were permanently assigned to their use; sufficient furniture was provided to make these apartments comfortable; and they were ordered to be kept with scrupulous attention to health and neatness.   The proctor was required to arrange with the nearest hotel for the supply of all meals that would be needed by the Visitors, during their stay, while shelter and fodder for their horses were provided in the University stables.[1]

The only section of the administrative machinery which bore the distinctive stamp of Jefferson's democratic genius was the Faculty, and this only on the side of the chairmanship. The Board of Visitors and the regular officers of the institution followed, in their general character and special functions, the lines customary with trustees and agents. This was so too with the Faculty in the larger duties which they discharged, as will be discerned in a subsequent enumeration. From a broad point of view, the relation of this body to the Board of Visitors was simply that of a small wheel within a big wheel, the small wheel revolving in the same direction as the big, and absolutely controlled in its motion by its greater fellow. It has been asserted [2] that, had Jefferson caught his inspiration from Teutonic, and not from French sources, he would perhaps have placed the Faculty upon a coordinate footing with the Board of Visitors; but this was hardly practicable as the University was a State and not a private institution. Jefferson was most solicitous that the Commonwealth's exclusive proprietorship in it should be patent at every turn; and this could only have been brought out most clearly by imposing all the responsibilities of its general government on one Board, and making that Board answerable to the State. The complete subordination of the Faculty's

[1] The Board assembled in the old library pavilion as late as 1849 This house had, during that year, been assigned to Dr. Davis, the demonstrator of anatomy, with the proviso that he should vacate it whenever the Board was to convene. In 1850, Professor Harrison, as chairman, suggested that the Board should meet in the house on Monroe Hill, at that time occupied by Major Broadus, the steward of the State students Letter to Cabell, Sept 10, 1850
[2] By Professor John B. Minor.

position is fully disclosed in the three great administrative duties of its members as a body: (1) they enforced the ordinances of the Visitors; (2) they recommended such changes in these ordinances as their experience and observation suggested as advisable; and (3) they adopted, with the Board's approval and consent, such by-laws as would enable them to carry out more successfully the purposes which the fundamental laws had in view.

The Board always exhibited jealousy of the smallest attempt on the Faculty's part to infringe upon the sphere of the larger wheel; and when they bestowed upon that body the right to enact a particular by-law, they raised around that right a spiked railing of the clearest and most specific restrictions   Such, for instance, was the character of their action in October, 1825, in authorizing the Faculty to adopt such disciplinary regulations as the alarming insubordination of the students at that time called for at once.   Imperative as these regulations were certain to be under the like circumstances always, they were only to become a part of the institution's permanent laws, should they be approved by the Board at their next meeting.   A comparison of the respective records of the Board and Faculty leads to the conclusion that the Faculty was really in a better position to form a just conception of what the University's welfare demanded than the Board, for its members were on the ground; the affairs of every department were always passing directly under their vigilant eyes; and their solicitude that the progress of the institution should not be obstructed, never slackened.   Moreover, they were far more frequently in consultation, with its consequent clarifying influence on their outlook   The Board was required by law to come together only once a year, and its meeting rarely went

beyond two or three annually. On the other hand, the
Faculty held in 1825 alone as many as twenty-seven meetings, although the session did not begin until March 7;
and in the years that followed, the number was often
even larger. It was through the Faculty that the Board
was able to get all its information; and, in most instances,
it adopted the Faculty's recommendations. It is quite
certain that the Visitors' point of view was, as a rule,
impartial and disinterested, and that their supervision
was generally valuable, and sometimes indispensable; but
many cases arose in which the institution would have been
served to more profit if the practical and discriminating
conclusions of the Faculty could have been the final word
in the decision.

The original provision for the chairmanship was precisely such as to make the Faculty of the highest use to
the University. It illustrated, in the most conspicuous
way, the deeply discerning thought which Jefferson had
given to the working organization of the institution, and
also his determination to enforce equality of privileges
and responsibilities By the rules of 1824, each member
of the Faculty was required to act as chairman in rotation; but his term was not to run beyond the length of one
year. There were, in Jefferson's opinion, two benefits to
spring from this regulation: (1) the personal distinction
which would attend the incumbency of the office would
fall to each professor in turn; and (2) each in turn, also,
would be in a position to acquire that extraordinary
knowledge of the affairs of the University which its executive guidance and control for one year would be sure
to impart. These advantages to accrue from the occupancy of the chairmanship would have been fully shared
by all when all had once filled it; and the burden of its
duties could not fall too heavily on any one so long

as a single year was set as the period for their discharge. The system was such as not only to perfect the Faculty's information about the University's affairs, but also to stimulate further their interest in those affairs, and to plant in the breast of each chairman in succession a competitive ambition to perform the duties in the most fruitful manner. Had Jefferson survived, his influence, which had created this system of rotation, would, doubtless, have been used to retain it.   But, unfortunately, perhaps, it lasted only two years after his death.

Dr. Emmet, it will be remembered, in writing to his father in 1824, declared that one word, repeated three times; namely, " lectures, lectures, lectures," summed up his daily life.   Probably, in the beginning when the overcrowded courses of instruction had to be relearned to some degree by the several professors, the burden of teaching was more irksome and engrossing than at a later date when these courses had become more familiar to them.   The addition of the heavy responsibilities of the chairmanship to this burden was indisputably a severe tax on the professor's powers, and a strong disinclination to assume them quickly showed itself when the controlling hand of the first rector was permanently withdrawn. As early as December, 1827, the Faculty requested that the tenure of the office should be limited to three months; and this, perhaps, led the Board, at their next meeting, to decide that, after the expiration of the term of the chairman then in office, the appointment should, for the future, be indefinitely reserved to their own body.   It is quite possible that the superior qualifications of some members of the Faculty to fulfil its duties, and the very small qualifications of others, was early perceived by the Visitors, and this was the chief reason that governed them in making the change, for the onerousness of the chairmanship would remain, whether the appointment came from the Board or the Faculty. The difference between the capacity of Professor Tucker and the capacity of Professor Blaettermann, for instance, as presiding officers, was too obvious to be overlooked.

But whether the chairmanship was filled by the action of the Board or of the Faculty; whether it was held by one professor for many years, or by a succession of professors for one year in rotation, in harmony with the original plan, the duties and responsibilities of the position remained the same. The relations of the incumbent with the other members of the Faculty were not altered. He was still *primus inter pares,*— at once the head of the body and its agent. The whole of the administrative machinery was not monopolized by him. Each member of the Faculty continued to feel that he shared in the University's management; that the piloting of its destinies lay still partly in his own hands; and that, as one of its guardians, he must begrudge neither time nor labor towards increasing its prosperity and enhancing its reputation. He could only shirk or ignore his obligation by running contrary to his sense of official duty.

It could not be said of the chairman, whether elected by the professors or appointed by the Board, what can be too often correctly asserted of a very able and zealous president; namely, that he reduced the Faculty to the status of cyphers, and took their place as the academic body himself. What were his principal duties under the original system? He was the spokesman of the Faculty on both public and private occasions; he saw to the execution of all laws adopted for the government of the institution; overlooked the proctor, the hotel-keepers, and all other subordinate agents; suspended, for a limited time, all delinquent students, or inflicted on them the minor punishments; sent out the monthly reports to their parents; and, finally, impowered them to change their boarding houses, or to use the public rooms. In relation to the Faculty itself, he was authorized to convene that body as often as the welfare of the University imperatively required; he presided at its meetings, with the right of voting once as a professor, and a second time, as the chairman, should there arise a tie; and he brought to its attention all matters bearing on the fundamental government of the institution which required a decision. In its turn, the Faculty could call on him for information about any subject upon which they had a right to deliberate.

It was one of his duties to keep a journal, in which all offenses against discipline were to be recorded for the information of the Board, at its next annual meeting; and that body, whenever it wished, could put upon him some task of an exceptional nature. Thus, under the enactments of 1831, he was directed to submit, at the end of every session, what was designated as a Consolidation Report, which was a summary of all the weekly reports that had been sent in by the professors during the previous session. This all-embracing report described the specific courses of instruction which had been given; how often, if at all, each professor had failed to lecture or to examine; how often too to make up his weekly report; and the number of times each student had been absent from his classroom. In the performance of this duty, the chairman was dependent upon the cooperation of the other members of the Faculty; and to an important degree, he was also assisted by them in the detection of the violation of the ordinances by the students. No such offense could be punished by the Faculty unless he had first brought their attention to it; but each member was required to report to him all delinquencies that had fallen under his own eyes.

In 1828, the dormitories were laid off into as many districts as there were professors; and as far as practicable, with an equal population of students. To each professor, a district was assigned for supervision. It was his duty to inspect its precincts from time to time; to enforce a rigid discipline by suppressing all noises and disturbances; to report the names of the incorrigible; to listen to special complaints against the proctor and hotel-keepers, and to protect the students in general in their right to comforts and conveniences in their dormitories and boarding-houses. This regulation was adopted under the influence of the turbulence which then distracted the University, and was suggested by the desire to lighten the burden of the chairman, now so hard pressed by novel additions to his ordinary functions. It turned out, however, to be a temporary expedient.

XXIII. *Administrative Organization, Continued*

The chairman was not the only officer of the Faculty. That body was also served by a secretary. At first, some member kept the record, but, in 1826, William Wertenbaker was appointed to the position,— which he, however, filled only temporarily at first.

The Faculty held their meetings under numerous roofs: in 1826, they convened in the library; in 1827, in the library or pavilion VII; in 1828, in the home of either Tucker or Lomax; in 1829, of Tucker or Emmet; and in subsequent years, either in the library, a lecture-room, or the residence of a professor. The customary hour of assembling seems to have been half past four in the afternoon.

There were four officers subordinate to the Faculty:

the bursar, the proctor, the patron, and the janitor.
The duties of the bursar were those commonly incidental
to that important office and require no description
This, however, was not true of the other three officers,
who played, in due proportion, a very conspicuous part in
the history of the institution.

Broadly described, the proctor was the master of police and inspector of buildings, lands and other property
of the University. He was expected to visit all the dormitories at least once a week, and all the hotels at least
once a month, and to draw up a report on their condition
for the information of the chairman. All fines imposed
on the occupants of these buildings for damage inflicted
by them were to be collected by him and deposited with
the bursar. He was impowered to employ laborers to
keep the entire area of the University in a sanitary state;
to head off trespasses, intrusions, and rows upon the
grounds; and to frustrate all other attempted violations
of the statutes He was required to acquaint the chairman with every breach of discipline that took place within
the limits, and to warn off former students who should return after being expelled. It was his duty to communicate
to the proper law officer, when instructed by the Faculty,
all knowledge in his possession that would bring about the
prevention or punishment of such acts within the precincts as the criminal court would take direct cognizance
of. It was his duty also to superintend all building operations that were in progress; to frame the contracts necessary to their right execution; to settle the accounts of
the undertakers, and to deliver to them drafts on the bursar in payment of such balances as should be in their
favor. It was his further duty to collect all moneys,—
including the rents of the numerous dormitories and the
several hotels,— that were owing to the University. It

was also his duty to receive the students' complaints touching their fare and report them to the chairman; to find out the justice of these complaints by personal attendance at meals; and to correct the shortcoming, if any, by a warning to the hotel-keepers. In the same way, all instances of neglect by these keepers in connection with the servants, the furniture, or the fuel of the dormitories were subject to his investigation and amendment. He was responsible also for the purchase of the fagots and lights which the students needed in their rooms.

At one time, a conflict of authority arose between the proctor and the Faculty touching certain points upon which the former asserted his right to exercise his own private judgment and discretion: such points related especially to health, the water supply, the state of the walkways and alleys, and the preservation of the buildings from destructive trespass. There was a divergence of opinion as to the measures which should be adopted to correct the unwholesome conditions that then prevailed in these particulars, and the order in which they should be carried out. The Faculty appealed to the Board of Visitors for support in their contention, and they were very properly confirmed in their superior authority.

The principal duty of the patron, so long as that office was in existence, was to take the funds of the students into his keeping so soon as they matriculated. These funds were first subject to his commission of two per cent. as his compensation for the responsibility of receiving and holding them. By the authority of the proctor's warrant, he paid to each professor the amount due him as fees for tuition; to each hotel-keeper, at the expiration of each month, the amount owed for the board

of the young men who obtained their meals at his tables;
to the bursar, all sums due by the students for the use
of the dormitories and public rooms, and by the hotel-
keepers for rent; and by the young men and hotel-keepers alike, for all other charges against them.   He was
required to pay the bills for books or clothes presented by
a merchant with the purchasing student's endorsement,
provided that they were legitimate; and also to cash all
drafts upon him by the young men for pocket-money not
in excess of a just proportion of the sum deposited for
that purpose; but he was impowered to refuse to honor
an order given by one student to another for an article
bought, unless the sale had been first approved in writing
by the chairman   He was also required, at the end of
the session, to return to each student the balance remaining to his credit after all the proper deductions had been
made; and likewise if the student should leave the precincts before the session closed, whether he had been expelled, or had withdrawn for unexceptional reasons
Finally, the patron cooperated with the proctor in enforcing the police regulations so far as to give aid when called
on to prevent breaches of the ordinances; and he was expected to report to that officer all offences that fell
within his personal observation   He assisted the proctor also in making estimates, and in drafting contracts
for building and repairs, and in verifying the accounts
of undertakers.   Like the proctor, he was entitled to a
house within the University precincts free of rent and all
other charges except for wear and tear.   He was also
impowered to open a book-store in an apartment on the
grounds which had been specifically assigned to him for
that purpose.   The prices of the text-books to be sold
by him, were, however, to be supervised by the Faculty;

and he was forbidden to fix them at more than fifteen per cent. advance upon cost.[1]

The person who entered most directly and incessantly into the daily lives of the students was the janitor, and for that very reason, perhaps, he was the one who most often was detested. In drafting the regulations of March 4, 1824, the Visitors authorized the Faculty to appoint some one who should be always near at hand during the meetings of both the Board and the Faculty, in order to perform such manual offices as might be called for. He was at one time, also, expected to be close by whenever a class was sitting, more especially in the Schools of Natural Philosophy and Chemistry when apparatus had to be handled; and also in the laboratory, whenever his assistance was needed in the experiments. It was he who was employed to run the lithographic press, and to keep the philosophical and chemical instruments in order; to wind up the clock; but above all, to visit the dormitories in the morning to report every case of violation of the ordinance that enforced early rising. Not satisfied with this exhausting range of duties, the enactments of 1831 required him to do such work as an artisan as he should be competent to do, provided that it was not in conflict with the discharge of the other claims on his time. In return for this extraordinary variety of services, he received two hundred dollars a year as wages, and was granted a house and firewood at the expense of the University.

The first janitor was William Spinner, a colored man, an unfortunate selection for the session of 1825, as that year was rendered very turbulent by the riotous spirit

---

[1] This privilege was originally granted to Brockenbrough, but does not appear to have been exercised.

of the students   It is probable that they would have
contemned the authority of a white janitor at that time,
but there was not the smallest likelihood of their being
overawed by the firmest and sternest negro.   William
Brockman succeeded him.   He too must have failed to
give satisfaction, for, in December, 1828, John Smith,
also a white man, took his place and remained in the University's service until his death,— a practical proof of his
competency and fidelity.   He was always addressed as
Doctor, a title derived from some slim pretentions to
knowledge of medicine.   A son of Professor Davis, who
has recorded his recollections of the traditions of those
times, declares that he was, in reality, a quack,— not con-
sciously or dishonestly so in intention, but by the purely
empirical character of his medical advice   He was
superficially versed in other sciences, but was acknowledged by every one to be a very skilful, diligent, and
conscientious officer   He had soon won the respect of
all, and in his blue broad-cloth coat, adorned with bright
brass buttons, and with a wide-brimmed white felt hat
resting on his head, he must have presented a very interesting, if not imposing, appearance, as he walked, with
great dignity, down the arcades to inform some delinquent student, with all the solemn authority of an English beadle, that his presence was sternly desired in the
chairman's office.   His own office was situated in the
basement of the Rotunda   He seems to have been popular with the young men in spite of the persistence with
which he aroused the drowsy ones at dawn, and the number of times he was compelled to carry disturbing mes-
sages to their dormitories; and if his blue coat and felt
hat occasionally suffered from a douche of water, as he
opened a door, it appears to have shaken only tempor-

arily the amity which existed between him and the unruly students.[1]

[1] "He was no ordinary man," the Faculty declared in their resolution of March 1, 1861. "Gifted with strong powers of observation, reflection and judgment, he was clear and constant in his convictions, always independent, and yet never offensive in the expression of them. His integrity was unimpeachable. Although his lot was an humble one, he was content with it, and rendered it reputable by a faithful discharge of his duties. Kind and unselfish, he was ever ready to render a service to his fellowmen, and exhibited no envy at the better fortune of others. Long a believer in Christianity, the old man has gone to the grave in peace, full of years, with the general esteem of the community and the well earned and hearty respect of the Faculty."

Lewis Commodore, the hired negro bell-ringer, was not warmly in sympathy with General Cocke's views on temperance. In June, 1846, the Board of Visitors passed the following resolution: "Whereas Lewis Commodore, the faithful and valuable servant of the University, with the exception of drunkenness, which has well nigh ruined him, having seen his error, and for five months last past maintained the steady and consistent course of a reformed man, be it resolved, that, during the vacations in future, Lewis shall not be required to work out in the grounds with the other laborers, but be confined only to the performance of such a reduced portion of the duties of his station as the absence of professors and students will permit, so long as Lewis maintains his pledge of total abstinence from all intoxicating drinks." In 1832, Lewis was exposed for sale in Charlottesville. "Professor Davis, myself, and the proctor," says the chairman of the Faculty of that day, in a report to the Faculty, "believing that to lose his services would be a real misfortune to the University, agreed to purchase him for the use of the institution, and he was bought accordingly." It was Lewis's duty to ring the bell at dawn.

FOURTH PERIOD

FORMATIVE AND EXPERIMENTAL STAGE, 1825–1842

1. *How the University was Reached*

Jefferson, it will be recalled, had not only confidently expected, but had publicly announced that the University would be in a condition to receive students on the first of February, 1825   This day was chosen because it was anticipated that the English professors would have arrived by then and be ready to begin their lectures.   Had all the teachers been on the ground, the institution was, by December 1, 1824, really prepared to start upon its active career, for, with the exception of the Rotunda in part, and the Anatomical Hall, in whole, the important buildings needed for the commencement of work were finished, whether pavilion, dormitory, hotel, or lecture-room, the courses of instruction had been laid off; the administrative officers, elected; and the ordinances for the government of the students, adopted.   It was due to the detention of Key, Dunglison, and Bonnycastle by the delaying mishaps of their voyage, that the University failed before March 7, 1825, to enter upon its first stage of operation, for which it had been equipping itself so assiduously, in so many ways, during the previous six years   This day of consummation must have been looked upon by Jefferson as one of the happiest in his long and illustrious life, and his deeply quaffed delight at that hour must have compensated him most acutely for all the vexing and distracting obstacles that had, so persistently,

arisen in his path,— only to be overcome in the end, however, by extraordinary energy and tenacity on his part,
and on the part of his loyal and unselfish supporters.

Hitherto, we have been describing the physical, institutional, and legislative history of the University in process of construction.   We have now to start upon its
history as a completed seat of learning.   The student,
who, up to this hour, has always been behind the wings,
now comes forward, and taking his stand at the centre
of the stage, never leaves the mild glare of the scholastic
footlights during the remainder of the story.   It was for
his benefit that those beautiful edifices had been erected;
for him, that those accomplished professors had been
brought from overseas; for him, that those varied and
extensive courses of instruction had been provided; for
him, that those disciplinary laws had been adopted.   We
must now begin to look at the entire setting, whether
physical, or moral, or intellectual, from the point of view
of its relation to his welfare.   Without his presence,
without his interests, it would all become a costly but
unmeaning show,— a house of splendor without an occupant, a comely body without a spirit.

The Board of Visitors, in order to obtain students
for the first term, were not content simply to let the public
know that the doors of the University were now open,—
notices stating in detail the advantages which it had to
offer were inserted in the principal newspapers of the
South as far as Milledgeville, in Georgia.   Jefferson
himself posted a shower of circulars with his own hands.
Before the session of 1825 had come to an end, the
session of 1826 was announced in the journals of every
Southern State lying east of the Mississippi River, and
also of the cities of Columbus and Cincinnati, in the State
of Ohio.   " It is better to diffuse advertisements through

many States and parts of States," Chairman Tucker shrewdly wrote, when instructing the proctor, "than to advertise longer in a smaller number."

How were the students who entered the University during the first years able to reach it? We have seen how slow and cumbrous were the means of transporting to that place so much of the material that was used in its construction. It was, of course, less arduous in those times to convey a person from one part of the country to another than to carry a barrel or a hogshead; but the only difference in the degree of difficulty was the difference in movement between a bulky stage and a lumbering wagon, each pulled by a team of four sweating and hard-breathing horses. Both creaked through the mud and over the stones, with almost equal sluggishness. The barrel and the hogshead had over the passenger at least the advantage of being insensible and unconscious throughout the long journey. Writing in 1824, Isaac Coles, Jefferson's private secretary, incidentally mentions that public coaches were then plying at intervals on the road between Richmond and the West. When Cabell went up to the University in 1819, he was conveyed as far as that place by one of these jolting vehicles, and thence, through the wooded countryside, jogged on horseback to his own house at Warminster. Stages, at this time, also creaked and rumbled on the highway that wound from Fredericksburg, through the bushy wilderness of Spottsylvania, to Gordonsville and Charlottesville.

In 1820, a lighter carriage was regularly provided for travellers passing from Piedmont to Tidewater or the reverse. During that year, Solomon Ballou [1] solicited the public patronage for a "hack," which, as he an-

---

[1] Ballou was afterwards found guilty of robbing the mail in his custody as a public conveyor

nounced in the columns of the *Jeffersonian Republican*, would set out from Charlottesville for Richmond on Wednesdays; and every Sunday would leave the capital on its return to Albemarle. The hack was the most ubiquitous vehicle on the streets of the little town so soon as the students began to pour in; and it was extravagantly patronized by them at all hours of the day and night, until, in 1826, it was shut out of the precincts between twelve o'clock noon and seven o'clock in the morning; and several years afterwards, there was a debate in the Faculty whether it should be suffered to enter the bounds at all. The only superiority which such a vehicle could assert over the ordinary stage coach, in a prolonged journey, was the greater speed with which it could be drawn over the public roads. It must have cut down the time consumed in such a journey; but like the coach, offered no comforts of any kind to the sleepy traveller, however luxurious it may have seemed to be to the tipsy and uproarious student returning to his dormitory not long before dawn.

In traversing the region between Richmond and Charlottesville, the passenger had to spend at least one night on the lonely road, either in the dark corners of the stage-coach itself, or in one of the taverns by the way that had been built for the baiting of man and beast. By 1838, the Central Railway had been finished as far as Louisa county. The journey could then be brought to a close in a single day. The student who lived in Richmond left that city by train at five in the morning, and descending from the cars at the raw terminus in the woods, entered the patient coach that was standing by for him and his fellow-travellers to transport them towards the Rivanna. He accomplished the remainder of his journey at a speed of six miles an hour, without counting the tiresome delays that resulted from the numerous stoppages.   By the new means of locomotion, he was able to save not less than nine hours of time, and to escape the rough discomforts of the primitive country inn at night.   The heavy coaches in which the passengers were slowly sent on to their common destination were owned by the railway company.

The student whose home was in Baltimore, Washington, or Fredericksburg, on the north, or in Norfolk, on the south, came, in the one instance, by rail, and in the other, by steamboat, to Richmond; and there, like the resident of that city, took a seat in the steam-cars for the Louisa terminus, travelling thence by coach to the University.   It was in this roundabout way that the young men from the northeastern, eastern, and southeastern regions of Virginia,— from the valleys of the Potomac, Rappahannock, York, and James,— could most conveniently reach Charlottesville.   It was not until 1849 that the railway was built as far as Keswick, which left only a short interval to be still traversed [1]   In 1838, the fare from Richmond, by consecutive rail and coach

[1] The students whose homes were situated in the counties below the James, travelled, about 1845, by canal to Scottsville, "and there took a road-wagon for Charlottesville," (Recollections of Charles S Venable) In 1846, Joseph C Cabell mentioned, in a letter to his wife, that there was "a night stage" from Charlottesville to Gordonsville He preferred, however, to travel to that place in the day time and by "hack" He expected to board the cars there In 1847, Dr James I. Cabell was detained two days on his journey to the University from Richmond by the railway in consequence of the interruption in the traffic by a heavy snow "This place," wrote Mrs Samuel H Smith from Charlottesville, about 1830, "is seventy miles from Fredericksburg, and by rising with the sun, we have performed the journey with great ease in two days, stopping to rest two hours at breakfast and two at dinner," (First Forty Years of Washington Society) John H B Latrobe, travelling to the White Sulphur Springs, also came by this highway A piano which the proctor sent from the University to Winchester, about this time, was transported by the following route to Richmond by wagon, thence by water to Georgetown, thence by canal to Harper's Ferry, and thence to Winchester by wagon

conveyance, was five dollars and a half, and from Fredericksburg, six dollars. During the times when the stage was the only passenger vehicle plying on the same road, the fare from Richmond was but three dollars,— which shows that the greater convenience following from the railway had led to a heavy addition to the original charge.

The students whose homes were situated in the Valley, or beyond the crest of the Alleghanies, travelled to the University by way of Rockfish Gap in stage coaches. These also, after 1838, were owned by the Central Railway Company. The same corporation was in possession of two important lines that ran from Staunton to Lexington and Buchanan respectively, and a third line that crossed the mountains by turnpike to Guyandotte. Direct and reliable means of transportation from points south and north of the Ohio River, and as far as Kentucky, Tennessee, Georgia, and Mississippi, was thus furnished through all the revolutions of the seasons. The students from Southwest Virginia, and the South Atlantic States, came up by stage from Lynchburg. In 1829, Alexander Garrett was appointed a commissioner to lay off a new bed for the Lynchburg highway; but his work was probably confined to the vicinity of the University. It seems that, in 1832, the road passed so near to the arcades of one of the Ranges that the idle young men who occupied the dormitories in that quarter amused themselves, when the coach slowly rolled in sight, with flouting and jeering at the passengers. This vociferous greeting they called the " family smile." In 1838, the Central Railway set up a line of public stages on the Lynchburg highway; but it was only on alternate days that a coach started from Charlottesville for that city or the reverse. The hour of departure was midnight.

II. *Beginning and Length of the Session*

The first of February, 1825, as we have seen, was chosen as the day for the first session to begin.   Would that date have been preferred had all the English professors been expected to arrive four months earlier? To start upon the work of each session in the midst of the most rigorous section of winter, when travel was very frequently halted by frost and snow, and to protract it through that part of the summer when the heat was most ardent and debilitating, seemed, on its face, to be an arbitrary and irrational arrangement.   But the cause of its adoption lay in the impression that Eastern Virginia, and the States farther south, were the regions most likely to patronize the University; and that the mountain climate in the dog-days would be certain to increase the number of students from those points of the compass   There were friends of the institution, however, who refused to accept this practical reason as a justification.   " Think of two hundred boys," exclaimed Gilmer, " festering each in one of those little rooms in August or July!   The very idea is suffocating."

July, with its scorching sun, had not yet arrived when the students pleaded with the executive committee, through the Faculty, for a holiday of ten days or more, on the perfectly sensible ground of the unusual length of the session and the stifling and wilting temperature that was then prevailing.   Jefferson, from the cool heights and airy apartments of Monticello, drily replied that " there was but one vacation in the year, and this extended from December 15 to January 31."   In the privacy of his own mind, he was probably astonished that these youthful students, with such novel and extraordinary opportunities for learning, should not have asked for the abolition of even the interval of rest which he mentioned. Ten and one half months to be given up to work and one month and a half to play seemed to him a rational proportion; but the boys, exasperated by the heats of August, responded to his veiled rebuke by breaking out in a rebellion that greatly angered and perplexed the authorities at first; but their obduracy softened; and on October 7 (1825), the Board of Visitors decided that, thereafter, the annual vacation should begin on August 1, and terminate on September 11, with a recess at Christmas, which was to continue for a period of at least two weeks. The second session opened on February 1, 1826. The Board, on October 4, of that year, resolved that the third session should begin on February 1, and end on July 4, and that afterwards the session should begin on the 20th of August, and end on the 4th of July. A recess of two weeks was to intervene at Christmas. On December 16 (1826) the Board made a second change: the session was to begin on September 1, and end on July 20. In July, 1828, September 10 was designated as the day of opening; in 1834, September 1, and the session was to terminate on the 4th of July. There was little alteration thereafter during this period.

In 1838, the Faculty objected so strongly to the Christmas recess that they asked the Board to abolish it. Although no holiday besides the twenty-fifth was allowed in December, 1830, at least forty of the students left the precincts; and the professors made no attempt to lecture, since the young men who remained at the University refused to attend. In 1834, it was formally announced that, should the students pointedly stay away from the classroom during the Christmas period, the lectures should be considered to have been delivered, and when the examinations were held in each school, the most searching questions were to be put on that part of the course which had been so flagrantly neglected by them. It was the adoption of rules like this,— which seemed to have their springs in a vindictive mood,— that partly explains the insubordination that came so violently to the surface so often during these early years. Taken with the refusal to continue the immemorial Christmas holiday, or to acknowledge, from the start, that the blistering hours of July and August were not the time for study, this regulation of 1834 demonstrated that the Faculty and the Visitors were at least partly deserving of the unpopularity which they aroused in those youthful minds.

There was at least one professor, however, who disapproved of these exasperating restrictions and punishments. This was Tucker, the oldest and the most experienced of them all. In 1835, he advised that a recess at Christmas should be formally granted, as the new rule, requiring the prolongation of the lectures through the holidays, had only left the classrooms as empty as in the foregoing years. He summarized the reasons for again conceding the recess, and it will be pertinent to restate them, as they bring out certain conditions that prevailed in the University during this period of its history. The grounds in favor were: (1) parents were willing for their sons to visit their homes at that time; (2) all public and private business was then suspended; (3) the season was given up to merry-making and relaxation; (4) it was impossible to force the students into disloyalty to customs which were cherished under every Virginian roof, and were shared in even by the humblest of the slaves; (5) the regular session was so protracted that a short vacation would turn out to be a relief; and it was at Christmas that it could be most conveniently allowed. In opposition to these reasons, it was said, (1) that the intermediate examinations were held in January, and a holiday in December was a poor preparation for them; (2) that the roads were so unfathomable in winter that there could be no regularity in the return of the absentees, and a recess of ten days at that season really signified the loss of a month; (3) that it increased the expense of college life; and (4) that the students from remote States, having no inducement to leave the precincts, would be tempted by idleness to fall into dissipation, which would be damaging to the good name of the institution.

The chairman's recommendation in favor of granting a recess failed to receive the Visitors' approval; but so numerous were the vacant seats in the lecture-rooms in December, 1836, that the Faculty were constrained to connive at the violation of the regulation. A student who was curtly summoned before that body to explain his refusal to be present at his classes, obtained an acquittal by proving that two of his professors had left the University for the holidays, and that the third had voluntarily discontinued his course for the time being.

III. *Origin and Number of Students*

What was the social origin of the young men who matriculated during these early sessions? We can only infer it from the names embraced in the catalogues. Let us consider those recorded for the year 1825, which, for some reasons, will always remain the most interesting in the University's annals. Among the students then present, we discover the youthful scions of such conspicuous Virginian families as Ambler, Bolling, Brockenbrough, Carter, Cary, Cocke, Eyre, Mason, Fairfax, Harrison, Hubard, Lee, Magruder, Marshall, Meriwether, Nelson, Page, Peyton, Preston, Randolph, Saunders, Selden, Scott,

Slaughter, Spotswood, Stuart, Tayloe, Tazewell, Wallace, Watkins, Wellford, Wickham and Yates   If we run our eye over the voluminous columns of names that follow 1825, in annual succession, down to the end of the period which we are now covering,— an interval of seventeen sessions,— it will be discerned that not a single mansion of distinction in the social life of Virginia, during those years, failed, at one time or another, to be represented in the person of a student within those stately precincts.   To call the roll of their names is to call the roll of families who have deeply stamped their virtues and their talents upon every aspect of the State's history during the long interval,— now serene, now stormy,— that followed the Revolution and preceded the War of Secession.   This is not so true of the young men who matriculated from the sister commonwealths of the South; but in proportion to their number, we discover among them also names of high social and political prominence in the broad region that lay between the Yadkin and the Mississippi River.

Indeed, these early rolls fully explain the prejudice which then existed against the University as the institution of the rich   "There are persons," said Thomas W. Gilmer, at that time a member of the General Assembly, and destined to become the Governor of Virginia and Secretary of the Navy, "who ask, why should the State bear so heavy an expense to afford means of education to those who can themselves procure it?   It is not enough to answer that it had diffused science more generally through the State, and elevated the standard of literary attainment amongst us"   However, it was not due to any haughty selfishness of class in Jefferson that the young men, in the beginning, belonged, as a body, to the social rank of the well-to-do citizens of the community, for it can never be forgotten that, in his plan for the district colleges, those sons of indigent parentage who should distinguish themselves there for their scholarship, were to be admitted to all the higher schools of instruction in the University at the public expense.

Thomas W. Gilmer, foreseeing that popular favor would be diverted from the institution to its damage, if not to its destruction, should it remain so indisputably the seminary of the wealthy, strove to conjure up the means by which it might be linked with the cause of primary education, and thus more directly contribute to the spread of knowledge through all the social grades of the State. He begged Cabell to submit some matured scheme that would assist him in his purpose. Above all, he put the same question to the proctor, Brockenbrough, — a man, as we have seen, fully competent to give wise advice based upon long and discerning observation on the ground. "Many counties of the State," the latter wrote in November, 1830, in reply to Gilmer, "have not sent a single student since the opening of the institution. Why is this? Is it because the expenses are too great for the resources of the people, or for want of taste for literature? . . . How would it do to propose, by way of remuneration to the several counties for the large annuity contributed towards it, that the University should receive and educate a student, or students, from each county or counties, equal to the representation in the House of Delegates, free of expense as to fees and rents,— the students thus educated to be employed as teachers, who would diffuse a fondness for literature throughout the State?" Such was the earliest recorded suggestion of the system of State students, which was to be adopted within a few years, and which was to silence the unreasonable reproaches leveled at the University, by adjusting it to a more democratical footing than it occupied at the start.

How many students were in attendance during the first period of growth, extending from 1825 to 1842 inclusive? " The letters I have received from almost every State south of the Potomac, the Ohio, and Missouri," Jefferson wrote to Cabell, as early as 1822, " prove that all these are looking anxiously to the opening of our University as an epoch which is to relieve them from sending to the Northern universities   And when we see that the colleges of those States considered as preparatory only for ours, have 1, 2, and 300 students each, we cannot doubt that we will receive the double and treble of their number.   I have no doubt that our accommodations for 218 will be filled within six months after opening; and for every fifty coming afterwards, we shall have to build a boarding-house and twenty-five dormitories."

Jefferson was so keenly elated by the enrolment in 1825,[1] that he sanguinely predicted that, in 1826, so many students would offer for matriculation that the capacity of the dormitories would be strained to lodge them; and " there would probably be," he said, " as many additional to that as Charlottesville can accommodate, which is expected to be about one hundred . . . As far as we can judge not one will go to Charlottesville as long as a dormitory is to be had " During the second session there were only fifty-four students beyond the number present in 1825. Jefferson had looked forward to at least three hundred   The list dwindled to one hundred and twenty-eight in the third session; and in 1829, it sank further to one hundred and twenty   During the seventeen sessions closing with the year 1842, approximately three thousand, two hundred and forty-seven

---

[1] The enrolment for 1825 numbered about one hundred and twenty-three students

young men were enrolled by the proctor, an average of one hundred and ninety-one only for the separate session. About nine hundred and forty-two remained two years; three hundred and ten, three years; ninety-two, four years; twenty-four, five years; nine, six years; and two, seven years. The students who tarried longest were sons of the professors, who, as we shall see, were admitted to the lectures at a very unripe age. It is a fact of some significance that the largest number of students who had been present during two sessions was in 1826, the second year in the scholastic career of the institution.

In the history of the attendance during these first seventeen sessions, we discover the existence of a condition which has always prevailed; namely, the failure of a large proportion of the young men to return after the close of their first year. This arose from the peculiarities of the elective system as compared with those of the curriculum. Under the curriculum, it was necessary for the student to pass through the four divisions of the freshman, sophomore, junior, and senior years before he could carry off his baccalaureate degree. The difficulties of the ascent were so nicely proportioned to each year that he rose by easy gradations, session following session, until he finally arrived in triumph at the top. As the young men in each division were engaged in exactly the same task at precisely the same hour, they were always able to assist and encourage a lagging brother on the road; and as all had the same goal in view, they felt that the discredit of not reaching it would be the more mortifying from the very number certain to succeed. But there was no justifiable reason for losing the degree; the previous preparation was apt to have been sufficient for the freshman class; and if there was failure in any grade higher up, the disappointed collegian had only to resume its course a second time, with renewed hope of receiving the prize at the end of his senior year.

On the other hand, in the elective system as adopted at the University, there was no preordained course for the student to pursue. He followed his own taste,— too often immature when he had any preference at all,— in the choice of his studies; and equally as often he was not really equipped to attend the lectures he selected. The standard of graduation was high; and in the largest number of instances, the student ended his first year in dejection. No influence beyond parental constraint existed to spur him to return,— no bachelor's degree, open to the majority, which it would have been an academic disgrace to him to lose; no spirit of comradeship to cause him to feel that his absence would be a disloyalty to his class. The loss, the second year, of two students of every three of those who had been present the previous session,— which was the proportion observable during the first seventeen sessions,— was primarily due to this acute impression of failure. It was also, to some extent, due, contradictory as it may sound, to success in traversing some special field which the elective system made practicable in one year, in spite of the requirement, from the beginning, that every academic pupil should, each session, pursue a course embracing three subjects. The languages or the sciences could be studied during a single year, and the alumnus might leave, after the close of one term, as much entitled to be called a " graduate of the University of Virginia " as if he had won diplomas under all the six academic professors.

In what proportion were the several States represented in the mass of young men present during the first seventeen sessions? Of the three thousand, two hundred and forty-seven who approximately comprised the whole number, two thousand, three hundred and forty-two were matriculated as Virginians. There were one hundred and seventy-nine South Carolinians, one hundred and seven Alabamians, eighty-two Georgians, eighty Louisianians, seventy-four Mississippians, sixty-five North Carolinians, forty-nine Marylanders, forty-seven from the District of Columbia, forty-one Tennesseeans, thirty-six Kentuckians, and eighteen Floridians,— a total of six hundred and sixty-four from these commonwealths. The students belonging to the States lying beyond the borders of the South embraced six from Ohio and New York respectively, fifteen from Pennsylvania, and five from Missouri. Apparently, Jefferson's sanguine expectation that the University would, at an early date, allure additional young men from the West and North failed to become a reality except to an insignificant and negligible degree. It is quite probable that the few who were admitted from the four Commonwealths named were the sons of Virginians residing either permanently or temporarily in those communities. The animosities that had always been smouldering between the Northern people and the Southern were fiercely rekindled by the political conflicts of 1820, when the questions leading up to the Missouri Compromise were under intemperate debate; and this mutual hostility continued to flare up throughout that period of the University's history which we are describing. This unquestionably tended to discourage the education of the sons of the North in its lecture halls.

Indeed, it was not until the session of 1834–5 that even the States of the South beyond the borders of Virginia began to send an expanding number of students to the institution. In 1825, of the one hundred and twenty-three young men on the ground, as many as one hundred and eight were from the Old Dominion; on the other

hand, in 1841–2, fifty-eight of the one hundred and
seventy present were from other Southern commonwealths,— a very perceptible rise in the proportion of
the matriculates belonging to them.   The extent of the
increase is shown in the following table·

	1825–1833	1833–1842
South Carolina . . .	36	143
Florida . .	3	15
Maryland .	25	24
Alabama	16	141
Louisiana . .	17	63
Kentucky . . .	13	23
Tennessee .	13	28
North Carolina	26	43
Mississippi . .	13	61
Georgia . . .	16	69
Total . .	178	610

The most remarkable expansion occurred in the attendance from South Carolina, Georgia, Alabama, and
Mississippi.   In Maryland alone was there a falling off.
Considered as a whole, the increase amounted approximately to three hundred and fifty per cent   The explanation of the change for the States of lower Carolina and
the Gulf lay in the augmented world-demand for their
principal staple, cotton, and the consequent advance in
its price.   There was no increase of importance in the
attendance of students from Pennsylvania, New York,
Ohio, the District of Columbia, and Missouri.   Thirty-
two for the first period, it was only forty-six for the second.

iv *Matriculation*

So soon as the student reached the University by one
of those stage-coaches, which, as we have seen, plied

through that region of country, he was expected to go promptly to the proctor's office, and submit to all the conditions of matriculation. The first was to give a statement in writing as to his age. If under sixteeh, he was refused admission, unless accompanied by an older brother, or was himself the son of a professor on the ground. Sometimes, the Faculty acted on their own discretion, if there was a good reason in a particular case why this rule should be partially relaxed,— thus in 1830, Carter W. Wormeley, who was under sixteen, was, in October, permitted to remain as a quasi-matriculate because he would reach the accepted limit in February, and was so well-grown already as to pass for nineteen. The second requirement was that the student, if an alumnus of some other incorporated seminary of learning, should hand in a certificate of good conduct from its authorities. The third requirement was that he should deposit with the proctor or the patron,— if such an officer had been appointed,— all the money, drafts, checks, and orders in his possession, which he had brought from home to defray his different expenses The total sum thus surrendered was to be subject to the following deductions: (1) the two per cent. commission payable to the proctor or patron; (2) the rent of his dormitory; (3) the charge for the use of the public rooms; (4) the tuition fees; (5) the amount which he would owe his hotelkeeper for the first period of three months; (6) the sum estimated to cover the cost of text-books and stationery; (7) a contingent fee, to compensate for any damage which he might do to the property of the University What probably made the deepest impression on his sensibilities was the requirement that he should give up all the loose contents of his pocket-book, which he had hoped to reserve for amusement or for petty expenses of every sort from day to day.

This was another of the pricking regulations for which apparently there was no sound reason; indeed, it was very nicely calculated to arouse that feeling of sharp hostility to authority so rampant during this period. The explanation offered by the Board of Visitors for imposing it was that the forcible limitation of the amount to be spent by the students would enable them to devote their time and energies more positively and conscientiously to their studies; and would assure a slower and more thoughtful enjoyment of the money through the measured disbursements of the patron, for he, by scanning the bills sent in to him, could soon detect the smallest indulgence " in parade and pleasure," and by curbing it, would leave the young men a larger opportunity " to acquire literature and science, useful habits, and honorable distinction." One can easily see in the mind's eye the wry faces with which this lofty explanation, with its slight smack of irony, was received by the students, already writhing under their pecuniary dependence upon an academic officer. Each one was required to take an oath that he had deposited the entire amount in his possession; and should it be afterwards proved that he had not done so, he was compelled to pay a commission of four per cent. instead of two. It was not simply the money brought by him to the University at the beginning of the session which had to be given up· all funds that subsequently came into his hands had also to be surrendered. The accounts for 1836 reveal that the average amount which the young men had in the patron's custody was seventy-four dollars, and in 1837, seventy-five; and this was a counterpart of the entire period. The largest sum that was withdrawn for pocket money at one time was ten dollars. It was rarely so much; indeed, five dollars was the modest amount which the patron thought sufficient to dole out in response to most of the applications.

The student could not evade this restriction by making purchases on credit except under a narrow limitation, for, in 1828, he was forbidden by the Faculty to run up debts in excess of five dollars, unless he could show the written consent of parent or chairman. Ten years afterwards, an Act of the General Assembly specifically curtailed the merchant's right to give credit to students; and under the authority of this law, the chairman declined to acknowledge the validity of any obligations of the young men unless contracted for necessaries. He used his own discretion even in the cases of those who offered their parents' written permission in justification. So soon as the abuse of credit by student and merchant was put under the ban of a statute,— which rendered it liable to be passed upon by the grand jury,— there was less difficulty in enforcing the Faculty's ordinance in restraint of that evil.

There were certain fixed charges, as we have seen, to be covered by the amount deposited by the student at the beginning of the session. These varied slightly from year to year, but throughout the first seventeen sessions remained substantially unaltered   If the matriculate announced his intention, with the proper permission, to attend the lectures of one professor alone, the fee was fifty dollars; of two, thirty dollars each; and of three, twenty-five dollars, respectively. After 1837, ministers of the Gospel, or future candidates of divinity, were relieved of this expense. A new charge of twenty dollars was, subsequent to 1834–5, imposed upon the student of law, in addition to the usual one for a single chair.   The young man who entered late, or departed early, unless prevented from stopping longer by sickness, was required to pay the tuition fee for the entire session.   It was only in 1825, — when the beginning and length of the session were rendered uncertain by the abnormal circumstances of the hour,— that the amount of the tuition fees was proportioned to the time of actual attendance.

During the first four years, one hundred and fifty dollars was always paid in by the student to defray the charge of his hotelkeeper for board; but, in 1829–30, the amount was lowered to one hundred dollars.   This sum entitled him to the use of the very plain furniture in his dormitory, and also to servants' attendance, and to laundry   The deposit for rent, when one room was to be occupied by two tenants, was eight dollars apiece for the session; the general cost of fuel and candles was fifteen dollars apiece; and of books and common stationery, about forty dollars.   The contingent fee was fixed at ten dollars.   The amount intrusted to the patron for clothing and pocket-money was in the neighborhood of one hundred and fourteen dollars; and for the use of the library and public rooms, fifteen dollars.   In 1829–30, it was estimated that, with clothing, pocket-money, and the contingent fee omitted, the student's annual expenses should not run beyond two hundred and eighteen dollars; and in 1834, with these two items counted in, beyond three hundred and seventy-five   But, in 1838, when the proctor calculated that the outlay ought not to exceed three hundred and fifty dollars, he acknowledged that the great majority of the young men spent at least five hundred in the course of a single session.

Having made the deposits with the patron as the enactments prescribed, taken an oath that he retained no funds in his possession, and that he would obey the ordinances,— a copy of which was given him,— the student then announced the courses of study which he wished to pursue.   It was now the patron's duty to pay the appointed fees to the professors designated, in return for which each delivered to that officer for transmission to the student a ticket [1] admitting him to his school.   The matriculate, without parental authority to the contrary, was required, as we have already mentioned, to choose three schools if he belonged to the academic department; and in 1827, he was granted the right to add still others, provided that he should state his desire to do so within one month after entrance.

What was the patronage enjoyed by each of the schools during the first seventeen sessions? In 1825, when the professorship of law was as yet vacant, the attendance was as follows: in the School of Medicine, there were twenty students; of Ancient Languages, fifty-seven; of Modern, seventy-three; of Natural Philosophy, thirty-five; of Mathematics, seventy-three; of Chemistry and Materia Medica, thirty-five; and of Moral Philosophy, fifteen.   Of the approximately three thousand, two hundred and forty-seven young men enrolled from 1825 to 1842 inclusive, the several schools were entitled to the following proportions: Mathematics, 1541; Natural Philosophy, 1122; Ancient Languages, 1112; Modern Languages, 976; Moral Philosophy, 804; Law, 705; Chemistry, 680; and Medicine, 630.   We are able, at a glance, to gauge the relative popularity of the different schools.   The School of Mathematics led the procession; the School of Medicine closed it,— the average annual attendance in the one was eighty-five students; in the other,

---

[1] This was the origin of the word "tickets" as applied to the different courses or schools

thirty-five.   During the period of seventeen years under review, the School of Medicine was at flood-tide in 1835–6, when fifty-five students were enrolled in it.   The attendance in the School of Law dwindled from seventy-two in 1839–40, to fifty-four in 1841–2; in the School of Ancient Languages, from one hundred and seven in 1825, when Professor Long occupied that chair, to thirty-nine, seventeen years later.   This decline was reflected in the School of Modern Languages, which fell from one hundred and thirty-six in 1838–9 to forty-eight in 1841–2. The figures for the School of Mathematics in 1836–7 and 1841–2 were, respectively, one hundred and thirty-five and forty-seven; for the School of Natural Philosophy in 1837–8 and 1841–2, one hundred and ten and forty-one; for the School of Chemistry in 1836–7 and 1841–2, seventy-five and thirty-six; and for that of Moral Philosophy in 1839–40 and 1841–2, seventy-eight and forty-six.   We shall be able to comprehend clearly the reasons for this temporary decay when we come to examine the other sides of the history of this period.

v. *School of Ancient Languages*

In the beginning, the rule was adopted that no student should be admitted to the School of Ancient Languages unless, in its professor's judgment, he was qualified to read the Latin and Greek classics of the advanced grades. It will be recalled that Jefferson was opposed to any portion of that professor's time being taken up in drilling a primary class, and it was partly the hope of devising a substitute which led him to advocate so earnestly the establishment of the intermediate district colleges.   So exacting was his standard for this preliminary training, that Chapman Johnson, his colleague on the Board of

Visitors, protested that he demanded that " the student should be a better scholar than most of our teachers before he shall enjoy the benefit of classical instruction in the University." " Whilst it is certainly proper," he added, " that the professor of ancient languages should not teach the elements, and should confine his attention to the higher aspects,— to critical dissertation on their beauties and defects, and to illustrations of their history, structure, genius, and philosophy,— yet care should be taken not to deprive too many of the benefits of his professorship by excluding those who lack attainments in the languages."

The only grades of instruction in Latin and Greek which Jefferson approved, disclose that he had really an advanced seat of learning in mind, whilst Johnson was satisfied that the new institution should occupy, in some of its important courses, the platform of an ordinary college. The superficiality in preparatory classical training, during these early years, was so great in the case of many of the students that the University was compelled to exercise some of the functions of a mere academy. A rigid test of admission to the School of Ancient Languages would have reduced the number of pupils to a very sensible degree, and its influence would, in consequence, have been very much contracted. It was to get around this that an elastic significance was given to the requirement that those entering should be familiar with the " higher works " of the Latin and Greek authors,— which was interpreted as meaning that the pupil had been carried through the *Metamorphosis* of Ovid, and the *Commentaries* of Cæsar, in the limited curriculum of a secondary private school, and was, therefore, qualified to be promoted to the next grade.

There were two influences that prevented the introduction of such unripe scholars from sinking the reputation of the chair.   The first was general, and also operative through a protracted series of years: it was the supreme attention that was paid to the senior classes at the very time that the junior were not neglected.   It was the senior classes in which the most fertilizing work was done; and it was this work, and not that of the junior classes, which gave the school its very high standing.   The other influence was the character for genuineness and thoroughness which the fruitful and contagious scholarship of Long stamped upon that school from the hour when its lecture-room was first thrown open; he was associated' with it during three years only; but he established for it a vivid tradition of exacting standards, which set a pace for its conduct that has never slackened throughout its history.   It was not his habit to deliver a formal expository lecture.   Generally at the meeting of his higher classes, he required one hundred lines from Virgil and Thucydides to be read, followed by translations from Horace or some other author, Greek or Latin; or he varied this programme by examinations in Greek or Latin grammar,— all answers being submitted in writing.   The grammatical constructions were illustrated by copious references to different authors   The students were directed to follow up each reference; and in doing so, they became familiar, not only with the special constructions which they verified, but with the general text of the authors thus used.   It was a course of study that called for close attention and indefatigable labor, " but," says Gessner Harrison, Long's most distinguished pupil, " it was most interesting."

Long commanded the respect but not the affection of all his pupils.   He was inclined to show his detestation of ignorance or shallowness in his classes, not by openly quarreling with the delinquents, but by quiet sarcasms that cut deep into the gristle of their conceit. No one, however, who was honestly concerned about his work, and endeavored to prepare for it with zeal and intelligence, was ever the victim of a severe reprimand, or even mild rebuke from him. Long was fully in harmony with Jefferson's thoughtful view, that the history and geography of a people should be studied simultaneously with its language. History, geography, language,— each formed a vital link in his comprehensive exposition of the two great courses embraced in his professorship. His capacity as a teacher was not confined to the instruction of University classes,— he drew up, at General Cocke's request, a plan for the education of Cocke's youngest son in the ancient languages, which brings out in the clearest light his practical insight into his calling down to the rudiments, as well as the thoughtful philosophy of his scholarship. The course which he was anxious for this boy to study was the one which he urged as necessary to the right preparation of every Virginian pupil who expected to enter the University after leaving the private school. How small was the knowledge of the Grecian tongue possessed by some of those who were admitted to his lowest class, was revealed in his statement that a youth who had read two books of Xenophon, with a teacher's assistance, in the manner which he had recommended for General Cocke's son, and had afterwards mastered the remaining books of that author, without such assistance, " would know more Greek than nine-tenths of the students who came to the University."

Gessner Harrison, Long's successor, caught his first inspiration from Long's example. In 1830, he divided the students in the Greek course into two classes. The first comprised those who were able to show a thorough

familiarity with Xenophon's *Anabasis* when they entered
the University.   The members of this class were, towards the end of the session, advanced to a play of Euripides, and, at the same time, grounded in metre and
prosody.   In the meanwhile, they had been required to
study the formation and composition of words.   The text
of each was illustrated by a running commentary on the
literature, arts, manners, customs, politics, and commerce
of that period; and also by the geographical divisions
which then existed.   The second class was composed of
the students who had passed the examinations of the first
year, or had entered the University equipped to pursue
the highest course in the language.   They began with
Herodotus, went on to a play of Euripides or Aeschylus,
and ended with the epic of the Iliad, and the dramas of
Sophocles and Aristophanes.   The fundamental qualities of these great writers; the differences in style which
distinguished each from the rest; and the light thrown
upon their text by contemporary history, literature, and
geography,— all were presented with care and thoroughness.

But Harrison was not satisfied with the work that was
done in his lecture-room   Not many authors could be
adequately treated within so limited a time.   He aimed
to inspire his pupils with such a thirsty taste for the language that they would ardently continue its study in their
dormitories by following out parallel courses of reading
in Thucydides, Plato, and the Athenian Orators, which
he had recommended, and which he himself undertook for
his own recreation   One who knew him in life [1] relates
that, among his vivid recollections of this venerated
teacher, was that of seeing him stretched at length on a
sofa as deeply absorbed in a Greek classic as some young

[1] Dr George Tucker Harrison, his son.

lady might be in the last sensational novel from the cir-
culating library.

His scheme of instruction in Latin followed exactly
the same line in general as it did in Greek.   The division
here was in two classes also.   The initial study of the first
class was confined to the satires of Horace and Juvenal, a
play of Terence, and certain *Epistles* of Cicero.   In the
meanwhile, tuition was given in prosody and metre, and
also a full description of the history, literature, religion,
civic and domestic institutions of the Roman people.   The
course of the second class embraced the *Epistles* of Horace
and the *De Arta Poetica,* the *Georgics* of Virgil, the plays
of Terence or Plautus, the *Annals* of Tacitus and the
Orations of Cicero.   The students of this class were made
familiar with the resources of the Roman Empire, its
colonial system, its military and civic establishments, its
arts, antiquities, commerce, and geographical divisions.
There was also, for their improvement, an exhaustive exposition of the principles of the language.   In the School
of Latin, as in that of Greek, they were urged and inspired to push their investigations beyond the normal tasks
of the classroom; and with that in view, specific courses
of reading were recommended to them in such authors as
Cicero, Livy, Lucretius, and Plautus, and in the *Epigrams*
of Martial.   A written translation of the text assigned
from day to day was expected of all; and, occasionally,
this translation had to be turned back into the original
tongue.   Harrison correctly looked upon this to be as
useful an exercise in teaching the English language as in
teaching the Latin or Greek; and the benefit which he
thus conferred on his students was one of the most fruitful that sprang from his memorable career as an instructor.

In 1836, the two classes of the Latin and Greek languages respectively came to be designated as senior and junior as more representative of their real character. Hebrew formed a part of this important school; but the demand for tuition in it seems never to have been sufficient to call together even a small number of pupils. Although Harrison had been so recently trained by one of the most competent of English classical scholars, he soon fell under the influence of the German method expounded in the first part of Bopp's epochal grammar, issued in 1833, a copy of which he received from Long. Bopp compared the Sanscrit language with the languages, not only of Ancient Europe, but of Modern.   He was the pioneer in that illuminating field of research.   Harrison was young enough to be susceptible to the spirit of innovation; and he seems to have seized upon Bopp's ideas with the most intelligent eagerness.   He introduced comparative etymology into his courses at a time when it was held in small esteem in the other institutions of England and America, and when it was neglected even in Germany itself.   In spite of the fact that the burden of his professorial tasks left him but slim leisure for gathering original data, he was able, by his own gleanings, to collect enough to form the basis of his excellent Latin Grammar.   This book was given by an American student to Curtius, the most celebrated master of comparative etymology then alive.   Curtius read it.   " This is a good book," he said, when returning it, " an excellent book for the time it appeared."

Harrison's manner of studying classical syntax has been pronounced by capable scholars to be, for its day, of very striking originality.   He rejected the deductive method of the German school and adopted the inductive. Having garnered and analyzed a mass of facts, he drew from them definite principles which appeared to comprehend them all; and using these principles like a chemical test, sought, through them, to offer a satisfactory explanation of such facts as subsequently fell under his notice. His enthusiasm in this work of exposition is illustrated by an anecdote that was told of him. A friend, who was as keenly interested as himself in philology, dropped in to dinner. When Harrison entered the room, he was so bursting with his last discovery, that he could scarcely stop long enough to thank the Lord for the meal. "I think I have found it, sir," he exclaimed, "I am about sure I have got the true explanation of meta in the sense of after."

We are indebted to Dr. John A. Broadus, one of his pupils, for a graphic description of his style as a lecturer: "He had not a ready command of expression, and his first statements of an idea were often partial, involved, and obscure. But he perfectly knew,— a thing not very common,— when he had, and when he had not, made himself clear. He would, by variety of expression searching for the right word or phrase, approach the thought from different directions, gradually closing in till he seized it; and when he reached his final expression, it was vigorous, clear, and complete. Then he would watch his audience with lively interest, and if he saw many clouded faces, would repeat his process with all manner of illustrations and iterations, till at last the greater part of them could see clearly."[1]   It was not very often that he,— who never joked with his class, though pleasantly familiar with them,— indulged in that form of pedagogical oratory which the collegians somewhat irreverently, but quite picturesquely, spoke of as "curling." But on

[1] "Under his original treatment," says Professor Francis H. Smith, a pupil, "the laws of syntax came to appear to us as a beautiful branch of practical psychology, and we finished our Latin and Greek courses loving those languages"

one occasion, he allowed himself to be so warmed up by his interest in his subject as to rise to a remarkable height of moving utterance   A student among those present who was listening, slowly turned his head and sarcastically winked at his neighbor.   The Doctor observed the act, and abruptly stopped in the full career of his discourse.   In the midst of an appalling silence, he then said, " Gentlemen, while I was trying in my poor way to set forth a historical fact, my effort provoked derision from one gentleman.   I am sorry that I failed to awaken his interest, and secure his respect "   The delinquent, so soon as the class was dismissed, offered a full apology.

But Harrison, as we have stated, was not often disposed to imitate his colleague, William B Rogers, distinguished far and wide for vivid eloquence in the classroom.   So unceasing was the labor imposed upon him by the duties of his double professorship, piled up on those of the chairmanship, which he so long occupied, that he was occasionally rather somnolent in giving his customary instruction.   On a certain day, he was lecturing to his Latin class, and there was a sudden halt in the current of his exposition,— the professor had dropped asleep,— but opening his eyes with a start, he excused himself to his pupils for his drowsiness, and, refreshed, resumed his subject with his normal vigor.

VI. *School of Modern Languages*

The course in modern languages was placed by Jefferson on a footing of equal dignity with the course in ancient.   This was an innovation that demonstrated, like so many of his educational convictions, his penetration into the future and his uncommon modernity of spirit. James Russell Lowell has recorded that, as late as his own youth, the French and German tongues were taught in so great an institution as Harvard by the professor who gave contemporaneous lessons in dancing and fiddling! Jefferson had a thorough relish for the beauty of the Grecian classics, but it was in the literature of Rome that he seems to have found the most unfailing pleasure, if the constant presence of Latin books at his elbow can be taken as a proof. And yet he early perceived that a modern language might have a value lying outside of its mere literary flavour. Being at bottom a statesman, a political philosopher, a civic prophet, he was clearly aware that all the powerful nations would, in time, be drawn into more intimate relations with each other than then existed; and that a knowledge of alien tongues would thus come to have a practical importance in its bearing upon the welfare of the American people. As education in general was expected by him to promote all the qualifications of true citizenship, so expertness in the principal languages of Continental Europe was, in his opinion, calculated to equip the American mind with a more correct understanding of international dangers and responsibilities. In other words, he was thinking, not only of the cultural and literary advantages to the individual of mastering those tongues, but also of the broader gain of turning that knowledge to the international profit of his countrymen.

Whatever may have been the personal defects of Professor Blaettermann, his acquirements as a linguist were indisputable. The School of Modern Languages, of which he was the first head, embraced courses in French, German, Spanish, Italian, and Anglo-Saxon; but he also announced that he was prepared to give lessons in the vernacular of Denmark, Sweden, Holland, and Portugal.

Like his colleague, Long, he was hampered by the necessity of teaching numerous pupils who had to be instructed in the lower grades, but his impatience, unlike Long's, vented itself, not in veiled sarcasm, but in naked brusqueness.   On one occasion, he ridiculed so roughly the exercise of a student who had just begun to learn the French language, that the outraged young man rose angrily from his seat and told him flatly to his face that he would refuse to write another.   The class in Spanish numbered as many as forty members, and yet he attempted to teach them all with three copies of a single grammar.   It was in protest against this sort of eccentricity, or else his chronic rudeness, that many of his own pupils patronized a private French school that was opened, in 1827, in the vicinity of Charlottesville.   Three years afterwards, at the instance of Madison and Chapman Johnson, the addition of a tutorship to his chair was debated by the Board, either because the courses of instruction were too extensive for one lecturer, or because the dissatisfaction with him had grown too acute to be overlooked.   The latter explanation seems to be the most plausible, for the proposal aroused his vigorous opposition,— it was said that he was thrown into a " fidget," for, on the one hand, he was threatened with degradation if he consented, and on the other, with collisions with the tutor, should the two have any difficulty in adjusting their respective functions.   The tutorship was established in the teeth of his repugnance to the change; but he appears to have been conciliated by the assignment of the junior to such duties only as the senior should specify.

In 1832, it was concluded that the subjects of the School of Modern Languages were too numerous to require that graduation in all should be necessary for the acquisition of a diploma.   The course was, during this year, divided into two classes; the Romance and the Teutonic. There were, in the instance of each, a junior and a senior year. The literatures of all the four nations embraced were the topics of tri-weekly lectures, while modern history, and the political relations of the principal countries, were also fully discussed in a separate course. The members of each class were furthermore permitted to receive private instruction in any one, or in all of the tongues taught in the school, on condition that it should be given by a native Frenchman or Italian, Spaniard, or German, who was willing to be governed by the rules laid down for him by the Faculty.

Jefferson, when he provided for an English section in the School of Modern Languages, seems to have had only the Anglo-Saxon branch in view; and he acknowledged that one of the main benefits which he expected to accrue from its study was the information about the principles of free government that was thus to be obtained. While, it is true, that belles-lettres and rhetoric formed, after 1830, a part of the School of Moral Philosophy,— which was in charge of Tucker, the most accomplished English scholar among the professors,— nevertheless the English language was the one great language which was neglected in the University's round of instruction. Jefferson, as we have already remarked, was well versed in the classics, and his letters and state papers prove him to have been an excellent writer in his native tongue; but he seems to have given slim attention to English literature,— a fact that has left a lasting impression upon the University of Virginia, so far as it has had any influence on the literary productiveness of the South. The early professors,— such as Dunglison, Key, Long, and Bonnycastle from England, and Emmet, Tucker, and Lomax from the United States,— were men who put a high value upon the study of the English language; and they were disposed to criticize the deficiencies in that study which lowered the institution in their day. " If the means of the University were more independent than they seem to be," Lomax wrote to Cocke, in 1828, " a professorship might be established, which there is many a clergyman well qualified to fill, if not in this country, in England. I mean a professorship of English literature, comprehending in it the study of the English language in its origin, its history, its character, a critical knowledge of its best writers, composition, and elocution. Such a professorship would be of incalculable utility; and would save the University from the disgrace which is reflected upon it by the ignorance of English literature which is to be discovered among some of our best students."

Lomax voiced the conviction of his own, and of a later time, too, in thus criticizing the absence of facilities for the study of the English tongue in a seat of learning, which had a right, in all other particulars, to claim the broad self-designation of university. In July, 1839, the Board of Visitors became aware,— apparently for the first time,— that this neglect was seriously damaging the reputation of the institution; and the Faculty were instructed to appoint a committee to find out the means of correcting it. The plan reported, in the following November, recommended that all the students should be divided into sections, and that each section should be placed under the supervision of a professor. Every student should be required to send in to the head of his section a monthly composition at least two pages in length. The compositions of each section, thus periodically accumulated, were to be carefully examined by its presiding professor, and those laid on one side as the best were to be handed in to the Faculty. The students who had failed to write, or had written with culpable slovenliness, were to be reported at the same time to the same body. As might have been predicted, this laborious scheme of stimulating skill in English composition was promptly tabled by the Faculty and was not afterwards heard of. The members of that body, as a whole, no doubt, thought that they were already sufficiently burdened by the demands of their regular classes.

In 1840, the new University periodical, *The Collegian,*— which was founded nominally to create for the students a field in which to learn how to write their native tongue with correctness and elegance,—complained that, in consequence of the fact that no provision was made in the courses of instruction for either composition or elocution, the graduates left the precincts with the wide province of English literature unexplored, and as ignorant of its history as when they were admitted. "There is a dearth of literary taste among them," it asserted, "and they are lamentably deficient in some of the very important parts of a liberal education." That this flaw went as far as grammar and orthography, was annually brought out in the failure of so many of the members of the senior classes to pass the English examination, to which they had to submit before they were permitted to offer for graduation in any of the regular schools. During many years, apart from lectures in Anglo-Saxon, rhetoric, and belles-lettres,— which were, of necessity, contracted in their scope, because they were simply the by-play of already overburdened chairs,— the only training in English composition which the major number of the students enjoyed was obtained from translations in the Schools of Ancient and Modern Languages; but they had no means whatever in these schools of acquiring information of English literature, although every facility was offered for perfecting their knowledge of the literatures of Spain and Italy, Germany and France, as well as of Greece and Rome.

VII. *Schools of Mathematics and Philosophy*

By the terms of the original enactments, no student was to be admitted to the School of Mathematics who was not "an adept in all the branches of numerical arithmetic." The whole round of instruction was divided into four classes. The first junior was occupied with the theory of designating numbers, the scales of notation, the derivation of the several arithmetical rules, and the first problems of algebra, analyzed with and without the use of letters to show the advantages of employing letters. The second junior continued the study of algebra, and began the study of geometry, and also of general trigonometry in its broadest applications. Spherical trigonometry was treated at length in its relations to practical and nautical astronomy and the projection and construction of maps. Then followed analytical geometry and the first part of differential calculus. The senior classes were engaged with the study of differential and integral calculus. There was also an extensive course in mixed mathematics.

In counting up the general subjects in which he gave instruction, Bonnycastle, Key's successor, particularized them as " (1) those simple elementary rules which do not aim to cultivate the powers of reasoning independently of numbers, but seek only to determine such numbers as occur in domestic economy, and the various departments of business; (2) those very general, extensive, and exact rules, of the nature of logic, which have suf-

ficed to reduce three-fourths of the propositions of which
the human reason is conversant, to propositions either
of pure number, or that can be solved by means of pure
number; (3) those rules of mere calculation which are
required in such branches of practical mathematics as
surveying, navigation, and astronomy." It was the second of these sections that was studied with the most
care in the University, because it bore so directly on general education by the enlargement of view which it fostered, and the more active exercise of intellect, and the
greater disposition to reason, which it encouraged.

It was altogether in harmony with Jefferson's practical and liberal mind that scientific studies should, apart
from other good reasons, have been held in esteem by
him because of the special qualities which they called for
in their prosecution   Experimental investigation has
been correctly described as a course in applied logic.   It
signifies accuracy in sense, perception, and calculation;
reveals the rigid relation of cause and effect; and reflects
an intellectual attitude that is free from the distracting
bias of prejudice, false pretension, and superstition.[1]
Jefferson's early environment in the remote country had
made him from youth a student of nature in all its
aspects; and this disposition, natural and acquired, had
been invigorated by his sojourn in France at a time when
experimental science was deeply interesting the inquiring
minds of that aroused nation.   There were chairs dedicated to the science in the Universities of Paris, Toulouse
and Montpelier.   The establishment of the Republic
only served to stimulate the more its pursuit in every
department.   The study of it on its mathematical and
physical sides had received an impetus in the English uni-

---

[1] There is an admirable discourse on this phase of experimental investigation by President Smith of Washington and Lee University (1920).

versities from the marvellous researches of Newton; but there was no course there in biology, and no employment of the modern scientific methods, until after the middle of the nineteenth century,— indeed, what is known in our own day as scientific education sprang up in England outside of the pale of her two greatest seats of learning, Oxford and Cambridge.

From an early period, scientific studies had been popular in all the influential American colleges.   Astronomy was taught at Harvard in 1642, and natural philosophy, in 1690; and instruction was also given there in chemistry, in 1760, and in botany about the same time.   King's College and the University of Pennsylvania, being purely secular in their organization, were disposed to encourage such studies with uncommon ardour.   By 1756, the latter had established courses in applied mechanics, astronomy, natural history, chemistry, and agriculture.   Chemistry formed a valuable part of the system at the College of William and Mary, in 1779, and there was a separate professorship for it at Princeton in 1795; at Yale, in 1802; at the College of South Carolina, in 1811; and at Williams College, in 1821   We thus see that, by the day lectures began in the University of Virginia, the study of the sciences had made respectable progress in all the American institutions of the highest grade, chiefly because there was a special need for such studies in a new country in the first stages of rapid development from the original state of nature.

The elective system, which has always prevailed at the University of Virginia, was more vigorously promotive of scientific courses than the curriculum of the older colleges   The popularity of such courses has arisen, in no small measure, from their direct bearing on vocational life.   It is not their disciplinary influence upon the mind

which gives them their principal value, but rather the
practical information which they impart; and it is this
sort of information which has always seemed the most
desirable in the opinion of the average American.   The
ascendency of the scientific studies dates, in the United
States at least, from the spread of the elective system,—
which the University of Virginia was the first to adopt
as a system appropriate to every subject in the round of
its instruction.

The School of Natural Philosophy was only open to
those students who had passed a successful examination
in numerical arithmetic.   During Key's occupancy of the
chair of mathematics, Bonnycastle delivered lectures on
the relations of mathematical science to natural philosophy, but after Key's resignation, Patterson, the new professor,— Bonnycastle having been transferred to Key's
vacant place,— was restricted to pure physics.   Upon
him also devolved the duty of showing the application of
physical science to the arts, which was justly considered
of the first importance in a country endowed with so
many natural sources of wealth, requiring a scientific
education for their utilization.   In 1828, the small oval
room situated on the first floor of the Rotunda was reserved for the reception of the philosophical apparatus.
The proper manner of safeguarding these invaluable articles was a perplexing one from the start,— when they
fell into bad shape, they had either to be sent to Philadelphia or New York for restoration, or skilful workmen
from those cities had to be brought on for that purpose
to the University, both of which courses of action inevitably caused delay and expense.   It was proposed, in
1826, that "two intelligent and willing lads" should be
trained to handle these instruments and repair the damage sure to result from wear and tear.   These lads too

were to be employed, instead of the janitor, to assist the professor with his experiments in the lecture-room. Apparently, this suggestion was not carried into practice, since no further reference to the plan is recorded. The course of instruction in this school was divided into two sections: the first embraced statics, dynamics, hydrostatics, hydro-dynamics, pneumatics, crystallization, molecular and capillary attraction, strength and stress of materials, and acoustics; the second, heat, electricity, galvanism, magnetism, electric magnetism, optics, and astronomy. The lectures in both sections were illustrated and enforced by experiments. During the session of 1839–40, the sciences of geology and mineralogy were transferred to this school. It was the relation of geology to our own country which received the foremost consideration; and only those branches of mineralogy were taught which had an economical value, or which merged in geology. '

The interest in natural history felt by all the American colleges had grown so keen by 1817, that it swelled to the volume of an academic craze. The collections of plants and minerals in their possession were already remarkable for size and value. As early as 1825, the University of Virginia had become the recipient of some of the fruits of this mania as exhibited by private individuals: Dr. Boswell, of Gloucester county, during that year, donated to it two large boxes of minerals which he had obtained in Germany; and Jefferson, by his last will, followed up this gift with his own museum of curiosities. In the beginning, the professor of natural history was charged with the tuition in chemistry, botany, zoology, mineralogy, geology, and rural economy. To him was also assigned the creation of the botanical garden to which Jefferson gave so much inquiring thought during the last months of his life; he had gone so far, indeed, as to instruct Emmet to lay off its various lines; and the proctor had been directed to supply the hired laborers who were to prepare the beds for the numerous plants. Every plant was to be of a useful, and not an ornamental, character. The area selected for the garden was irregular in surface and strewn with the débris of the brick-kilns. A hill had to be terraced, and the grounds along a branch underdrained.

Emmet seems to have looked upon the project with impatience, although, it will be recalled, he was so soon to experiment at Morea, his home, with so much ardour, in the same province. In October, 1826,— Jefferson having passed away,— he asserted that the requirements of his chair were so laborious and so exclusive that he would be unable to give the garden the protracted and discriminating attention which was imperative; and moreover, he acknowledged that botany and rural economy were sciences with which he was only "superficially acquainted"; that they demanded a "thorough practical knowledge"; and that this could only be gathered up at the expense of his other duties. At his request, the Board of Visitors relieved him of the task of establishing the garden   They were either convinced that the School of Natural History contained too many subjects for instruction by one man, or they perceived that some of these subjects, being unpopular with the students, could be safely dropped from the course, for, at their meeting in July, 1827, they confined Emmet, for the present at least, to chemistry, materia medica, and pharmacy, and directed that the school thereafter should be known as the School of Chemistry and Materia Medica. If any instruction in any branch of natural history was given by him before 1836, it was suspended, after that date, as inconsistent with the proper discharge of his obligation to his leading topics.   The same obstruction discouraged the transfer of the main divisions of this science to any other of the chairs, but, as we have seen, geology and mineralogy became, in 1839–40, a part of the course in natural philosophy.   The Board of Visitors, however, were fully aware of the need of the original school to complete the required round of the academical department; " but its introduction," they declared, " cannot be advantageously effected without the establishment of a separate professorship, accompanied by its appropriate attributes,— a botanical garden and a museum of mineral and geological collections. . . . The Visitors are prevented from carrying out these views by the want of sufficient funds and by the existence of debts acquired for more useful purposes."

In the beginning, the School of Moral Philosophy embraced the subjects of ethics and metaphysics; but, in 1826, political economy was added to the chair; and in 1830, rhetoric and belles-lettres, which had previously been taught in the School of Ancient Languages.   During the first half of the session, the junior class received instruction in rhetoric, belles-lettres, and logic, and the senior in mental philosophy; during the last half, the junior class was occupied with belles-lettres and ethics, and the senior with political economy.   There were also lessons in English composition; but they reached too small a number to be of benefit to the entire body of the students.

VIII. *School of Law*

It would seem that, at first, the School of Law, like the School of Medicine, in the University of Virginia, was

designed to open up to its students the means of obtaining
the broadest education rather than mere professional
knowledge for practical use in earning a livelihood. We
have seen how keenly interested, if not fanatical, Jefferson was in prescribing the text-books to be taught on the
political side of that school. In 1829, a conviction
sprang up that the chair of law should be reorganized
in order to meet more fully the needs of such young men
as intended to become active members of the bar. The
imputation had been cast upon it, that, whilst other prominent colleges embraced all the subjects of professional
jurisprudence in the studies of one session, the courses
of the school at the University of Virginia were so extensive that properly two sessions should be consumed in
mastering them. This was a stumbling block to the student who was compelled, by a narrow income, to confine his preparation to one session. In order to remove
it, the course of the first session was made an epitome
of all the important branches of municipal law. This put
the student of the University school who wished to has-
ten, or whose income was small, on the footing of the
students of the schools in other States. Should he decide
to remain during a second session, he would have the principles learnt by him during the first more profoundly
analyzed and more voluminously diversified in their application.

Lomax was not, by his previous training, in sympathy
with the spirit which made this alteration unavoidable;
but he candidly acknowledged to Cabell that he had hardly
entered upon his duties when he perceived that it was
beyond the Visitors' power to force down the throats of
his pupils a system of legal instruction that was distasteful to them   " The day has gone by," he wrote in 1830,
" when any person was ashamed to appear at the bar

under a period of less than three years' study. The necessities of some, and the impatience of others, urge most modern students into their profession after one year's study, or at most, two years'. They are eager that the period shall be devoted to such instruction as may practically fit them for their profession. Their demand for the law is as for a trade,— the means, the most expeditious and convenient, for their future livelihood. I found myself irresistibly compelled to labor for the satisfaction of this demand, or that the University would have no students of law. . . . I have selected what, after much deliberation, I deemed the most approved and suitable English text-books."

This list consisted of (1) Blackstone's *Commentaries,* (2) Cruise's *Law of Real Property;* (3) Selwyn's *Abstract of the Law of Nisi Primus,* and (4) Muddock's *Chancery.*

In the lectures which Lomax delivered on the principles set forth in these volumes, he cited, as supplementary to the text, numerous dicta found in the appellate reports, not only of Virginia, but also of all the other States of the Union. As a complement to this professional course, which formed the normal work of the school, he recommended to the Faculty the adoption of what he designated as an "academic course of law." This should treat of American jurisprudence in its broadest scope. With this new branch added, he was convinced that the facilities for legal education at the University would be unsurpassed. The Faculty, in their turn, recommended it to the Board of Visitors.

There were, at this time, several causes for discouragement which tended to reduce the number of pupils in the School of Law. First, the regulation that subjected the students of every school indiscriminately to public exam-

inations, and then, as a supposed reward for tested efficiency, required that the names of the successful should
be published in the newspapers. Lomax declared that
the young men under him had, as a rule, arrived at that
period of life when they disdained the prizes which
these examinations held out to boyish emulation; but
above all, they deprecated the effect upon their own standing at the bar,— which they would so soon join,— of a
failure to obtain these prizes, however much they might,
in reality, contemn them. Secondly, the uniform was
offensive to older students such as made up the membership of his classes. Many of them had entered the University only for a single year, and their expenses were
sensibly increased by the necessity of purchasing new
suits of clothing for use only during a few months.
Thirdly, it was revolting to his pupils' self-respect that
they should be expected to submit to the patron's financial guidance at an age when, in the eyes of the law, they
were mature enough to manage their own affairs, and
dispose of their own money. " Invested with this competence by law and sustained by the consciousness of his
own powers," he asserted, " the student at that period
of life when unnecessary restraint is particularly irksome,
was required to live within the precincts, and living there,
was denied all discretion in his minutest pecuniary con-
cerns; was compelled to put his purse in the hands of the
proctor, and to pay him for keeping it out of its unfortunate owner's reach." Lomax counseled that every pupil
in the School of Law above a specified age should be permitted to reside in an approved boarding-house situated
beyond the precincts; and that he should also be relieved
from all pertinency to himself of the regulation so justly
excepted to. This wise recommendation was adopted by
the Board, with the result that the worst grounds of

complaint were done away with for all those students of
law who were willing to vacate their dormitories.

Whilst Lomax was as inflexible as his successor, Davis,
in advocating a strict interpretation of the Constitution,
— a conviction held by him as a disciple of Jefferson and
Madison,— nevertheless he did not give as much time as
Davis did to the exposition of that part of his course
which embraced those principles of government that were
of such keen and fundamental interest to his great exemplars.   In the junior course as taught by Davis, after
Lomax's resignation, there were comprised numerous subjects which were, not only necessary to be studied for
practice at the bar, but, owing to their universal significance, were also of the highest value as the solid ingre-
dients of a liberal education,— such subjects were the
law of nature and nations, the science of government,
constitutional law, the history of the common law, and
the elementary principles of criminal and municipal law.
The text-books of this class were *Vattel*, the *Federalist*,
Resolutions of 1798–99, Blackstone's *Commentaries*, and
a treatise by Davis himself.   The attention of the senior
class was concentrated upon the theory and practice of
law as a profession, as illustrated in different works on
common and statute law, equity, maritime, and commer-
cial law.   In 1833, there was organized a law society,
the members of which, at first, assembled, at regular intervals, in the basement of pavilion VII, but afterwards
in one of the lecture-rooms of the Rotunda.

IX. *School of Medicine and Anatomy*

When the medical school at the University of Virginia
opened its doors, there were already to be found in other
parts of the United States the like schools, which during

many years, had been in the enjoyment of a large and lucrative patronage. The most popular of these were situated in Boston, New Haven, New York, Philadelphia, and Baltimore,— cities standing north of the Potomac, and, therefore, for Southern young men so far away as to entail both expense and discomfort in reaching them. Many Southerners of fortune, desirous of a medical education, turned their footsteps towards London and Edinburgh; but the greater number sought the offices of local surgeons of repute, who gave their lessons in the intervals when they were not riding about the country or town in order to visit their patients,— a provincial system that had its exact counterpart in the training which so many callow lawyers of the South were receiving during the same period.

Jefferson, in forecasting a medical school for his projected institution, certainly took into account the loss and the inconvenience which the Southern communities had so long suffered from the absence of such a school. The need of it, indeed, was too patent to be blinked. But when the chair at the University was established, no measure was adopted by him to convert it at once into a practical one; its chief aim, at first, was not to give a professional education, but simply instruction in a branch of liberal culture which every accomplished gentleman was presumed to have studied. He held this view solely because he was under the impression that, in the absence of all clinical facilities, the lessons of the new school must be confined to mere theory. Charlottesville was a small village; the contiguous region was rather sparsely inhabited; and the jolting conveyances of that day shut off invalids who might have come from a distance. There was no material to justify the erection of a hospital, and without a hospital, how was it possible to qualify students for active practice after leaving the University?   At one time, Jefferson seems to have thought that this obstacle could be got over by transferring ·the school, not to· Richmond, but to Norfolk, where he expected that the promiscuous and vagabond population of a seaport would furnish a plenitude of anatomical subjects for dissection, an extraordinary number and variety of diseases for observation, and many accidents for surgical operations   He was compelled to acknowledge that, until such clinical facilities could be created, those of his medical students who wished to practice must seek the finishing touch in institutions situated in other parts of the country.   It was his recognition of this grave handicap which prompted him to block the perfectly legitimate plan of the College of William and Mary to re-establish itself in Richmond, and to associate there with its existing departments an additional department in practical medicine.   Jefferson anticipated that this combination would be the ruin of his own school, or at least would so throw that school into the shade as to bring it into public discredit; which, in its turn, would lower the prestige of the entire University.   It is disputable whether this would have followed; but Jefferson was honestly apprehensive of it.

In the beginning, the course of study embraced the subjects of anatomy, surgery, the history of the progress and theories of medicine, physiology, pathology, materia medica, and pharmacy.   Ostensibly, there was but one teacher in charge of the school, but in reality, there were two, for Emmet, as the professor of natural history, gave instruction in the medical subjects of chemistry, botany, and comparative anatomy, while Dunglison lectured to the classes in anatomy and medicine.

After Jefferson's death, there was a natural disposition on the part of those in charge of the medical school to advertise its unique course of theoretical tuition as offering certain advantages that counterbalanced its practical deficiencies It was pointed out, for instance, that, in all other colleges, the medical instruction did not extend beyond a term of six months at most, while, in the University of Virginia, it was spread out over nine at least.   Furthermore, in the sister colleges, the medical professors were permitted to go on with their practice; in the University, on the other hand, this distracting privilege was denied them beyond its precincts, unless they were simply called into consultation.   The only object of this exception seems to have been to give the instructors of the school a wider opportunity to become familiar with the characteristic diseases of the climate and country.[1]

The Board of Visitors had soon perceived the benefit that would follow from the establishment of a separate chair of anatomy and surgery; and they were only prevented from making this addition at once by the necessity of paying the University's debt, now that the General Assembly had positively refused to assume it.   As the most practical step, they determined to shift some of the studies of Dunglison's school to the shoulders of Emmet, who, with that purpose in view, was relieved of a large part of the course in natural history, as we have already stated; but this was not done until July 19, 1827, when materia medica and pharmacy were taken from Dunglison and assigned to him.   One motive for this important change comes to light in a conversation which took place between Cabell and Dr. Chapman, of

[1] In 1825, Dr Dunglison was permitted to teach a small number of private pupils Minutes of Board of Visitors, Dec. 11, 1825

Philadelphia, early in the spring of that year. It seems that Dr. Chapman had, on this occasion, intimated that, if the University of Virginia would appoint a second professor in its medical school, the University of Pennsylvania might be willing to accept a course of medical lectures there as equivalent, for graduation, to one course in her own lecture-halls. Cabell, on his return to Virginia, found that both Emmet and Dunglison warmly approved of this tentative proposal, and he, therefore, wrote to Dr. Chapman to obtain the formal sanction of the University of Pennsylvania "I would willingly call home and educate here all our medical students," he said in this letter. "In a long time to come, however, every such effort would be abortive, and the wiser course seems to be to cooperate with institutions already organized in other States, and possessing the peculiar advantages of large cities and extensive hospitals. The practical result of the change now contemplated in our medical school will be to draw to it, in the first instance, some of the more wealthy medical students of Virginia, and to send them on much better prepared than they are generally at present. As our society advances and our population augments, we may gradually become more and more independent of foreign assistance."

It would seem that the University of Pennsylvania did not sanction Dr. Chapman's proposition until June, 1829; but that institution had no reason afterwards to regret this liberal policy. "I was told some time ago by a medical student of Philadelphia," R Y. Conrad wrote to Dr. Magill, "that the medical school of your University (University of Virginia) stands there in high estimation, and that the students of one year from your University school almost invariably graduate in Philadelphia the second year at the head of their classes, being much better prepared in the science than if they had attended the first year at Philadelphia."

In July, 1827, a demonstrator of anatomy and surgery was appointed with the understanding that his duties were to be defined by the professor of medicine. The new instructor was required to teach what was technically entitled particular anatomy, in contradistinction to general anatomy, and also operative surgery as distinguished from surgical pathology. Upon him also fell the task of forming an anatomical museum in illustration of the courses in physiological and pathological anatomy. The departments of the medical school stood now as follows: (1) professorship of medicine, which comprised all the courses in the history of the progress and theories of medicine, physiology, pathology, obstetrics, and medical jurisprudence; (2) professorship of chemistry, materia medica, and pharmacy; and (3) the recently erected demonstratorship of anatomy and surgery. The only two branches of study that had been added to those previously taught were obstetrics and medical jurisprudence.

In 1830, Dr. Johnson, the demonstrator, was asked by some of his own students, backed by citizens of Charlottesville, to deliver a series of lectures on the subject of dentistry, a department of surgery which was then ordinarily abandoned to ignorant itinerants. There were several of his pupils who had made up their minds to follow the practice of this science as a vocation in life; but Johnson refused to bring it into his existing round of studies unless a class of at least ten could be formed, and apparently that number failed to offer.

At first, the demonstrator did not enjoy the privilege of a seat at the Faculty table; but within a few years after his original appointment, he was admitted to its deliberations, with the right to cast a vote on a footing of equality with his associates.   One of the difficulties confronting him, in these early times, was the procurement of cadavers for expository dissection.   Those picked up were generally the corpses of negro slaves, and in many instances had been snatched away by students under the blanket of darkness; but some of the subjects were white, and had been brought from a distance; in November, 1831, permission was granted to six medical students to go as far as Prince George county on what was described as an "anatomical expedition."   An excursion of this kind to the cemeteries around the University always bristled with serious risks.   A student taking part in one, in 1831, was shot while in the act of raising a body from the grave.   The members of the demonstrator's class very frequently joined in contracting for shares in a cadaver, which, in 1833, at least, does not appear to have been expensive, for we find, in that year, five students subscribing only three dollars and a half a-piece for an equal proportion in such a subject   At this time, there was a small brick building standing in the little ravine situated just below the anatomical theatre, which was used as a boiling house for the dissipation of the remnants of the dissecting table.   In 1832, the demonstratorship was merged in the chair of anatomy and surgery, a new department.   Physiology was transferred to this professorship two years later.

As the number of students in the medical school did not increase, the popular impression spread that this lack of success was due to the provincial remoteness of the University.   In 1834, Dr. Magill, in a letter to Cabell, after voicing this conviction in incisive language, boldly asked whether the Board of Visitors would consent to the school's removal to Richmond, where it would be in possession of every clinical facility enjoyed by its Northern rivals. It was nearly impossible, he said, to impart at Charlottesville knowledge of practical anatomy, in spite of the fact that the class was still so small that each member could be personally reached,— (1) the procurement of cadavers at all was so costly at best that the expense thrown upon the medical student, in consequence, was fast mounting; and the supply came to an end altogether when a long spell of wet or harsh weather set in; (2) the absence of a hospital shut the medical students off from the illustrations of different maladies, and prevented the acquisition of practical skill in the use of the surgeon's knife. "No amount of closet study, no book learning," exclaimed Dr. Magill, "can qualify a man to contend with disease." The room for practice at the University, he added, was too narrow to afford either profit or improvement to its medical professors. Without opportunities of treating cases belonging to their respective branches, neither the surgeon nor the physician could become an entirely satisfactory expositor. Richmond possessed a large hospital and also a poor-house, and as a medical school would soon be founded there, the corresponding department in the University was certain to be damaged, even if it should not be totally destroyed.

Dr. Warner, a colleague of Dr. Magill, fully concurred in these views; but apparently, Dr. Emmet was averse to the proposed change of location.

About three years afterwards, Dr. Warner again advised that the medical school should be uprooted and transplanted to Richmond. He condemned its present working for two reasons: first, each professor was expected to lecture upon more courses that he could teach with thoroughness; and secondly, the demonstrator was too much pressed for time to be able to improve the means of dissection. He urged that the school should be divided into four courses: (1) anatomy and surgery; (2) medicine, embracing the theories and classifications of diseases; (3) physiology, pathological anatomy, and medical jurisprudence; (4) chemistry, materia medica, therapeutics, and pharmacy. Dr. Griffith emphasized the need of anatomical and clinical facilities on the ground. The first could be secured by the appointment of an agent in Richmond who could forward weekly by wagon four or five cadavers. But he thought that it was not practical to erect a hospital. In 1825, a dispensary had been established as an adjunct to the Anatomical Hall. The single professor of the school, at that time, lingered half an hour after lecture, on alternate days, to give medical and surgical assistance to the indigent without charge, and at the rate of fifty cents a person for all patients who were able to pay it. The medical students were required to attend and assist in diagnosis and ministration. The money accumulated from fees was expended in the purchase of the necessary supply of drugs. This dispensary was of such small dimensions, and was so devoid of clinical advantages, that the professors of the medical school refused to look upon it as even a moderate substitute for a hospital.

So acute was the alarm caused about 1837 by the rumor of an independent school of medicine to be set up in Richmond that the Board of Visitors were impelled to take steps to allay it by improving the medical course at the University. As the institution was not in possession of sufficient means to build a hospital, even if it could be supported by the limited patronage which it would receive at so distant a point, it occurred to them that something in its stead could be effected by adding another professorship. And this, perhaps, would have been done, had not Dr. Dunglison, who was now living in Philadelphia, when consulted, expressed hostility to the proposition on the ground that a fourth chair would not increase the facilities for dissection and hospital service,— the only deficiencies against which there was a just cause for complaint. He was inclined to deprecate any alteration in the system as adopted in the beginning. "One of the great advantages of the University of Virginia as a medical school for a first year," he said, " is that the student is not overburdened with lectures, and has plenty of time to study the various subjects. This recommendation of the school I frequently hear." He, therefore, very emphatically advised that supplementary subjects should be taught without calling in the assistance of a fourth professor; and this counsel seems to have impressed the Board of Visitors favorably, for, during the ensuing session, the requirements for the existing school became more extensive and more elaborate. Dr. Emmet lectured to two classes on chemistry and materia medica, and twice a week he demonstrated the practical application of chemistry to pharmacy and medicine. Dr. Griffith gave instruction on the subject of medicine. His courses also were divided into two classes: (1) theory and practice of medicine and obstetrics, and (2) medical jurisprudence. Dr. Cabell filled the chair of anatomy, physiology, and surgery. His instruction was made more lucid by the use of splendid colored plates which had been procured from Paris.

The depression prevailing in 1836 and 1837 over the prospects of the medical school, in competition with the projected school at Richmond, had, by the session of 1839–40 passed away; the cheerful attitude of an earlier date had returned; and there was now a spirit rather of boastfulness than of dejection. The following were the points of special merit which were now claimed for its departments: first, the session was the same in length as that of the academic schools; namely, ten months instead of six at the most, which made up the session of the Northern medical colleges. This prolongation, it was said, put the student in possession of " unusual facilities for gradually acquiring, and thereby digesting the information conveyed to him by oral instruction, without that confusion of thought and fatigue of mind which are inevitable, when, as always happens in city schools, he has to encounter daily six or seven lectures delivered in rapid succession." Secondly, before each lecture, the medical student at the University was required to answer questions bearing on the subject of the previous lecture, or portions of text-books that had been given out to be mastered. The professor's explanatory comment supplied each of his hearers " with the most valuable means of fixing in his mind correct information, while it had the incidental advantage of familiarizing him with the mode of trial to which he would be subjected in his first examination for graduation." Thirdly, the length of the session gave the student ample time within which to cover the elementary branches of medical science before he was called upon to listen to discourses on the advanced branches. Fourthly, any student of approved character was permitted to offer himself as a candidate for graduation, and to receive the doctor's degree, without reference to the period which he had devoted to the study of medicine, provided that he had passed his examinations satisfactorily. Fifthly, there were open to him the anatomical and pathological museum, the infirmary,— which was expected very soon to create opportunities for clinical instruction — and the library. Sixthly, he had to pay only a small fee in the class of practical anatomy;

and seventhly, the expense of living at the University was moderate, its site, healthy, and its climate, salubrious, whilst its remoteness from cities, and even large towns, removed all temptation from the student to grow indolent, or to fall into a bog of dissipation and self-indulgence.

x. *Military Exercises*

Jefferson, as President, was not disposed to increase the strength of the military arm of the Government,—indeed, his natural bent was to whittle it down to a point which would leave only the narrowest margin of national safety. Suspicion of military encroachment was, in those times, as constantly flaming up in Republican minds as suspicion of centralizing intrigue,— perhaps because they were presumed to be in sympathetic collusion. Jefferson, as we know, had no toleration for anything that winked at either the form or the spirit of royalty; but he so far curbed his aversion for swords and muskets as to think that a military training of some sort could be made serviceable to the individual and the State alike. He was not so sure of the supremacy of the civil power in all emergencies that he could blind himself to the possibility that the day might come when the only protection for that power would be the skill which every able-bodied citizen had acquired in the use of military weapons. He gave, in the Rockfish Gap Report, the fullest expression of his matured convictions on the subject of education in all its various departments; and in the light of his naturally pacific tendencies, it is worthy of particular notice that, in this epochal document, he recommended that the students in the projected university should, in their hours of recreation, be required to spend some of their time in obtaining a practical knowledge of manual

exercises, military manoeuvres, and tactics in general.   It
was his opinion that such training should be imparted at
an early period of life,— for this was the period of apt-
ness, docility, and emulation, when lessons of that nature
were, not only the most quickly learned, but also the
longest remembered.

In October, 1824, the Board gave the Faculty the
authority to appoint a military instructor, who, from half
past one to half past three, on every Saturday, should be
required to drill the entire corps of students   The course
which he was to cover was to embrace field evolutions,
manoeuvres and encampments.   He was to follow the
strictest military rules in his command,— the roll was to
be regularly called, and every absentee, and every other
delinquent besides, was to be reported to the Faculty, who
were to inflict such punishment as their judgment approved.   The guns to be used were to be numbered by
him; and he was also to distribute them, receive them back,
and carefully preserve them from damage.   They were
really to be wooden dummies, with iron locks, half barrels of tin, and wooden ramrods.   As the students, during the first year, did not exceed one hundred and twenty-
three, only one company was organized at the start, under
the provision of this ordinance.   William Matthews, a
resident of Everettsville, in Albemarle county, but formerly a cadet in the Military Academy at West Point,
was chosen to fill the position of military instructor.

In April, 1826, the original rule that every student
should take part in the drill was modified,— only those
who were willing to volunteer should be enrolled.   In
order to ensure a sheltered spot for the company while
training, one of the gymnasia joined as wings to the Rotunda was reserved for that purpose.   This space would
seem to have been too contracted for actual manoeuvres,

except by very small single squads; and it was probably used chiefly as a lecture-room. Matthews was to be liable for any damage to it which might occur during the hours of drill. The instruction was continued throughout the summer of 1826, for the limits of the session had not yet been altered. There were serious difficulties to be overcome in giving it. Fifty-five to sixty students participated in the exercises, but in Matthews's opinion, it was impossible to train them properly without real guns. That these had not been procured was not to be imputed to him; he had written to Jefferson a few weeks before the latter's death calling his attention to the pressing need of muskets to replace the dummy weapons; but Jefferson had replied that the funds were too low to permit of a purchase, and that he disapproved of an application to the State armory for a supply. Matthews, not to be discouraged, begged Cocke to solicit of the Governor the number of muskets wanted. "I wish to have the arms as soon as possible," he said, " as my engagement with the University will expire shortly, and it is my wish to instruct the attending classes in manual exercises." He suggested that the guns should be spiked before they were withdrawn from their present place of deposit, as this would prevent their being afterwards turned to dangerous uses.

Matthews's term came to an end on September 1, and he petitioned the Faculty for reappointment. In a letter which he wrote to the Board of Visitors in the course of the same month, he advised that the system of tactics then employed in the American Army should be adopted; and that every student in the University, whether he volunteered or not, should be compelled to enter his name in the roll   In addition, he recommended that, when this enlistment had been completed, the whole number should be divided into four squads, and that each squad should be required to attend sixty minutes, at least, every week, to learn the theory of the military art; and he also suggested that the reveille should be sounded at sunrise,—a very politic proposal, as such a rule would foster a disposition to rise early, which the Faculty was already endeavoring to enforce.   Matthews seemed to think that the call of the roll, at this unwholesome hour, would be a " preventive to habits of idleness, dissipation, and improper conduct."   There was no intention, however, of discontinuing the drill on Saturday afternoon.   It was his ambition to obtain the Board's permission to found a School of Military Art comparable with the other schools already established in the University,—a plan which the Faculty seems to have received at first with favor; but they declined to convert his existing course of instruction into a permanent school until the Board should have determined the amount of his emolument.   In the meanwhile, he had procured the endorsement of the Superintendent of the West Point Military Academy.

Towards the end of December (1826), Matthews wrote to Madison, the new rector, to express regret that the Board should be so dilatory in coming to a decision upon the proposition of establishing a permanent military school, although, in anticipation of it, the Faculty, he said, had permitted him to continue his previous course of training   He solicited Madison's approval of his plans; and he again dwelt upon the necessity of procuring one hundred and fifty muskets and carbines from the State.   These, when not in actual use, might remain in the proctor's custody.   He announced his willingness to assume the responsibility of cleansing and repairing the guns.   It was his opinion that a School of Military Art would be influential in protracting the stay at the University of many students, who would not, with the present schools only, tarry longer than one year, or a couple of years at most.

Madison was of a more pacific cast than Jefferson, and no project to teach military science on an imposing scale commended itself to his approval. Writing to Cocke several weeks after the receipt of Matthews's practical letter, when he had had ample time to consider the proposed school in all its bearings, he calmly questioned the utility of military training in general. " Certainly for physical purposes," he said, " the gymnasium is incomparably superior. It would be well if the two branches of instruction could be united in a competent individual." But as Cocke had served with distinction in the last war, and was, he knew, in sympathy with a reasonable plan for military training, Madison did not venture to condemn the proposal further; on the contrary, he closed his letter by recommending its adoption, and suggested that a pavilion should be reserved for the instructor's use, apparently both as a home and a lecture-room.

Madison and Cocke, in their public capacity as the executive committee, seem to have been willing to consent to the erection of the School of Military Art, should the Faculty's approval be first obtained. A formal school on a footing with the others was, however, never established; nor did the future course of instruction take a broader scope, or assume a status of greater dignity. This is explained by the fact that the Faculty, on receiving the committee's communication, although formerly more favorable, were now satisfied with simply renewing the limited privileges which Matthews had enjoyed during the preceding session. The suggestion that all the students should be required to drill was again rejected;

only those who volunteered were to be enrolled for the military exercises; and these exercises were not to begin until the first of April, and were to go on then for only one hour in the early morning of every Tuesday, Thursday, and Saturday.   Arms were to be obtained from the State.   All these different prescriptions were carried out. Matthews continued to reside within the precincts, and was allowed the use of the library on the footing, not, it is to be noted, of a professor, but of a student.   He was still an instructor during the session of 1827–28. The company, at this time, was commanded by Captain John Preston, and among the officers were Philip St. George Cocke, a son of General Cocke, and afterwards a graduate of West Point and a General in the Confederate Army, William Daniel, a famous judge of a later period, and Patrick Henry Aylett, a descendant of the orator.   No weapons were given out to the squads until they were on the point of entering the drill; but the officers were permitted to carry their muskets to their dormitories for practice.

Matthews had much ground for dejection.   " On account of the uncertainty of my success here," he wrote Cocke, in July, 1828, " I have thought it would be advisable for me to abandon the military school unless the Visitors could assure me a school of one hundred students at five dollars each. . . . The number of students diminishing yearly is but a poor encouragement for any one.   I am disposed to continue here two or three sessions if I can do it on better terms than heretofore.   I wish to study natural philosophy, engineering, and the higher branches of mathematics.   If I do not remain here, it is my intention to make an effort to get attached to the Topographical Corps of Engineers."

Matthews withdrew from the University before October, 1830, for, during that month, the students assembled in one of the rooms of the Rotunda, and decided to form a company, to be instructed by Mr. Ferron, the French fencing-master, who had probably received a military training in his native country. The Faculty gave their consent; but when the students returned at the beginning of the following session, and reorganized the corps, Captain John Carr, the proctor, was appointed by the Faculty to the position of military instructor, and arms were asked of the State. Carr's relation to the corps appears to have been altogether nominal,— he was simply its honorary colonel. He admitted that he had little power to control its movements, and whatever power he did possess, he never attempted to exercise. After Matthews's departure, the military instructions seem to have been confined to a weekly drill carried out by youthful officers, who, in some instances, had only the impoverished military knowledge of self-taught amateurs The company had now really sunk to the position of a body that had been organized chiefly for the amusement of its members; there was no room open to them for acquiring information about military science in its larger aspects; but there were numerous opportunities for showing a lively partizanship in the election of the officers. The occasion of such an election was always accompanied by tumult and dissipation.

On November 12, 1831, one hundred muskets were received, in correspondence with the number of men enrolled. The company, from the time it was furnished with firearms, was a noisy participant in the various patriotic celebrations which enlivened each year, the foremost of which occurred on July 4, February 22, and April 13. On February 22, 1832, the captain obtained permission for his corps to parade on the Lawn and deliver

several rounds of *feu de joie,* and afterwards, to march
to Charlottesville to serve as an escort for Alexander
Rives, who was to deliver an oration in the Episcopal
Church   A salvo was fired at the conclusion of the
speech, and the company then returned in the same formal
order to the University   Criticism of the organization
increased in emphasis, as its more or less frivolous conduct, in the absence of a trained instructor, became more
manifest. First, the expensiveness of the membership
was censured,— the epaulets of the officers, it was said,
cost eight dollars; and their smallest outlay, during a
single year, amounted to sixteen dollars.   But a second
objection rested upon a more reasonable ground than
this,— not only were the fusillades on the Lawn disturbing to the peace of the precincts, but a bullet or two had
been known to be fired; and the natural alarm which this
had caused, was further aggravated by the rebellious
spirit, which, in those times, so frequently burst out like
a flame among the students   The rollicking entertainments periodically given by the company encouraged the
taste for drinking already prevailing in the University,
while the ambitious blare of the young soldiers' wind instruments was so crude and inexpert as to irritate the sensitive nerves of the professors, and seriously distract the
attention of the young men engaged with their studies in
dormitory or lecture-room.   The captain claimed no
power to control his men except during the drill,— so soon
as the corps stopped to rest his authority ceased, and the
youthful volunteers were free to indulge in any form of
pleasantry, however annoying to others, which their impish wits might suggest

The ordinance requiring a military teacher for the
University still remained unrepealed, and in December,
1832, the company asked permission to appoint their own

captain, Thomas L. Preston, to this responsible post. The Faculty admitted their inability to secure, at this time, an instructor of a higher competence than an intelligent student, and as Preston was a young man of uncommon force and distinction of character, and some experience of military discipline, they finally assented to his selection. The arms which had been loaned by the State were delivered to him on condition, (1) that they were to be surrendered whenever the Faculty demanded it; (2) that they were only to be used in the military exercises; (3) that no ordinances were to be violated during the drill; and (4) that no firing was to take place within the precincts. As the company had been assigned a parade ground of its own, the fusillades were to be restricted to that area.

By July, 1833, the corps had become so disorderly in its general conduct that an irritated public feeling demanded its disbandment. When an application for its reorganization was made the ensuing October, Dr. Emmet urged that a positive refusal should be returned; but it was again permitted to form,— with definite restrictions, however, upon its independence of action. A sentiment was now springing up in favor of putting in practice again the original enactment that authorized expert military instruction in the University. Captain Partridge, of Vermont, a thoroughly competent officer, was, in response to this sentiment, employed to give such instruction; but, unfortunately, on the same limited and hampered footing as the one which Matthews had occupied,— that is to say, his pupils must be volunteers, and he must look to them alone for his remuneration, a slim reliance which foreshadowed the early ending of the course of lectures on military subjects which he agreed to deliver. His connection with the University apparently continued only

through a single term, for at the beginning of the following session (1835), Penci, the fencing master, asked
permission to organize a military company, which he
offered to drill; and the Faculty consented on condition
that he should give his services gratuitously, and conform
strictly to the ordinances.   This arrangement was perhaps unsatisfactory, for his instruction was discontinued
at the end of the session.   In October, 1836, the corps
was reorganized, and it was this body that was guilty of
the most indefensible outrage against order which was
recorded even in those years of riot and rebellion.   To
this lawless outbreak, we shall refer at a later stage in our
narrative.   Its conduct on that occasion very naturally
brought the students' military company into a discredit
which lasted for many years.

XI. *Minor Courses of Instruction*

Jefferson was one of the first Americans to discern the
value of manual training as a minor feature of a liberal
education.   Before the University was opened, he had
provided in the ordinances for the erection of workshops
within the precincts, or on sites sufficiently near to be
convenient to the students.   Here all who so desired
were to be free to acquire skill in the use of those mechanical contrivances which generally are only employed
in the pursuit of a trade.   In order to reduce the expense of the shops, they were to be offered to respectable
workingmen, who were to be relieved of the payment of
rent on condition of their consenting to the students handling their tools; and they were also to have the right
to sit under any professor without paying a fee, if his
lectures bore upon the mechanical and philosophical principles of their art.   There exists no proof that this

scheme, which has become so common in our own times, was put in practice.

In 1833, the Board of Visitors determined to introduce a course in civil engineering as an adjunct to the one in mathematics. Bonnycastle endeavored to carry out their purpose by delivering a series of lectures on the subject; but the plan did not, apparently, at this time pass beyond this rather barren initial act. He continued, however, to urge that this professorship should be created. Again, in 1836, he informed the Board that he considered its establishment as entirely practicable, and Professor Rogers, of the School of Natural Philosophy, now offered his assistance to bring it about. This combination assured the chair; the new school was designated the School of Civil Engineering; and one lecture was delivered weekly by each professor belonging to it. Seventeen students attended during the session of 1836–7; and in 1839, four graduates received diplomas.

It will be recalled that a room was reserved in the Rotunda by Jefferson for instruction in those arts which are employed to embellish life. One of these was music, and in April, 1825, the Faculty required the proctor to advertise in the journals of New York, Philadelphia, and Richmond, for a teacher, who was to be " a good practical performer on more than one instrument, and well versed in orchestral performance and the science of composition " At least, one candidate for the position was turned down. In fact, there was much difficulty in filling it properly. The Board of Visitors asked the Faculty to give the reason of this, and that body replied, that, unless some additional inducements were offered, no competent person could be engaged; this, they advised, should take the form of a moderate salary for at least one year, — which would indicate that fees had previously been relied upon to support the incumbent.   Mr. Bigelow applied for the situation; but it was not until November, 1828, that he is found giving lessons in music, and at the same time, occupying a room within the precincts   His only reward was the fees which he received from his pupils.   He remained at the University as late as the year 1833, and quite possibly longer.

In 1828, Dr. Barber obtained the Faculty's permission to deliver a course of lectures on the subject of elocution.   His place, in 1832, was taken by Donald McLeod, who also occupied a dormitory; and he was succeeded by at least two others.   Lessons were also given in penmanship and stenography.[1]

As far back as 1803, Jefferson expressed an interest in agricultural education, and when he came to draft the Rockfish Gap Report, he recommended that a course in the science of agriculture should be comprised among the general courses to be adopted.   But the suggestion failed to secure the countenance of the Legislature.   It was the popular opinion in Virginia in those times that the young farmer could be trained for his calling by learning from his own slaves all the methods used in the past; and that these were sufficient for the undiversified crops which were grown in the soil of the State.   Jefferson philosophically consoled himself with the hope that the professor of natural history,— whose principal course was chemistry,— would be able to give agricultural instruction along definite general lines at least.   But Cocke, — who, it will be recalled, was not inclined to balk at the most radical innovations unless they took the form of bringing in foreign teachers or building Roman temples on American hilltops,— was determined to establish at

[1] The teachers of stenography were Hezekiah Davis, in 1831, and Richard E Johns, in 1839

the University, if practicable, a professorship in this science. He is said to have advocated the incorporation of the Agricultural Society of Albemarle principally because it would be the most feasible means of raising an endowment for this agricultural professorship; and other bodies in the State of a like character were urged to join in swelling the fund. A letter was drawn up by the President of the Society and circulated far and wide through the rural parts of Virginia, with the result that a large sum was collected; but, unhappily, the person to whom it was loaned fell into bankruptcy, and the investment was irrevocably lost.

William C. Rives was solicitous, in 1835, that the Board of Visitors should at once petition the General Assembly to establish a new professorship at the University to take " charge of the principles of agriculture," along with the kindred sciences of botany, geology, and mineralogy. A model farm, he said, should be laid off as a department of the school, and the whole subject taught at once practically and scientifically. The hour, however, was not yet ripe for the project.

XII. *Methods of Instruction and Examination*

There were three methods of teaching employed at the University from the start: (1) the lecture; (2) the daily examinations in class; (3) the written exercise. The professor was theoretically at liberty to give preponderance to whichever one of these he considered to be best adapted to the character of his own course, but the lecture, in practically every instance, was the chief means of instruction The system, as a whole, had been introduced by Jefferson, and had been derived by him from the example of William Small, under whom he had sat when a student at the College of William and Mary.   Previous to Small's professorship, the method of instruction at that college had been confined to recitation from the text-books.   Jefferson was convinced that teaching by lecture rather than by text-book would stimulate independent thought in the student, create a desire for original investigation, and discourage mere memorizing.   Whatever danger of incoherence and desultoriness might accompany this manner of tuition, would, in his opinion, be corrected by the careful oral examinations, which were required to follow the next day   So unusual a system, however, was not approved by all, in spite of his endorsement of its principle as correct.   First, it was asserted that the notes of the student were necessarily imperfect and disconnected, and that no daily oral examination could remove the unfortunate effect of these deficiencies. This examination, indeed, would be largely a repetition of the original lecture in order to fill in the vacant gaps in the student's memoranda.   Secondly, however brilliant that student might be, an undue proportion of his time would be consumed in the mechanical effort to get these memoranda into shape; and finally, only a few professors, with all their learning and experience, possessed a marked power of exposition.

In reality, the lecture method imposed as extraordinary a burden on the professor's capacity as on the student's. It demanded a more thorough knowledge of his subject, and a greater talent for communicating that knowledge. It was not enough that he should be able to explain lucidly single points in the text: he was also expected to grasp the principles and the details of his theme,— the abstruse and the simple elements of it alike,— so clearly and so surely that he could present it as a whole with perfect perspicacity to his pupils.   Nor was it sufficient that he should voice the thoughts and theories of others; he must be capable of reaching his own independent conclusions and enforcing them with his own reasoning, logically and firmly expressed. Such a method did not shut out text-books, but it presupposed that the professor was so discerning that he could discover what was improper in these books and reject it. It was correctly said at the time of the adoption of the system of lectures at the University of Virginia that it could not be carried out with inferior instruments; and that its benefits were in proportion to the efficiency of the teachers in imparting knowledge.

It seems to have been foreseen as early as 1826 that some mechanical means must be devised to lighten the labor of both professor and student by incorporating in print a brief syllabus of each lecture. A lithographic press was purchased during that year, and each member of the Faculty was permitted to have the use of it for a period of two days in succession. The press must have proved, on the whole, unsatisfactory, for we find that frequent applications were made to the proctor to increase its working usefulness. In 1828, the professors complained that they had been long deprived of its aid, although it had been put in place in a room, a man employed to manipulate it, and the proper quantity of paper bought to supply it. In the following year, two dormitories were assigned for its accommodation. For sometime, it had been housed in an outbuilding. As late at 1835, a Mr. Tompkins was directed to remove it to Charlottesville in order that he might have a chance of acquiring there the art of handling it, and it was hoped that, in this way, " it might render some service to the University." It would be inferred from this protracted discontent that the press had, throughout this period, afforded the student little assistance in securing an accurate copy of his professor's lectures.

The rule appears to have been for the instructor to deliver his lecture first, and to follow this up with an oral examination on the last lecture but one. With the lecture of the day, and the recapitulation of the preceding lecture, the student received the benefit of the substance of two lectures at every meeting of his class. By the enactments of 1825, each class was to continue in session during at least two hours on at least three days of the week. The first class to assemble in 1826 did so at seven o'clock in the morning; it broke up at eight, and spent half an hour at breakfast; and at the close of that interval, re-assembled, and remained in session during an hour. In July, 1827, the Board of Visitors required lectures to begin at half past seven in the morning until the end of the following April; and after that date, the hour for coming together was to be half past five o'clock. The adoption of this inconvenient time was perhaps one cause of the discontent that so irritated the spirits of the early students. This rising by dawn in the humid air of early spring, and attending lectures at that hour in damp and chill recitation rooms before breakfast, was thought by some members of the Faculty to have had a distinct influence in bringing on the epidemic of 1829. The young men had a right to dispute the wisdom of a Board that imposed on them an ordinance as senseless from a practical point of view as it was dangerous from a hygienic. In 1832, one of the students, Mr. Winfree, who was charged with rising late, excused his conduct on the ground that he was called upon to be present at lectures five times each week at half past five in the morning. The hour of assembling for the first class was, in 1838, set at six o'clock; but by 1841, the original hour

of half past seven was again in force. The last class of
the day broke up, at one time, at half past three; at another, at half past four.

The professors were under as close supervision in the
work of the class-room as the students themselves. The
chairman of the Faculty was expected to report: (1)
how often each instructor had failed to lecture as required; (2) how frequently he had neglected to question
the members of his class; (3) how much time had been
consumed by him in delivering lectures and making his
examinations; and (4) how often he had omitted sending in his class report to show the number of his pupils'
absences, and the degree of their attention and progress.

There were, from the start, two general examinations:
the intermediate and the final During the first three
years, the intermediate began on the first Monday in
December. The Board of Visitors were expected to
attend in person, but no strangers were permitted to do
so. This examination took place in the "elliptical
room" of the Rotunda in 1826; but it seems that the
intention had been, except for "the unfortunate state of
the books," to hold it in the library. The final examination came off in the presence of the students and professors during the week that preceded the "commencement" of the vacation; and this also took place in the
"elliptical room" of the Rotunda. In 1828, the date
of the intermediate examinations was transferred from
the month of December to any month near the middle of
the session which the Faculty might select. The final
examinations this year lasted from July 10 to July 16.
The time consumed in one day in the examination of a
single school was two hours in the morning and two in the
afternoon. The examination in ancient languages was
finished in three days; in mathematics, in four; and in

modern languages, in five.   The briefest, anatomy, was completed in one day.   The remainder did not, in any instance, spread over three days; and several fell short of that length of time.

A change in the manner of holding the general examinations was proposed at a meeting of the Faculty held in April, 1829.   A committee of this body recommended, on that date, (1) that the chairman, at the close of the session, should appoint for the examination in each school, a committee comprising the professor of that school and two of his colleagues; (2) that the former should draw up in writing a series of questions to be propounded, and that to each question there should be appended a valuation in numbers, the highest of which was to be one hundred; (3) that the chairman should choose the date of examination; (4) that the class should assemble with pen and paper, and that, for the first time, the questions should then be given out; (5) that the majority of the committee should be required to be present at the examination in order to supervise it; (6) that the professor of the school should value the answers numerically; (7) that a report embracing all these details should be handed in to the Faculty; and finally, (8) that the students should be arranged in three divisions according to their merit as demonstrated by the examination. The one who obtained a marking of three-fourths of the valuation of his replies was to be listed in the first class; if less than three-fourths but more than one quarter, in the second class; and if less than one-fourth, in the third.

The manner of proceeding on the part of the several committees is illustrated in their action in 1832.   The entire Faculty assembled that year in the lecture-room of natural philosophy.   Harrison announced the result of the examination in the School of Ancient Languages.   He was the spokesman of that committee, and his report was adopted by the Faculty; and he was followed by Blaettermann as the representative of the committee appointed for the School of Modern Languages; by Bonnycastle, of the one for the School of Mathematics; and so on in turn by Patterson, Emmet, Johnson, and Davis, as the heads of the committees of their respective schools.   No report of the numerical valuations for the different divisions of the intermediate examinations was made by these bodies until the valuations for the final examinations had been submitted.

The preliminary English examination, which, in 1833, went before the intermediate, was held by a committee of three professors, appointed by the chairman.   Unless a student, before this examination, gave notice of his intention to become a candidate for graduation, he was not permitted to stand it afterwards without the Faculty's consent.   The proportion of those who, from year to year, succeeded, or did not succeed, in it, demonstrated the necessity for holding it,— in 1838, fifty-one passed and twenty failed; and in 1841, the corresponding numbers were forty-one and twenty-nine.   This English examination seems to have consisted of a rigid test of the candidate's qualifications in his mother-tongue,— he was required to write at least twenty-five lines in that language touching some phase of the course in which he was seeking a diploma; and when this had been read, he was questioned in English syntax and orthography.   Originally, the candidate for graduation was required, not only to pass an English examination, but also to prove his ability to read the works of the principal Greek and Latin authors; but this last provision was subsequently discarded as tending to cut down the number of pupils in the law and medical schools.

XIII. *Degrees*

It was announced in 1831, that no diploma was to be given for less proficiency than a student of fair talents could acquire after a course of two years' study.   In the beginning, this award was restricted to those who had reached the first grade; the medals to those who had risen to the second; and books to those who advanced to the third.   The diploma was the token of two degrees,— the one, the doctorate, academic or professional; the other, the plain graduate.   In a very limited sense, the doctorate was the degree of a curriculum, as a fixed though short series of studies had to be mastered before it could be won   This was especially true of it when vocational   The term " graduate " was also considered to have the character of a degree [1]   A student who had successfully passed the examination in ancient languages, or any other separate school, was as much entitled to the designation " Graduate of the University of Virginia " as if he had carried off diplomas in all the schools.   It was Jefferson's intention to confine the academic award to the graduate diploma,— the academic doctorate diploma was simply an advanced graduate diploma,— as the one most in harmony with the conception which he had of the University's purpose; namely, that it was to be restricted to graduate work.   No academic degrees in the usual sense, and no honorary degrees, were to be bestowed.   In no particular, in our opinion, did his judgment touching the affairs of the institution show greater weightiness than in his determination to shut out all the old degrees except the doctrinate, academical or vocational.   The academic degrees subsequently intro-

---

[1] In 1837, Professor Tucker spoke of the " Graduate of the University," as a " quaint title "   He wished to substitute " bachelor of arts " for it.

duced,— especially the mastership of arts,— were incongruous with the spirit of the elective system, for they, like the professional degrees, required a fixed curriculum, and the industry of several years for their acquisition. But beyond this, their practical influence on the mass of students was unfortunate, for they tended to raise a small number of them to a position of superiority over their fellows, and thus accentuated the comparative failure of the great majority.   This influence was not without responsibility for the extraordinary disparity in numbers already pointed out between the students who had attended one year and those who had attended two,— a disparity which had its springs mainly in discouragement and depression.

There was a perfect simplicity in Jefferson's arrangement of awards for the vocational schools and the academical schools.   It is true that, in the beginning, the only vocational degree given was the doctrinate of medicine, but this inevitably set the precedent for the introduction of the entire list of professional degrees, from that of bachelor of law to that of civil engineer.   It did not, however, necessarily foreshadow the degrees of master and bachelor of arts, and the numerous other academic degrees that, from time to time, have been established at the University.   Had the academic award been permanently limited to the diploma of graduation, whether ordinary or advanced, it would have conferred on that award a dignity which would have waxed with the constantly increasing reputation of the institution; nor would this dignity have been curtailed by the fact that it rested as much upon the student who had acquired one diploma as upon the student who had acquired ten, for both would have stood upon the same high platform, inasmuch as both would have been equally entitled to be called a

" Graduate of the University of Virginia."   The academic doctor would have been simply an advanced graduate of the same institution.

The denial to the Faculty of the right to confer honorary degrees is not so easily approved.   The idea which Jefferson had in mind was that every degree bestowed by the institution should be a proof of merit which had been exhibited in its own class-rooms alone.   So long as that was the rule, there would be no temptation whatever for it to confer any degree except on the ground of what had been laboriously acquired, and also of what was acknowledged by all to be deserving of recognition.   On the other hand, in conferring purely honorary degrees, there seemed to him to be room for the display of a far less praiseworthy spirit   Political enthusiasm and sectarian zeal might govern the Board in their choice rather than disinterested appreciation of extraordinary talents and achievements   A military hero and a sectional Congressman have received the chaplet of the doctrinate in many American institutions for accomplishments that lay far outside of the scholar's pale.   It is possible that Jefferson was apprehensive lest the dignity of his new seat of learning should, in the future, be lowered by an occasional false step of this nature; but he was probably more anxious to shut out the doctrinate of divinity than the doctrinate of letters or laws.   His distrustful attitude towards honorary degrees was characteristic of a man who had struck fiercely at all artificial distinctions, and who was suspicious of men's disposition to create them where they did not already exist.   There was possibly too an aristocratic flavor about honorary degrees which made them distasteful to him.   In reality, there was no legitimate objection to such degrees if bestowed, — as doubtless they would have been at the University, —

with the normal discernment and discretion. They are awarded by all the world's greatest seats of learning in a spirit which has only occasionally provoked censure. The influence and prestige of the University of Virginia would have been very much enhanced, and not at all lessened, had Jefferson's revolutionary, and, in this particular instance, eccentric, spirit not led him to reject so old and so honorable a custom.[1]

Although the enactments of 1825 specifically provided for a diploma, yet, during several years, the highest award seems to have been a certificate of proficiency. General John S. Preston, who was a student at the University in 1828, tells us that, at this time, there were no academic diplomas or degrees conferred. He received, in the autumn of that year, certificates "which," he said, "I presented at Harvard, asking the position of resident graduate. The rule required a diploma, but with flattering compliments to the younger university, I was installed as a resident graduate with the privilege of a master of arts." William Wertenbaker, writing of Poe, mentions that the poet obtained " distinctions at the final examinations in Latin and French," and that, at this time (1827), this was the highest honor that a student could win. "Under present regulations (1868)," he adds, " he would have graduated and been entitled to a diploma."

Jefferson had not been dead more than fifteen months when the Board of Visitors,— probably in response to a rising sentiment in the Faculty,— instructed that body to

---

[1] Dr Walter Reed was the most famous graduate of the medical school of the University of Virginia Whilst numerous Northern colleges were bestowing on him their highest honorary degrees as a reward for his discoveries touching the origin of yellow fever, his own alma mater was compelled to restrict the expression of her appreciation of his achievements to an obscure resolution of her Faculty and Board of Visitors

consider the advisability of altering the rule relating to
degrees, so far as to sanction the introduction of the
" ancient denomination of bachelor, master, and doctor."
Jefferson's plan of academic awards had been in harmony
with the Continental practice, about which he had learned
during his sojourn in Europe.   On the other hand, the
tentative plan suggested by the Board was in unison with
the long established rule of Oxford and Cambridge; and
as there were four natives of England, and one former
subject (Tucker), among the members of the Faculty,
it is quite possible that these professors had earnestly advocated its adoption some time before it was first considered by the Visitors.   Several years of debate and
agitation passed before the alteration was actually made.
Thus, in 1829, we find the Faculty, after prolonged deliberation, recommending (1) that the graduate should be
one, who, by rigid examination, should demonstrate his
proficiency in any of the University courses; (2) that the
graduate in the School of Medicine should be awarded
the degree of doctor of medicine; (3) that there should
be an academic and a professional degree in the School of
Law,— the academic graduate should be entitled " graduate of the School of Law," but his diploma should state
that the amount of information required to win it was
not sufficient to authorize the holder to become a member
of the bar; on the other hand, the professional graduate
should be entitled " barrister of law "; (4) that, if the
graduate in one or more schools should afterwards prove
that he had, by later study, become more highly versed
in such school, or schools, as the Faculty should designate,
he should receive a title of a higher quality.   What was
to be the name of this new degree?   Probably, the Faculty had in mind a passing suggestion of Lomax's, who
recommended that the graduate in four schools should be

called " bachelor of science." None of these proposed innovations, however, were adopted, at this time, by the Board.

On July 9, 1831, Dr. Dunglison submitted a resolution at a meeting of the Faculty urging the introduction of the degree of master of arts. The two reasons which he gave, in advocating this revolutionary addition, were, that the proposed degree would (1) " afford parents and guardians a guide in the selection of subjects of study "; and would (2) " keep the student longer at the University." A few days afterwards, the Board, following the expressed wish of the Faculty, but with a perceptible feeling of uncertainty as to the wisdom of their own act, authorized the use of the new degree,— not permanently, but " for the present." The system of degrees as established by the *Enactments of 1831* stood as follows: (1) the graduate,— the student who had proved his mastery of an entire school, like mathematics, or a branch of a school, like chemistry; (2) the winner of a certificate of proficiency in some section of a school; (3) the doctor of medicine; and (4) the master of arts,— the student who had been awarded diplomas in ancient languages, mathematics, natural philosophy, chemistry, and moral philosophy. In 1833, modern languages was added to this list, with the right reserved to the student to make his choice of any two. The degree of bachelor of law had not been adopted as late as 1839; indeed, it does not seem to have been introduced until July, 1840.

XIV. *Public Day*

The first elaborate commencement apparently took place in July, 1829. During these early years, it was spoken of generally as the Public Day, but we discover an incidental reference to it as the Exhibition.   In October, 1828, the Faculty were authorized by the Board to require the students to read to the audience on the next Public Day the written answers which they had submitted in their final examinations; and the occasion was to be further illuminated by the delivery of orations and the reading of essays.   The programme for that commencement (1829) was arranged at least two months and a half before the close of the session, and under its provisions, the students were to assemble on the last day of the term " in the Rotunda,"— which, doubtless, meant the library-room,— and the public were also to be admitted.   Each professor, at the call of the chairman, was to announce the result in his own school; and he was also to read aloud the questions which had been propounded to his pupils, one or more of whom were to be named by the chairman to read such replies as had been selected beforehand by the committee of that school   If necessary, a blackboard was to be used in their exposition. Speakers and essayists,— also chosen by the chairman,— were then to enliven the audience; and this was to be followed by the delivery of certificates and diplomas.   If the winner of a diploma failed to be present to receive it, the Faculty subsequently decided whether or not they should confer it at all.

In June, four young men were appointed to deliver the orations and one to read an essay.   The Faculty very considerately decided to omit the examination papers from the programme, because they would either consume too much of the limited time, or would add too sensibly to the solemnity of the occasion.   The following was the order of proceedings adopted for what was apparently the first real commencement in the history of the University, and for that reason, it is of sufficient interest to be repeated in detail: (1) oration by George P. Beirne, of Monroe county, Va.; (2) list of the students who displayed, in the final examinations, the highest proficiency in their studies; (3) oration by W. F. Gray; (4) essay by John H. Gretter; (5) announcement by the chairman of the names of the graduates, and the delivery to them of their diplomas; (6) oration by William Daniel, of Lynchburg; (7) oration by Charles Mosby, of Powhatan county.

In July, 1832, the proceedings began and ended with an oration. There were only two delivered instead of four, as in 1829, but there was an additional essay to take the place of one of the two orations omitted. The students had always disputed the Faculty's right to appoint the orators and essayists, and in March, they had elected,— apparently, however, with the Faculty's approval,— the entire number to serve in the following July. This they again did in 1833; but in 1834, at least one of the orators, and also one of the essayists, was chosen by the Faculty. This change aroused a storm of disapproval among the students, and they openly declared that none of their number should, with their consent, accept from the Faculty an appointment as orator or essayist; that should any one do so, they would decline to be present to hear him speak or read; and that when they assembled, it should be, not in the proctor's office, as ordered, but wherever they should prefer to convene. It is plain that the result of the students' election was as little satisfactory to the Board of Visitors as to the Faculty, and, in 1835, they introduced a different method of selection. In each November, the entire number of young men were to be set off in nine divisions. Each division was to name an elector; and the nine electors thus chosen were to hold a meeting, at which they were to'

nominate six orators and essayists.   It was confidently
expected that these nine representatives would, like the
members of the Federal electoral college, exercise a wise
discretion in making their choice.   But the students were
determined that they would not allow this shrewd device
to deprive them of what they looked upon as their right:
we find them assembling in April, 1837, and solemnly receiving the pledge of the electors that they would vote
only for the candidates whom the entire body of the
collegians desired, and whose names were then submitted
for acceptance.   The chairman complained that the
young men were so much interested in canvassing the
claims of the prospective orators and essayists that their
attention was diverted from their studies, and their dislike of disciplinary restraints sensibly heightened.   It
was noted too by him, with dissatisfaction, that these
candidates sought to increase their chance of election by
criticizing the Faculty.

The Visitors, in the end, revoked the resolution creating the board of electors, as that method had failed to
repress the violence of partizanship, or do away with the
confusion that accompanied the canvassing.   In 1840,
the two orators selected among the students for the Public Day were picked out under a new plan: at the beginning of the session, all the young men were invited to
prepare written discourses to be submitted to the chairman by the first of May.   The two among them which
were determined to be the most meritorious were set
aside to be delivered at commencement.

XV. *Successors to the First Professors*

We have now described the general courses of study
pursued by the young collegians who attended the dif-

ferent schools.   Who were the professors who taught them?   In a previous chapter we mentioned the most salient events in the lives of those who made up the first Faculty.   Before the period which we are now examining had ended in 1842, every member of this original body, with the exception of Tucker, had either died or retired. It will be pertinent now to supplement the details already given with a statement of the circumstances of these deaths and resignations, and some description of the men who were chosen to fill up the gaps thus created.

The first of the professors to leave was Key.   His resignation was not sent in until March 10, 1827, but at least five months earlier, he seems to have announced his intention of returning to England, for in the preceding October, the Board had recorded their regret that he should harbor such a purpose.   Both Key and Long had, on October 6, 1825, indignantly vacated their chairs, in consequence of the rebellious spirit displayed on the night of October 1, but had been persuaded to remain.   That the repetition of this commotion on a later day caused Key to revert to his original decision is indicated in the minute adopted by the Board on October 10, 1826, in which they state as an incentive to him to stay on, that " they are endeavoring to introduce some radical changes into the government " of the University, which " will secure more order than has heretofore prevailed."   As an additional inducement, they promised that the professors, thereafter, should be relieved of some of their irksome duties   The following winter would prove how far the projected reforms could be carried out.   The Board declared that Key's request for his release was so temperately and so feelingly expressed that it would be improper for them to hold him to his contract; but they asked him to give his professorship another trial, and if, on the first of March, 1827, he should be still discontented, they would leave him at liberty to withdraw at the close of the session.   Key, it will be recalled, had been filling his chair only nineteen months when he offered his resignation.[1]   Cocke, who seems to have had a provincial dislike of all foreigners, had always looked at him askant   His final comment upon him showed some acidity.   " I have just received a letter from Mr. Madison mentioning Key's resignation," he wrote Cabell, " but with the modest request that we will permit his salary to run until the last of August in order to suit the departure of a London instead of a Liverpool packet, as the latter would subject him to the expense of a journey across the island of Great Britain."

The vacancy thus created was filled by the translation of the professor of natural philosophy.   Madison would have preferred a different incumbent, for he was afraid, as he expressed it, lest Bonnycastle should become " seized with the same malady " as the one that had caused the severance of Key's official connection with the University; but Bonnycastle remained in the chair until his death, and gave it a reputation which it has never lost [2]   He seems to have been of a quiet and taciturn temper,— the impressions of which, however, were conflicting.   " Amid his grave occupations," we are told in the Faculty's resolution in his memory, " he had a keen relish for the pleasures of social intercourse, and few men were equal to him in combining innocent mirth with

[1] It has always been traditionally said that the principal reason which Key gave for his early return to England was, that the climate of Virginia was injurious to his health

[2] " The examinations set by Bonnycastle," says Professor Charles S Venable in his *Recollections,* " were years ahead of any mathematical instruction given to any college classes in the United States   He introduced the use of the ratio method, the trigonometrical function first used by English Universities in 1830 "

useful and solid instruction." In spite of these social qualities he is known to have been morbidly shy,— in fact, he had been seen to climb a fence and walk in the mud in order to avoid passing students on the pathway. Like Long, he married a Virginian lady. An arbor which he built for his children behind his pavilion was locally famous for the masses of roses and honeysuckle which he had trained to grow over it. He was remarkable alike for his capacity for abstract speculation and for imaginative production. All his English colleagues having withdrawn, it was not unnatural that he too should have nursed the hope of passing his last years in the land of his birth. "Some of my English friends," he wrote Cabell, in 1837, "are employed in procuring the means of my returning to them. The post they desire is not yet established, and, perhaps, never will be."

The earliest intimation that we have of Long's desire to return to England is found in a letter written to Cabell by Cocke in September, 1827. It appears that he had just been appointed to the Greek professorship in the projected University of London, but he did not ask to be released from the obligations of his contract with the University of Virginia — this having still three years to run,— because he anticipated that this length of time would be consumed in erecting the buildings of the new institution. Before a week had passed, however, he discovered that he was wrong in this expectation. He again wrote to Cocke, as the head of the executive committee, to tell him that he had received that morning a request from the Council of London University to take up his new duties on October 1,— it was already the tenth of September,— and there was barely three weeks left to him to close up his affairs in Virginia and make the voyage to England. It seems that he had been urged by Dr.

Briggs, of Liverpool, as far back as December, 1826, to become a candidate for the chair, but he had refused to do so for two reasons: (1) he was offered no positive assurance of success; and (2) the new institution might be put into operation before he would be at liberty to leave the University of Virginia.   By the ensuing March, however, he had made up his mind to adopt Dr. Briggs's advice; but he was still under the impression that, after all, the London University would not open its doors as early as July, 1829, after which time he would be entirely untrammeled.   When he informed the Council of his willingness to become a candidate, he frankly announced that his services belonged to the University of Virginia up to that specific date; and subsequently, in accepting the professorship, he had reiterated this statement.   He now wrote to Cocke to learn whether the Board of Visitors would consent to cancel his contract at the end of the term in July, 1828,— an interval of one session only. " My securing in England the comfortable means of subsistence," he said, " is an object of the greatest importance for my future happiness."

Brougham was the chairman of the London University Council, and through him, Madison, as rector of the University of Virginia, requested a postponement of the offer which had been made to Long; but an inattentive ear was turned to this: and in the following March, 1828, Long received a second summons to London   His resignation was accepted by the Board of Visitors in July in a reluctant but generous spirit.   " They would not estimate properly their obligations to the distinguished professor," they said, " if they insisted on retaining him against his will, or opposed any obstacle to the pursuit of a more eligible situation in his native country; nor would they act with becoming liberality to-

wards a sister institution if they did not feel some consolation in the reflection that what is loss to the cause of
science here, will be gained to a seminary which promises
no ordinary usefulness in the great work of instructing
the rising generation, and extending the limits of human
knowledge." In conclusion, they declared that Long had
acted throughout "with candor and propriety," and his
perfect integrity of conduct, added to the fidelity with
which he had discharged his duties, had led them to give
the release he asked for.

Long, a man of many excellent qualities, was sensibly
touched by this liberal treatment. He was clearly aware
of the awkward position in which his retirement would,
for the time being, place the University, and its attitude
of unselfish consideration for his interests rather than for
its own, may well have made a grateful impression on
his mind. The kindly feeling which he had expressed
for the institution when he first thought of withdrawing,
was, doubtless, heightened by this generous conduct of the
Board when he actually resigned. Madison, in a letter
to Cabell, written the following month, asserts that
Long looked forward to his departure with regret; and
this is quite probable, for he had married, as we have
seen, a Virginian lady, a tie that must, in itself, apart
from the duties of his professorship, have done much to
bring him into sympathy with the community. Madison
testifies to his popularity with his pupils; and Long himself, towards the end of his life, spoke with praise of
their manly qualities. But he does not appear to have
been valued in the practical affairs of the institution beyond the threshold of his classroom. Madison stated
privately that he was an "embarrassing member of the
administrative body,"— a somewhat vague expression,
but one that perhaps meant that he was pertinacious of

his own opinions. There is no evidence, however, that he was a man of an aggressive or obstructive disposition; on the contrary, he seems to have been quiet and amiable; and it is possible that the embarrassment which he caused in the Faculty may have sprung from the fidelity of his friendship for Key, who never seemed at all satisfied after his translation to Virginia.

On several occasions, following his removal to London, Long exhibited his continued interest in the University. In December, 1828, he saw an opportunity for the library to complete its set of Valpy's edition of Stephenson's *Greek Thesaurus,* and he personally called the American minister, Mr. Barbour's, attention to it. He wrote frequently to Gessner Harrison, his successor, and was very often helpful in sending him the latest European contributions of value to the science of philology. His correspondence with the other of his two most distinguished pupils, the scholarly Henry Tutwiler, which lasted until his own death, contains many evidences of his kindly impressions of his life, work, and friends at the University of Virginia He won a high reputation after his return to England Indeed, by his subsequent writings and teachings, he exercised, during nearly half a century, a most fruitful influence on the classical scholarship of his native country; and he edited numerous classical texts with such acumen that some of them, in spite of the modern advance in research, remain in use down to the present day. He was the principal English authority on Roman law and ancient geography; and through the *Quarterly Journal of Education,* was very instrumental in furthering the success of the Society for the Diffusion of Useful Knowledge.

There was one member of the Board of Visitors who, at first, was averse to accepting Long's resignation, unless a substitute could be found at once to fill the vacancy that would follow. This was Chapman Johnson. He was not sanguine of their ability to secure an American of the proper acquirements for the place; his preference was for an English incumbent; and who more competent to lay hands on him than Long? He thought, therefore, that Long should be required to obtain this new professor as the condition of his own release from his contract. Johnson, unlike Jefferson, was a sound churchman, and now that the " old sachem " was not alive to protest, he asserted that a scholar from Oxford or Cambridge, who had been educated for the ministry, would be acceptable,— some young episcopal clergyman who could submit such a brilliant credential of his attainments as a diploma from one of these ancient universities. " Tell Cabell," he wrote Cocke, " it is time to give up his old prejudice upon this subject, the offspring of the French Revolution, long since a bastard by a divorce of the unnatural alliance between liberty and atheism."

It was the opinion of Alexander Garrett, a man of uncommon shrewdness, that the most suitable persons to appoint were " young Virginians, when they could be obtained unusually well qualified, with fine talents, studious habits, ambition to excell, and unexceptional moral deportment." A young man of this cast, if elevated to a professorship in the University, " was not so likely," he said, " to be invited to other situations, but would remain for years, constantly improving, and would become so closely identified with the institution of his own State that it would be difficult to induce him to leave it." When this conviction was uttered, two of the chairs had been filled in harmony with it,— those of law and ancient languages,— and time enough had gone by to demonstrate its soundness. Long also had held the same view.

For some time after his removal to London, he seems, under the influence of Madison's earnest solicitations, to have given Brougham and Barbour, the American Minister, all the assistance in his power to obtain the services of an English scholar, but he nevertheless continued to advise that the choice should be limited to America. Nor did he do this because he thought that it would be impossible to find a competent man, who, as Barbour expressed it, was willing " to leave England for a distant land." When, in September, 1827, he had written Cocke that he intended to resign, he was under the impression, as we have seen, that he would remain in Virginia until the end of his term in 1829; he calculated that this interval would be sufficient to allow him " to qualify one of two or three of his students to succeed him more able than any one the University would be likely to get "; and he said to Madison, in the same month, that he would " gratuitously and gladly spare no pains in procuring a proper succession by an extra assistance to one or two of his pupils, whose capacity and proficiency were singularly promising, and whose disposition was favorable to such a career."

The first applicant for the vacant chair was Jesse Burton Harrison. In December, 1827, he visited Charlottesville, and talked with Long in person, who told him that, so far, he had not suggested to any of his pupils the plan of preparation which he had proposed in his letter to Cocke. He seems to have given his approval to Jesse Burton Harrison's candidacy in consequence of this interview. " He allows me to say," wrote Harrison, " that he desires my success, and he favored me with such a letter to the rector as I could have exactly desired " Long counseled him to pursue a course of philological study in Germany; and he decided that, should the Board appoint him, he would leave Virginia for that country at his own expense, and return in the following September, unless Long should find himself in a position to tarry longer at the University, or a temporary instructor could be employed, who would assume charge of his classes until the following January. Long had made Harrison's acquaintance very soon after his arrival in Virginia, and had come to hold him in high esteem, both as a man and a scholar. Professor Tucker, who had probably known him when a resident of Lynchburg, the home of Harrison's father, the friend of Jefferson, also recommended him warmly in a letter addressed to Cocke.

But not Jesse Burton Harrison, but a student of his · own was to become Long's successor, which was to fulfil his earnest wish that his mantle should pass to some one of his pupils. If his advice should be followed, the choice was certain to fall on one of the two among them, whom he had, from the beginning, regarded with the most affection and respect; namely, Gessner Harrison and Henry Tutwiler, a couple of youthful scholars united to each other by the memories of early association, the same literary tastes and pursuits, and the close and loyal comradeship that springs up in collegiate life. They were the most distinguished graduates of the first two years. ·

Harrison was the son of a father who was warmly esteemed in the community in which he resided, the county of Rockingham, which lies in the most beautiful part of the Valley of Virginia. The most famous body of men who ever assembled in the State was the Convention ·of 1829–30. It can be justly said of it as a whole that it was the gathering of all the talents that then adorned the ancient commonwealth. Madison and Marshall, Monroe and Randolph, were the most celebrated figures in that brilliant council, but hardly second to them in ripe experience and long public service, were man after man who had come up from the different counties, with the unwritten credentials of their constituencies that they had been selected because they represented, in the most eminent degree, the civic virtue and wisdom of their several communities. No higher badge of personal usefulness and distinction could be possessed by any one in those times of thoroughly trained public men than the record of membership in this great convention. Gessner Harrison's father took his seat in that body hardly a year after his son's appointment to fill the vacancy caused by Long's resignation and return to England. He was a physician in active practice, whose literary bent was reflected in the choice library which he had collected, and whose strong partiality for the life of the country gentleman was indicated by the well-ordered and teeming farm on which he resided. His admiration of the liberty-loving Swiss prompted him to name his son Gessner after the famous Helvetian hero.

Gessner's precociousness of intellect was so phenomenal that he was able to begin his education at the age of four; and at eight, he was learning the rudiments of the Latin tongue. From his earliest boyhood, he was devoted to general reading, and a volume was rarely absent from his pocket. This book, in the intervals of wood-chopping on the farm, he would pull out and devour; nor was this habit simply one for passing amusement and recreation,— Horne Tooke's *Diversions of Purley*, an authoritative treatise in those times, was mastered in the like intervals of leisure, and to it, he always attributed his keen relish for philological studies.

When Gessner entered the University, he was required to stand an examination. "I was much surprised," wrote Long, many years afterwards, "to find that he knew so much and knew it so well." [1]   He was accompanied by his brother.   The two young men had been taught by their father to observe the Sabbath with Puritan strictness, and they could not be tempted to run counter to this parental lesson.   Jefferson, it will be recalled, was in the habit of inviting the students in succession to dinner at Monticello on that day, as the only one on which they were released from their class-rooms. When the turn of the two brothers came, they politely declined, with the ingenuous statement that they were unable to make up their minds to neglect their absent father's wishes and teachings.   Jefferson, so far from being displeased, was delighted with their candor, and heartily commended them for their filial piety, which, he said, was "a consolation to meet with in an age when the young were much inclined to disregard the advice of their elders."   He asked them to dine with him on another day, and they gladly accepted.   No doubt, he exerted himself to put at ease these youthful guests, who had won his particular respect and attention by their sturdiness of character, for they returned to the University with charming recollections of his courtesy, and with an impression of his versatile powers which was never erased from their minds.

On July 24, 1828, after the Board had acted on Long's resignation, they authorized the rector, Mr. Madison, to appoint to the vacancy, during one year, any one of the following persons: Gessner Harrison, M. L. Tracie, and R. Reynolds.   It seems that the Board was not sure that any one of the three would accept, for Madison was instructed to report at once should all decline.   Harrison

[1] Long spoke with equal praise of the preparatory training of Harrison's brother, who accompanied him to the University, as stated in the text.

had just graduated in Greek, and had also received the degree of doctor of medicine. He was apparently the first spoken to, and he promptly consented Writing to Madison in March, when Harrison had been occupying the professorship on probation for six months, Long said that he was convinced that his pupil was far better suited for the place than any one who might be procured in Europe. Madison himself was doubtful as to whether the new incumbent would be willing to remain in the chair. He thought it quite probable that Harrison would prefer to follow the calling of a physician; but this apprehension was soon removed, for Harrison intimated to him confidentially that " he was desirous of having his appointment made permanent." Possibly, he had been influenced by his former preceptor in reaching this decision, for Long had never tired of pressing upon the Board the wisdom of choosing him. "After a year's experience of his success as instructor," Long wrote to Madison, " I do not think the Visitors will have reason to repent of what they have done, and I hope they will not find it necessary to apply to England for that which they already possess. If I may venture an opinion of what I know of the people of this country (England), I believe no person will leave it who is so well qualified for the situation as the diligence and increasing experience of your present instructor will undoubtedly render him."

Harrison was elected permanent professor of ancient languages, on July 15, 1829. He was now in his twenty-second year. He was at this time a great teacher, not *in actu,* but *in potentia.* In his choice a step was taken, which, as we have seen, was warmly urged by astute Virginians, like Alexander Garrett and General Cocke, but which would hardly have won the approbation of Jefferson himself. Madison, comprehending fully his prede-

cessor's views, had, at first, endeavored to obtain a distinguished and experienced scholar from England to fill
the place vacated by Long, but there was now no Gilmer
to rely upon to make the search abroad that would be
necessary. It was useless to expect as much interest
and energy of Barbour, Long, and Key The obstacles
that so soon discouraged this trio were precisely the same
as those which Gilmer had surmounted with such conspicuous success. Full of promise as Gessner Harrison
was, it could not be correctly said of him that he, as a
young graduate of twenty-two, conferred any distinction,
in the beginning, on the chair. His appointment carried
a risk with it in spite of his acknowledged talents; but
that appointment set a precedent which, in numerous instances,— among which may be mentioned specially those
of Harrison himself, William B. Rogers, Basil L. Gil-
dersleeve, James L. Cabell, Francis H. Smith, and
Charles A Graves, of our own day, has furnished the
University with some of its most successful instructors,
whose genius for their calling was, perhaps, in a large degree, attributable to the very fact that they were college
professors from their youth, which gave them that much
more time in the highest academic atmosphere to round
out the more completely their native aptitude for teaching. Long, no doubt, remembered that he had begun his
fruitful career at the University with as little positive
experience of his profession as Harrison, and this quite
probably made him more lenient in his views of his successor's rawness, and more sanguine of the ever-increas-
ing competence which was to follow from that successor's
uncommon abilities and acquirements. He received the
news of Harrison's permanent appointment with keen
satisfaction. "It is a measure," he wrote Cocke,
" which I sincerely hope and believe will promote the in-

terests of your institution.   In whatever way, I and Mr.
Key can cooperate with him, by sending private papers of
our proceedings, or by attending to any commissions with
which we may be intrusted, we will endeavor to do it with
all dispatch and faithfulness.   The Universities of London and Virginia are the same in their general plan.
. . . We allow, for instance, students to choose their
own classes, but the Council, who correspond to the Visitors, recommend a certain course to those who enter at
an early period of life.   Our experience then, and the
suggestions which we are daily receiving from friends
and enemies, may not be without use to your classical
teacher."

XVI. *Successors to the First Professors, continued*

Blaettermann, who occupied the chair of modern languages, was, from the start, unhappy in his relations with
the students and professors alike.   In 1829, the privilege
of residing without the precincts was granted him, and
he was relieved of the obligation of attending without interruption the meetings of the Faculty.   The minutes of
that body disclose that he carried no weight with it; he
rarely offered a resolution; and whenever he did, it was
almost invariably voted down by the majority of his
colleagues as worthy of scant consideration.   It is possible that the right which he received to appear with
irregularity was suggested by the unpopularity of his
presence.   In 1830, he was called upon by the Board of
Visitors to make his weekly reports promptly and ac-
curately; to instruct his senior classes in the literatures
of the languages taught by him; and to resume his lectures
on modern history and geography.   It is clear that he
had hitherto been slighting the discharge of all these

duties.   In 1833, a resolution was actually submitted to abolish the chair of modern languages until further order, this being an indirect method of removing him, but it was finally rejected.   He was still in possession of it in 1835, for, during that year, it occurred to him to paint the front wall of his pavilion,— which also he seems to have retained,— in a color not in harmony with the red brick of the rest of the buildings.   The perplexing question arose: did a professor have the right to paint his pavilion in whatever tints his taste, or lack of taste, might prefer?   Did he have the right to paint it at all? The chairman thought not.   " I suggested to him," this official reported, " that if he painted the wall of his house, the Board of Visitors would probably require him to restore the uniformity he had destroyed, by painting, at his own expense, all the pavilions and dormitory walls on the Lawn."   This dry but alarming intimation banished his brush to the waste basket at once.   Several months later, he was complained of for building a second smoke-house in a vacant corner of his back-lot.   At the meeting of the Faculty, on the following day, this knotty question was debated: Should Blaettermann be required to pull down the obnoxious structure?   Or should the task of demolition be left to the proctor?

Blaettermann was very often at loggerheads with the students.   Those occupying dormitories near his pavilion averred that, while bending over their books, they were distracted by the ear-racking squeaks of violins, on which the boys in his house,— one of them a youthful negro slave,— were always practising.   " When I complained," reported Archibald Cary, " they only played more loudly and frequently."   Blaettermann refused to interpose his authority to stop this noise, and the chairman of the Faculty was compelled to step in.

But the friction with students under the arcades was of no consequence in comparison with his tumultuous intercourse with the members of his own school. It was said that they, not infrequently, withdrew from his lecture-room as many as a dozen at one time. On the night of March 29, 1836, he delivered a lecture which seems to have been accompanied by extraordinary disorder. Many of the young men who had come either to listen or to scoff belonged to the classes of his colleagues. Handfuls of small shot were thrown at him by some as he attempted to go on, whilst others shouted and beat frantically upon the doors. At the request of several of those present,— who, being more temperate than the rest, resented this unseemly commotion,— he withdrew to the drawing-room of his own pavilion, and there took up his discourse again. A crowd rapidly gathered, and pelted the walls and windows of the house with showers of stones, which they had brought with them for that purpose. In 1838, a formal petition for his dismissal was sent in by a section of the students. Two years later, the chairman of the Faculty felt constrained to report to the rector that, during the week just over, Professor Blaettermann had twice cowhided his wife,— once in the public road, directly under the eyes of several witnesses,— and that it was the " general opinion that Mrs. Blaettermann had done nothing which could, in the slightest degree, extenuate the enormity of the act." " It is generally believed," added the chairman, " that few, if any, students will enter Dr. Blaettermann's school in consequence of the notoriety of his misconduct and the general indignation which it excited." The Board convened on September 14, and after calmly listening to a long statement from him, in his own defense, removed him, by a unanimous vote, from his professorship. He soon, thereafter, retired to his farm situated in the county; and here, while passing alone along a road that led to a neighbor's, suffered a stroke of apoplexy that killed him on the spot. His wife, a lady of English birth, and of many accomplishments, opened a young ladies' seminary in Charlottesville, which enjoyed a fashionable and remunerative patronage.

That Blaettermann's services to the University had been of substantial value, in spite of his constant spleen, and harsh and tactless manners, was indicated in the appreciative resolution which the Faculty adopted when informed of his death; and they readily consented to the interment of his body in the University cemetery. The churlishness of his humor, in his intercourse with his colleagues, is illustrated in the following example of it which has been recorded. He was always very much interested in the history of old or unusual words. Tucker, in spite of his personal charm and fine literary taste, was thought to be slightly prosy as a lecturer. " Professor Blaettermann," he said on one occasion, when the two happened to meet, " what is the meaning of the word rigmarole? " " I don't know whether I can give you the exact meaning of the word," was the brusque reply, " but if one will go to hear one or two of your lectures, he will have a good idea of its meaning."

Owing to the voluminousness of his course, or to personal disqualifications, Blaettermann was the only member of the Faculty who during this period was assisted by tutors. The first of those associated with his school was Colonna D'Organo, who remained but one session (1830–31), and then went back to Europe. He was succeeded by I. Hervé, a citizen of France, who had been a successful teacher of his native tongue in Richmond.

When Blaettermann was dismissed, Charles Kraitser,

a Hungarian wanderer, who was master of many
European languages, was elected in his place.   Kraitser
had taken part in a Polish uprising against Russia, and
when appointed, had been residing in the United States
during seven years.   The income from his chair,—
which was then chiefly dependent on the fees,—fell off so
" enormously," to use his own expression, that, in 1843,
he was brought to the necessity of making some new provision for his subsistence.   Writing to the rector, Chapman Johnson, to this effect, he asked that his resignation
should be accepted at the close of the session in the following July.   But the purpose which he had in view was
not really withdrawal from the institution, but the acquisition of a higher salary, which he was convinced could be
forced by this device.   He was ready to remain, he
said, if the Board of Visitors would pay him five hundred
dollars additional for the present session, and guarantee
his income against fluctuations in the future.   Johnson refused to assent to this proposal,— doubtless because he
had reason to think that the decline in the fees was due
to Kraitser's unpopularity as a teacher.   Kraitser, influenced by the advice of Tucker, Harrison, Rogers, and
Dr. Cabell, who were friendly to him, finally withdrew
his resignation, but the majority of the Board were inflexible, in spite of an earnest petition in his behalf submitted by prominent citizens of Charlottesville.   He is
principally remembered, in the history of the University,
for a rueful remark which he is alleged to have made
after his practical dismissal.   " The Board of Visitors,"
he said, " were gentlemen whom it was hard to please.
They had kicked Dr. Blaettermann out because he had
whipped his wife, and they have kicked me out because
I have been whipped by my wife.   What did they really
want? "   Mrs. Kraitser, we are told, was a stalwart and

irascible woman of very humble beginnings, and constantly turned her husband, a man of diminutive stature, out of doors in the middle of the night.[1]

Bonnycastle, who followed Key in the chair of mathematics, was expected to continue lectures in natural philosophy until a new professor should be chosen. Probably, the additional task now imposed on him did not allow of this, for he neglected his old course so flagrantly that Madison complained that he had brought about an " awkward and unpleasant state of things " at the University. Numerous students, who had come on to attend that course, had left the institution in disgust. Madison was anxious to fill the vacant chair of natural philosophy with an English professor, because he knew that Jefferson would have preferred such an incumbent. Mr. Gallatin, the minister to the Court of St. James, was

---

[1] On September 4, 1844, Kraitser wrote the proctor, Colonel Woodley, the following pathetic letter. He was then in Richmond, with the intention of going on to Baltimore by steamer "Please send me ten dollars,— I am compelled to beg you once more, (how many times did I beg!) to help me along,—that I may float off to Philadelphia Please write me a few lines if you can do no more, informing me of your health and of that young friend's (probably Woodley's child); and write me also, without failing, the name of that friend who has given you $5 00 for me, that I may know to whom I owe them, together with my gratitude. I cannot now promise anything positive for fear of being again cheated out of my hopes, wishes, and expectations I am entirely afraid to have any wish any more"

How bitterly Kraitser felt is shown by the conclusion of the same letter "I may write to the Board of Visitors of the University of Virginia to ask them to express some opinion about my services of three years, but I am so scared with regard of any thought concerning them that I always feel convinced that they are pedantically formal, punctual, systematic, and careful in trifling and preposterous affairs and things, but quite informal and headless in everything that is just, bold, and serious. The scrap of dirty paper on which my nomination or appointment to the ill-fated professorship was written or scrawled by Frank Carr is verily a beautiful document given by a serious body of old men to a person newly appointed to a University. And of what kind of character must the certificate of dismission (of 'character,' as the negroes say) be? I will probably intimate to them the propriety of saying something concerning my nothingness." Proctor's Papers

warmly enlisted in securing one, and Key also endeavored to make the search successful; but nothing resulted; and the same upshot followed the appeal to Mr. Brown, the minister to the Court of Versailles.

The names of several Americans were then canvassed. One year after Bonnycastle's transfer to the chair of mathematics,— during which time the chair of natural philosophy must have received slim attention,— Robert M. Patterson was appointed to it. Patterson's father was a distinguished professor of mathematics in the University of Pennsylvania, and had also, at one time, occupied the position of Director of the Mint. The son had first made the most of all the advantages which the former institution had to offer, and had then completed his education at the feet of Gay Lussac, in France, and Humphrey Davy, in England. During his stay in Paris, he was appointed the American consul-general for that city, but Napoleon, under the impression that he was a relative of Betsy Patterson, his grossly injured and abhorred sister-in-law, declined to recognize him in that office. After his return to the United States, he was elected to a chair in the medical department of his native university, and, finally, to the professorship of mathematics and natural philosophy in its faculty of arts. Afterwards, he was called to the influential post of vice-provost. His practical talents were indicated in his being selected, after the British dash on Washington, to build the fortifications needed for the defense of Philadelphia.

Patterson was married to a beautiful and charming woman. She and her husband, after their arrival at the University, found an unfailing pleasure in throwing open their drawing-room to students and professors alike; and their pavilion soon became the scene of a hospitality

as graceful as it was overflowing.   Patterson himself was
not only a man of uncommon learning, but also one of
many personal qualities that endeared him as well to his
pupils as to his colleagues.   Distinguished for polished
manners, he paid his classes the compliment,— which, no
doubt, was gently laughed at rather than praised,— of
dressing for every lecture delivered by him as if he were
afterwards going on to an elaborate dinner party.   He
was the intimate and constant companion of Dunglison;
and when the latter's name was considered for the professorship of anatomy in the Baltimore Medical College,
he himself became a candidate for the professorship of
chemistry in the same institution, in order not to be separated from his friend.   But both failed of appointment.
Patterson resigned his chair after a few years' tenure,
and on his return to Philadelphia, was nominated to the
directorship of the Mint, in succession to his brother-in-
law, Dr. Samuel Morris.   This he held during a period
of sixteen years.

Professor Joseph Henry was selected as the next professor of natural philosophy, with the proviso, that,
should he decline, the place was to be open to Professor
William B. Rogers of the College of William and Mary.
Henry was already in too comfortable and congenial a
berth to accept the offer, but he earnestly recommended
Rogers.   " He is one of those," he said, " who, not content with retailing the untested opinions and discourses
of European philosophers, endeavor to enlarge the boundaries of useful knowledge by experiments and observations of his own."   Rogers was only thirty-one years of
age when chosen, in 1835, to succeed Patterson.   Then,
as throughout his later life, he possessed an almost trop-
ical imagination, and a disposition of poetic susceptibility.
His temperament, in fact, was that of a great orator;

but although so highly qualified for a political career, he chose that of a scientist without hesitation, and remained constant to it, with a loyalty that only increased in intensity to the end.   As early as his twenty-third year, he delivered a course of scientific lectures in Baltimore; and at twenty-four, was filling the combined chairs of mathematics and natural philosophy in the College of William and Mary.   Like Emmet, he was the son of an Irishman of genius, who had sought to better his condition by emigrating to the United States, and who, after lecturing on scientific subjects in Philadelphia, had accepted a professorship in the old seat of learning at Williamsburg.

It was fortunate that the science of geology now formed a part of the natural philosophy course at the University of Virginia, for it was in his exposition of this science, then rapidly springing up in importance, that Rogers, the son, had already won his greatest distinction. Indeed, our first personal glimpse of him is associated with his zealous devotion to his work in that department.   A few weeks before his final election, he is found inspecting the gold mines of Buckingham county and the rocks of Willis Mountain, with a note-book and rough hammer in his hands, and a pair of well-worn saddle bags thrown over his horse's back to hold his scanty clothing and his mineral specimens.   So supremely valuable were his explorations considered to be, that in, October, 1836, he was permitted to suspend his lectures in order to complete the vast Appalachian survey in which he was then engaged, under his commission as State geologist   This survey had begun very informally many months earlier " I have, for the last three years," he wrote Cabell in December, 1834, " devoted much of my leisure time to collecting valuable details relating to the geology of the State, and during the four months I have recently passed among the mountains, I have greatly enlarged my store of information.   In case a survey is authorized by the Legislature, I should feel a strong desire to undertake its execution."   His first report as State geologist was remarkable for its accuracy at a time when the knowledge of geology was often ludicrously defective.   Thus Dr. Eaton, the author of one of the early manuals, admitted that he was unable to decide whether a certain plant of the coal measures was a vegetable or a rattle-snake! The two brothers, William and Henry, were the first to describe with completeness the order of rock strata in the Atlantic States.   Henry had undertaken the exploration of New Jersey, while William was similarly engaged in Virginia.

There were two courses on which Rogers lectured that gave him a very congenial field for the display of his extraordinary gift of exposition, and also of the breadth and profundity of his scientific knowledge; namely geology and astronomy,— the first bearing upon the composition of the earth, one star; the second, on the composition of the remaining stars of the universe, as well as on the stupendous laws that control their vast revolutions.   All the witnesses testify with enthusiasm to his mesmeric dominion over this audiences   "Who can forget," says the venerable Francis H. Smith, his eloquent successor in the same chair, "that stream of English undefiled, so smooth, so deep, and yet so clear, that passed from point to point with gentle touch, that commonly flowed along with the quiet of conscious power, yet sometimes became tumultuous with feeling, and then came the music of the cataract and the glory of the rainbow!   Like Turner, with his one dash of carmine, so Rogers with one happy adjective could illuminate the whole picture."   Nor was this impassioned power of speech simply the vibration of a single musical key. During his attendance at a meeting of the British Association, one member was overheard to say to another, who belonged to an altogether different section, "You ought to have been in our room yesterday to hear Rogers, the American geologist." "Oh," was the reply, "you ought to have been in our room this morning to hear the other Rogers, the American physicist." They were both speaking of the same man!

Edward S. Joynes, describing Rogers's eloquence, as recalled by him in after-life, said that it was "a spell and an inspiration," and that "there was nothing like it in the University." It was only once a week that he discoursed on geology. The lecture room was situated in one of the wings of the Rotunda, and the hour of delivery was three o'clock in the afternoon, the most inconvenient of all for the majority of the students, and yet the addition to his own class from the other classes was so great that the apartment could not hold the surging crowd that fought to gain admission   "Old Bill," says Professor Joynes, "really liked this proof of popularity, and would find occasion to let himself go. He would walk backward and forward behind the long table, speaking without notes, and borne along by the sympathy of his audience. He had a way of passing his right finger down the side of his nose, and whenever that happened, a murmur would run around the room, ' Look out, boys, Old Bill is going to curl,' and curl he could and did as no other man could." Rogers, however, was not always in this inspired humor. Aware that so many of his hearers, in their eagerness to push and elbow their way into his lecture-hall, had shirked their recitations, he, at intervals, made a point of reducing his remarks to the last residuum of scientific aridness. Some soaring topic,

instead of being treated in its lofty phases with illuminating rhetoric of the highest order, would be discussed only
on those sides that were entirely devoid of popular interest. "I was once present," writes Dr. Ruffner,
"when it was thought he would deliver one of his great
astronomical discourses, but he took his seat and announced that he meant to deal with the cold mathematics
of the solar system; and added that this view would
affect a truly scientific mind more than any verbal pres-
entation of the grandeur of the system." This aptitude
for dry irony sometimes cuttingly revealed itself in his
intercourse with his own upils. Once, during a lecture,
he quoted the opinion which a Greek philosopher had
ventured as to the geological origin of the earth. At
the ensuing meeting of his class, he asked one of its
members to restate this view. The latter, having forgotten it, glanced hastily at a note-book which his comrade in the next seat held up accommodatingly to give
him the information desired, and then stuttered out in
confusion, " He regarded the earth as a whale." A profound silence, either of astonishment or apprehension,
followed, which was broken by Rogers saying, in his
coldest manner, " You should use your eyes more carefully, sir."

By 1842, Dr. Emmet's health, always delicate, had become so enfeebled that he was forced to leave the University,— temporarily as he supposed,— in the hope of
restoring it by a residence in a milder climate; but he
died before he was able to resume the duties of his chair.
He was succeeded by Henry Rogers, who was as accomplished in his department as his brother, William, was in
natural philosophy. Indeed, as a practical chemist and
expounder of chemical laws, he stood in the very front
rank of his profession.

XVII. *Successors to the First Professors, continued*

In 1830, John Tayloe Lomax, the first professor of law, was compelled, as he expressed it, " by justice to his family," to accept a judgeship from the General Assembly, as that office would afford him a more lucrative income " Nothing," he wrote Cabell, " would have induced me to relinquish the scheme of utility which my labors for four years has been consummating, had not the expense of that period, and the future prospects, warned me that my revenues could not but be less than what my family were entitled to claim at my hands." He offered, in January, when he first mentioned his intention of retiring, to continue the discharge of his old duties until the close of the session, should the Board permit him to attend the terms of his circuit, which would only consume six weeks altogether spread over the whole interval   This proposal must have been assented to, for his successor, Davis, apparently was not appointed until the ensuing July.   Madison acknowledged, in a letter to Cabell, that it would be useless to try to obtain the services of Judge Tucker, Philip P Barbour, or some other lawyer of their exalted standing, for the reason which had led Judge Lomax to resign, would, in turn, discourage men like these,— who were in possession either of a large practice or of seats on the bench,— from accepting the same position   The only candidate of prominence who seems to have applied directly for the place was William Maxwell, of Norfolk,— who, however, enjoyed a literary rather than a legal reputation.

John A. G. Davis, who succeeded Lomax, was a native of Middlesex, and a graduate of the College of William and Mary.   In 1824, having removed to Charlottesville, he became a member of the bar of Albemarle, but for some months also attended a course of scientific lectures at the University. He soon married a great-niece of Jefferson   Like most of the talented and aspiring young men of that day, he had concentrated an important share of his energies upon local politics.   As secretary of the convention which met in Charlottesville, in 1828, he won Madison's commendation by the conspicuous ability with which he discharged the duties of that position.   At this time, he was associated with Thomas W. Gilmer and Nicholas P. Trist, in the editorship of the *Advocate,* a local journal of recognized influence.   He had also served with efficiency as the secretary of the Board of Visitors.

Like Gessner Harrison, Davis was elected to his professorship at the start for a period of one session only, but his incumbency was made permanent at the close of his first term as a reward for the unmistakable aptitude which he had shown for the demands of his exacting chair. So steadily did he rise in the solid esteem of all, that, at the time of his unhappy death by the pistol of a masked student, he had come to be considered the most useful member of the Faculty.   Charles L. Mosby, an early graduate of the University, and an astute lawyer, gave the following reason for this advance: " Some of the professors," he said, in a letter to Cocke written in 1844, " who probably had the largest and most varied attainments in their respective departments, have been the least valuable to the institution, from the fact that they were personally unknown beyond the precincts, and so made no good impression on the public mind by free and familiar intercourse with the people.   Professor Davis was an exception. . . .   To dignity of character, he happily united a certàin freedom and familiarity of manner which made him as acceptable to the public as he was valuable to the University." This suavity of tongue and demeanor was also dwelt upon in the resolution adopted by the vestry of his church after his murder; and that body also referred very feelingly to the serenity of his temper, the gentleness of his disposition, his kindness of heart, faith in friendship, firmness of mind and purpose, solicitude for the wants of others, and promptness in the discharge of duty.

It was said of Davis by a distinguished pupil that he taught the science of jurisprudence as a code of principles, and not as a code of precedents, in the manner of his most prominent successor   In his view of his subjects, constitutional law formed by far the most vital part of the course. The *Federalist* and the *Resolutions of 1798–99* were the great fountain-heads of his political doctrine, and through his exposition of these classic texts, his pupils learned to deny the supremacy of the Federal courts when the latter sought to define the rights of the States according to their own interpretation of the Constitution.   He was, in other words, a consistent and inflexible disciple of Jefferson and Madison.   His loss was a heavy blow to the prosperity of the school, which was not softened by the appointment of his temporary successor, N. P. Howard.   Mrs Ward, who had charge of one of the hotels, complained to the Board of Visitors that, in consequence of Davis's death, sixteen of her boarders, who attended his classes, had withdrawn from the University.

Dunglison resigned at the close of the session 1832–3. "I have many fears," he wrote Madison, "that this mountain air, which is proverbial rheumatic, does not agree with Mrs. Dunglison, and this dread makes me disposed to embrace any offer which may be sufficiently advantageous." He had acquired such reputation in his profession, that, by 1830, he was receiving invitations to enter the faculties of other institutions. During that year, he was elected to a chair in the Medical School of Cincinnati, but he refused to accept it on the ground that the site of that town lay too far inland to be conven- ient for any one either to go to it or to depart from it. He was asked to select any chair in the Jefferson Medical College, in Philadelphia, which he should pre- fer, but this invitation he at first declined, because that in- stitution, he said, had been founded in a spirit of oppo- sition to the other colleges of the city, and not as the result of any real demand for its creation in the urgent needs of the community. He seems to have been dis- posed to accept the chair of anatomy in the Medical School in Baltimore; but he suffered his candidacy to come to nothing without apparent regret. He finally received with favor a call to the chair of materia medica, therapeutics, hygiene, and medical jurisprudence in the Faculty of the University of Maryland.[1] So high was the esteem in which he was held that Madison was anxious that the " door should be kept open for his re- turn " in case the new post should prove disappointing to him   He did not sever the tie with the University at once, but from the beginning of the session of 1833–4, down to October 15, he delivered his regular lectures on obstetrics. The thoroughness of his system of teaching was illustrated in his course on materia medica, his prin- cipal topic: he first discoursed at length on the virtues and uses of the different articles, and then recapitulated the whole lecture; or else he recapitulated, equally as fully, at the end of the description of each article. In addition, he examined his pupils once a week on the sub-

[1] Subsequently, he became a member of the Faculty of the Jefferson Medical College

jects of that week's lectures,— not, as he said, to cate-
chise them, but to bring back again whatever might have
been forgotton.

Long, it will be recalled, boasted of the quickness and
readiness with which he moulded himself to the domestic
habits of the Virginians. Apparently, this did not go far
beyond the acquisition of a taste for the humble but
wholesome corn-cake Dunglison, on the other hand,
went much further. He had been residing at the University only four years when he bought a negro for his
own household service,— an act the more remarkable as
his wife was an Englishwoman, who could have had but
little tolerance for the institution of slavery. As the
price was small,— two hundred and forty dollars,— the
negro was probably under age; and after his purchase,
occupied perhaps the general status of an English appren-
tice.

Dunglison was succeeded by Alfred T. Magill. His
appointment had come about in a way that would hardly
have been thought by Jefferson to be sufficient justification of it, or in harmony with the reputation which the
chair had acquired through its previous incumbent. A
member of the Board of Visitors had been pleased with a
prize essay by Magill on the subject of typhus fever, and
he sent it to Dr Johnson, the professor of anatomy and
surgery, for him to pass final judgment upon its merits.
In writing of his favorable impression to Magill, Johnson
said, " I read your essay very attentively . . . and so
entirely was I satisfied with your ability that I did not
hesitate, though you were personally unknown to me,
to urge your claim in the strongest language." Judge
Henry St. George Tucker, Magill's father-in-law, was
equally enthusiastic about the essay " For style and
manner," he said to Cabell, " it is not inferior to anything

I have ever seen." Apparently, the genuine excellence of this single casual production alone brought Magill the appointment.

He had received his medical education in Philadelphia; but his active practice had been restricted to the county of Jefferson, where he resided; and it had been spread over four years only. The Board of Visitors limited his first appointment to a single session in order to test his ability to fill the chair acceptably. His introductory lecture was delivered to a packed audience, which had gathered in curiosity to hear the new and untried professor. " I must confess I was not a little alarmed and agitated," Magill modestly reported afterwards, " but I have reason to believe that I acquitted myself tolerably well." And this was the history of his incumbency of his chair. He entered upon its duties with a very moderate preparation in comparison with his predecessor, Dunglison, but he soon displayed aptitude of a high order; and when compelled, four years later, to seek relief from ill-health in a temporary rest, he received a sympathetic letter from the pupils in his classes, in which they dwelt with emphasis on his excellence as a teacher. In addition to his learning, he possessed an unusual charm of character. " He is gentle in his manners and free from austerity," said his father-in-law, in recommending him to Cabell; and this, with his fine native talents, pure and conscientious spirit, and superior attainments, has caused his memory to remain one of the most fragrant in the history of the University. He withdrew in May, 1837, and died in the course of the following month. His last act was to lift himself up with great pain in his bed, so that a picture might be taken of him for the solace of his children. Of the stoutest Revolutionary stock, he endured the ravages of his disease, consumption, with all the fortitude of a dying soldier   " This affliction," he wrote to his father, " has made me see more clearly than ever before the inestimable value of our religion, and my belief in it has been to me the source of unspeakable consolation "

Augustus L. Warner, of Baltimore, succeeded Dr Johnson in 1834 as professor of anatomy and surgery; R E. Griffith succeeded Dr. Magill.   He withdrew in 1839, and in his turn was succeeded by Henry Howard as professor of medicine.[1]   The chair had been offered first to Dr. Gross, and afterwards to Dr Harrison, of Philadelphia; but both, being agreeably situated already, had declined it.   So much delay was caused by the effort to find an acceptable tenant for it that the medical students openly threatened to desert the precincts in a body if it was not filled forthwith.   In June, 1837, James L. Cabell was a candidate for the professorship of anatomy and surgery, which had become vacant through Dr Warner's resignation   Cabell was a master of arts of the University, and after leaving its lecture-rooms, had pursued his medical studies in a hospital in Baltimore, which enjoyed the distinction of being the only one in America in which students were permitted to perform the surgical operations.   At the time of his election, he was walking

[1] Dr Henry Howard was a native of Frederick county, Maryland   In his eighteenth year, he began the study of medicine in Philadelphia, and after the completion of his course, practised for a period of twenty-four years in Montgomery county, was professor of medicine for a term of two years in the University of Maryland, and was then elected to the chair of medicine in the University of Virginia, with which institution he was associated until 1867, when he resigned and became the president of a bank in Charlottesville   The resolutions adopted by the Faculty on the occasion of his voluntary withdrawal dwell upon " his faithful services to the University through alternate periods of depression and prosperity "   He was equally valued in his private character   " This community," said the *Charlottesville Chronicle* in July, 1867, " never had any citizen more universally esteemed and respected "   Dr. Howard died in 1874

the hospitals of Paris. His term of service began with the session of 1837–8.

Cabell was a nephew and protégé of Joseph L. Cabell,[1] and in his case, the first sharp issue of nepotism, in the history of the University, was raised. The criticism aroused by his appointment had undoubted pertinency, for the new professor was a very young. man whose capacity as surgeon or physician had not been proven in actual practice. Indeed, at the hour of his selection, he had not progressed beyond the stage of studentship himself, and yet he became, almost on the threshold of his service, one of the most valuable of all the teachers embraced in the distinguished circle of the Faculty. At the start, he seems to have felt some aversion to the particular department in which he was called upon to lecture. He was so thoroughly educated that he was fully competent to instruct in more than one course. As a young man, he had been the mathematical tutor in the Napton Academy in Charlottesville; and on the professorship of moral philosophy becoming vacant in 1846, by the resignation of Tucker, he came forward as a candidate for the place, with a very learned and influential backing. When Dr. McGuffey, who was elected, died many years. afterwards, Dr. Cabell, in association with Dr. Witherspoon, the chaplain, undertook the duties of the chair until a successor to McGuffey was chosen. At one time, he considered very seriously the plan of withdrawing

[1] Judge William H Cabell wrote in August, 1829, to his brother Joseph as follows· "Our nephew, James L. Cabell, will be sixteen years old in a few days. He is the finest boy I ever saw To an excellent capacity, he adds the most remarkable assiduity. In returning home from parties, I have frequently found him at his studies at twelve or one o'clock at night. I think he bids fair to be one of the cleverest men in the country" "I am so well pleased with his habits and progress," Cabell wrote Cocke in September, 1832, "that I am determined to give him a finished education"

from the University and establishing a boarding school of a high order for young ladies. His wife's health was then infirm, and he thought that the change to the country proposed would be likely to restore it. In 1847, he was elected to a professorship in Richmond Medical College, and actually sent in his resignation of the chair of anatomy and surgery, which he then occupied in the University; but so anxious were the Board of Visitors to retain his services that the advertisement for his successor was deferred for a period of two weeks in the hope that he would, in the interval, be induced to alter his purpose. The resignation was withdrawn, and until his death, Cabell continued a member of the University Faculty. ·

Not a professor in the institution was more esteemed and valued than he, and there was not one more capable of original work. In 1859, he published the *Testimony of Modern Science to the Unity of Mankind,* in which he drew, in support of his conclusions, upon all the resources of physiology, zoology, and comparative philology, so far as they had been opened up by research and observation Many of the laws of biology, which were then unknown, were stated in this remarkable volume, and instances to illustrate them adduced, which, only a short time afterwards, were brought forward by the great English protagonists of the Doctrine of Evolution. The central point of his thesis was, that, as the lower organisms had shown the power to develop variety without the intervention of supernatural agencies, man himself might have reached his present form by the same process of natural selection and elimination. Many of the most serious objections to the theory which the English scientists foresaw, and more or less successfully combated, Cabell also anticipated, such as the difficulty of differentiating species from variety, the supposed sterility of hybrids, and the absence of indispensable links. The outburst of the War of Secession not only diverted him from further investigation in this new field, but also obscured his share in revealing those biological facts which have given so much celebrity to the names of Darwin and Huxley.

It might have been easily predicted of a man who could produce such a work as this that he would not fail to keep abreast of every great advance in his profession. It was noticed that he received all the new theories with eager but discriminating hospitality. Instead of rejecting, it was said, the remarkable revelations of the microscope and chemistry, when applied to biological studies, he accepted them in a spirit of wise enthusiasm. The antiseptic treatment of Lister found in him an earnest advocate before its merits had been generally recognized. He was then seventy years of age, a period of life not always friendly to innovation in any province of human affairs. But it was in preventive medicine that his principal achievement lay. The great movement on this line which has accomplished so much, began just about the time that he was chosen a member of the University Faculty. Its inauguration enlisted his interest at once. His name is found in the small list of the earliest members of the American Public Health Association, the first organized effort to introduce a reform in the laws relating to hygiene; he became the President of this body in 1879; and as chairman of its committee on legislation, was chiefly instrumental in drafting the measures which culminated in the establishment of the National Board of Health, of which he was appointed the first executive. He took the foremost part in the work of that Board, especially as directed to the suppression of yellow fever in the Southern States by revolutionizing the methods of quarantine; and it was admitted by his colleagues that it was due, in large degree, to his peculiar qualifications for the post that so much success was won.

Of Cabell, it was said that he had the courage of a lion, tempered with the tenderness of a woman.   He was a man of extraordinary personal independence of character, and yet full of consideration for the sensibilities of others; firm and decided in the expression of his own convictions, yet tolerant of differences of opinion.   In his personal bearing, he showed all the finished courtesy of the old school, made more impressive by his natural air of distinction; but nevertheless, when occasion arose, no one could give sharper tongue to disapproval.

"One winter's morning," says Dr. John C. Wise, " when Cabell's class in surgery awaited him, scanning and noting the neat clear syllabus of the coming lecture, it grew weary, and some impatient spirit going outside, gathered a huge mass of snow, and returning with it, inaugurated a ball contest, that soon waxed fast and furious.   Window lights were broken in plenty; the syllabus was hit; and long irregular lines coursed down the board.   All was riot and confusion, when, in a moment, the forgotten majestic Cabell was on the platform.   He arranged his notes on his lectern, took from his pocket an immaculate kerchief, glanced about him and seemed to shiver; he then saw the wrecked glass, the disordered floor, and alas, his ruined syllabus.   In a moment, it was all clear to him; his wrath swept him as a typhoon lashes the China Sea, yet he controlled it, and in a voice of suppressed emotion he flayed us! ' For boys, yes; but for men engaged in the serious and dignified study of medicine to engage at such a time and in such a place in sport destroying the property of a school afflicted with the direst poverty, such conduct is incomprehensible and unmanly!' Needless to say, there was no repetition of the offense."

XVIII. *The Professors' Fees*

In the description given of the circumstances of the English professors' selection and appointment, we referred incidentally to the emoluments that were definitely promised them for their anticipated services. As was then stated, their principal reward was to consist of the tuition fees. A specific sum was also to be paid, but only to assure a fair remuneration, should the fees of any chair turn out to be small and inadequate in amount. The rule adopted at the University was really the one that prevailed at the College of William and Mary when Jefferson was a student there: we learn from LaRochefoucauld that each instructor in that institution, at the time of his visit, received four hundred dollars as a fixed salary; and that he was also allowed to appropriate all the fees derived from the young men who had entered his classes.

It has been generally presumed, on the authority of Jefferson himself, that his object in assigning the tuition fees to the professors was to prick and stimulate them to greater energy by making it directly to their interest to increase the number of pupils seated in their several lecture-rooms. It is not improbable, however, that the University's poverty at the start was the true reason for the rule. Had the first session showed an enrollment of one thousand students instead of a hundred and twenty-three, is it likely that he would have been willing for the enormous fees, which would have resulted, to become the personal property of a little coterie of men who could lay no claim to having swelled the volume of those fees by the influence of their own reputations? It was the small attendance that was expected at first which made his plan of remuneration not inequitable either to the University or to the instructors   This was the only safe method to follow until the institution should become popular and prosperous.   It is true that it worked more profitably for the institution than for the professors at first; but Jefferson was fully justified in thinking, that, as between the two, the interests of the University should be paramount.   The original rule was, afterwards, with great persistence, held up as a precedent, which not even the Board of Visitors, it was asserted, could validly slight; but this view was not frankly advanced until the number of students had increased so much that the fees of the most important classes had begun to grow highly profitable to the professors who taught them.   The Board, as we shall see hereafter, very properly refused to acknowledge that there was any partnership between the University and its instructors, or that the relation of the latter to the institution was one of private gain at all.   In time, they quietly and resolutely abolished the right to the fees as a part of the remuneration of the members of the Faculty; all were placed upon the footing of an equal salary; and this at once removed that suggestion of sordidness and self-advertisement which was so unworthy of a seat of learning no longer forced to rely upon shifts to preserve its solvency

After the War of Secession, when there was a return to the original system, in consequence of the fear that poverty would hamper the institution for some years to come, the unexpected accumulation of fees in the hands of many of the professors from the large attendance of students became so great that they themselves proposed to contribute out of their own pockets to the establishment of certain imperative scientific courses which the Uni-

versity was unable to introduce, owing to the diversion
of these fees from its treasury.

During the first years, it was the instructors in law and
medicine who complained that the prevailing system bore
more harshly on them than on the other members of the
Faculty; and as this was shown to be true, they were permitted to charge a higher single fee than the rest of the
schools, so as to counterbalance the disparity. The
Board, anticipating a steady increase in the number of
the students, sought to light upon a rule that would,
without injustice, assure the maintenance of practical
equality in the remuneration. It was finally decided to
allow the fixed salaries of the original teachers to remain
as they were, but, after 1835, to restrict those of the
new to one thousand dollars, which was five hundred dollars less. No general alteration in the system of fees
was attempted at this time, which left the disparity un-
changed. The following table indicates the relative
profit, in the form of fees, of the different professors during the years 1835, 1836 and 1837:

	1835	1836	1837	Average
Ancient Languages . ..	$2,180 00	$1,950 00	$1,944.00	$2,031.00
Modern Languages . .	1,580 00	1,735 00	1,607 00	1,640.66
Mathematics	3,045.00	3,065 00	3,493 00	3,201.33
Natural Philosophy	2,105.00	2,210 00	2,897 00	2,404 10
Chemistry	2,815 00	3,145 00	3,090 00	3,016 66
Medicine	943 00	1,045 00	1,395 00	1,114.00
Anatomy and Surgery ...	1,130 00	1,500 00	1,465.00	1,365 00
Moral Philosophy .	1,280 00	1,710.00	1,195 00	1,395 00
Law	1,475 00	2,755 00	2,135 00	2,121 66

It was reasonable enough that Tucker, the incumbent
of the chair of moral philosophy, the fees of which had
shrunk so sensibly, should have complained to Cabell of
the flagrant inequality in the remuneration. Four of
the schools, he pointed out, received from one thousand to
twelve hundred dollars above the average, and four oth-

ers, from four hundred to nine hundred above it.   The
difference between the largest and the smallest income
from fees was annually in excess of twenty-one hundred
dollars.   The establishment of the School of Engineering
had greatly swelled the profits of two of the schools, which
had already reached a very high figure; namely, of the
Schools of Mathematics and Natural Philosophy.   " I
have always felt it an injustice and a humiliation,"
Tucker remarks in the letter quoted, " that I receive so
much less compensation than several of my associates,
who perform no more laborious services, whose experience was no greater than mine, and who incurred no
greater responsibility. . . . I am sure that there is no
professor here whose place could not be readily filled, or
whose loss would make the difference of five students to
the University.   I have felt the disparity the more too,
as well as those circumstanced like me, because there is,
perhaps, no other college in the United States in which
the pay of the professors is grossly unequal, and except
in the case of the president, is not precisely the same."

Tucker proposed that each member of the Faculty
should receive a fixed and uniform salary out of a joint
fund to be made up of the annual appropriation by the
State and the fees paid by the students.   This plan was
in harmony with the one which all the other colleges had
adopted.   Moreover, he predicted that it would nourish
a feeling of concord and fraternity among the professors;
and furthermore, by rendering them independent of the
fees of their classes, increase their ability to maintain
discipline and preserve order.   Tucker suggested that,
should this solution be acceptable to the Board, the fixed
salary should remain as at present, and that all the fees
should be thrown into a general pot, with the exception
of ten dollars of the amount paid by each pupil, which

should be reserved for the professor of the class to which that pupil belonged. These sensible proposals led to no change in the system of remuneration at that particular time; but, as we shall see, they were adopted in principle at least, at a riper hour.

In spite of the inequalities that prevailed in the professors' incomes, the social ties uniting them seemed to have been, on the whole, kindly and agreeable. We have already quoted Tucker's pleasant impressions of the social life of the University. In 1834, Bonnycastle wrote to Cocke that the members of the Faculty " held private meetings for the exchange of mutual good feelings," and for the discussion of " the most interesting topics of the day." These parties were composed of the instructors, the clergyman, the proctor, and visiting strangers invited by the host. Dr. Magill spoke very gratefully of the politeness and hospitality that were lavished on him after his arrival. " I have either dined or supped with most of the professors," he wrote his wife, who lingered in Winchester. He sent her word to purchase twenty or thirty pounds of butter before she set out, and to bring it along with her in a jar as a part of her baggage. There was, however, he said, no necessity for her to encumber herself with pickles and preserves, for Mrs. Davis, Mrs. McKennie, and Mrs. Emmet had already filled the storeroom in his pavilion with condiments and sweetmeats,— all made with their own beneficent and skillful hands. Some other amiable friend gave him a barrel of vinegar; but this, unfortunately, burst, and flooded the entire floor of his cellar with its acrid fluid.

XIX. *The Library*

How were the students supplied with the books which they required for their regular courses or for supplementary reading? There were, in the interval between 1825 and 1842, several book-sellers established in the immediate vicinity of the University, who were ready to furnish all the volumes that were called for in the class-room. The principal one seems to have been C. P. McKennie; and next to him were Street and Sanxey, a Richmond firm, who, during many years, were represented on the ground by William Wertenbaker. The collection of articles temptingly arranged in these two stores was large and varied; indeed, the polite shopmen endeavored to satisfy every need of the student in the way of the toilet as well as of the lecture-room. A pair of morocco pumps would be displayed in close proximity to the *Federalist* and the *Resolutions of 1798–9*, and a bundle of cigars or roll of violin strings would half cover an ornate copy of *Don Quixote* or *Gil Blas*. Soap, shoes, quills, sealingwax, bear's oil, hose, snuff-boxes, powder, razors, brushes,— all were for sale with the latest text-books in law, medicine, natural philosophy, and the ancient languages. Whether the student sought to gratify his taste for smoking, letter-writing, or foppishly adorning his person, or whether he wished to add to his collection of books for study or private reading, it was to these accommodating stores that he first directed his foot-steps.

It would be presumed that, with the University library at his service, he would not have been forced to spend much money in purchasing for the pleasure of independent reading, but, as we shall now see, the volumes of that library,— at first, at least,— were reserved for consultation only. It was not a storehouse of literature for pastime; on the contrary, it was originally gathered up with the most inflexible reference to its practical usefulness in complementing the work of the lecture-room. The plan for its formation was drafted by Jefferson himself. This plan, like the one for the extension of the buildings, allowed of the library's indefinite expansion along the same general lines. The collection was to embrace: (1) books of great reputation which were too costly for the average purse; (2) the most authoritative volumes in exposition of each science; (3) tracts marked by special merit; (4) books that were valuable because written in rare languages; (5) several editions of the same classic, which were esteemed each for its own excellence; (6) translations of superior elegance in themselves, or opening to readers works in an abstruse tongue; (7) books that were valuable as relating to some subject that had been but little treated.

There were two conspicuous features in this scheme which were highly characteristic of Jefferson· (1) all volumes that were designed for amusement only were to be shut out; (2) the only religious books to be let in were to be those that were so free from controversial taint that persons of every sect could read them with approval.   Indeed, so jealous was he of all ecclesiastical interpretations that he refused to accept any work on geology that could be made the basis of theorizing on the evolution of the globe through purely material agencies. The subdivisions adopted by him show how thoroughly he had, in his own mind, considered every section of the field which the volumes of a university library should cover.   They are worthy of repetition as offering further evidence of the breadth and exactness of his practical intellect.[1]

[1] In one of his reports, as Librarian, to the Faculty, Wertenbaker inti-

History		Philosophy	
Civil	*Physical*	*Mathematical*	*Moral*
1 Ancient	6 Physics, Pure	17 Arithmetic	19 Ethics
2 Modern, Foreign	7 Agricultural	18 Geometry	20 Religion
3 British	8 Chemical		21 Law–Nature and
4 American	9 Anatomy and		Nations
5 Ecclesiastical	Surgery		22 Law–Equity
	10 Medical		23 Law–Common
	11 Biology		24 Law–Merchant
	12 Botany		25 Law–Maritime
	13 Mineralogy		26 Law–Ecclesiasti-
	14 Technology		cal
	15 Astronomy		27 Law–Foreign
	16 Geography		28 Law–Civil Polity

Fine Arts

29 Architecture	35 Tragedy
30 Gardening, Painting, Sculpture, Music	36 Comedy
	37 Dialogue and Epistolary
31 Epic Poetry	38 Rhetoric
32 Romantic Poetry	39 Criticism in Theory
33 Pastoral Poetry	40 Bibliography
34 Didactic Poetry	41 Philology

The largest number of volumes in the library, as provided for by Jefferson, related to the two subjects, in which,— if we leave out natural history and natural philosophy,— he felt the most penetrating interest; namely, ancient languages and the science of law. There were, in the first list submitted by him, four hundred and nine titles touching the classics, and three hundred and sixty-seven touching jurisprudence in all its branches. Modern history followed with three hundred and five; religion and ecclesiastic history, with one hundred and seventy-five; pathology, with one hundred and sixty; philology and literature, with one hundred and eighteen; and the remaining subjects in dwindling proportions.

There were certain aspects of this original catalogue which revealed very plainly the bent of Jefferson's tastes

mates that Jefferson obtained the hint of this classification from Bacon's subdivision of knowledge.

as a student and as a reader.   The number of volumes which it contained relating to ancient history were nearly double the number of those relating to modern,— only 'seven titles bore on English history and only six on American   The former included the works of Hume and Smollett; the latter, of Robertson, Marshall, and Botta.   Only one of the six volumes bearing on natural history and zoology was written in the English language; only two of the nine bearing on botany; and only two of the nine also bearing on the mechanical arts. All the volumes descriptive of architecture, painting, sculpture, and music, were written in Italian.   Of the twenty-five titles relating to astronomy, five only were written in English.   All the works in epic poetry belonged to foreign tongues.   No copy of the *Paradise Lost* is to be found in the original list.   Was this because that great poem was, in his opinion, tainted with the spirit of ecclesiastical, not to say, sectarian, aggressiveness?   It was perhaps too orthodox and too controversial in its flavor to be really palatable to him.   The numerous volumes containing odes and pastorals were, with one remarkable exception, written either in the Latin or the Italian tongue; B. M. Carter's *Poems* was that exception, for this provincial author seems to have rushed in where Milton's angels had feared to tread. All the didactic poetry was in the Greek or Latin language.

Shakespeare gained an entrance under the head of Tragedy, but no English author enjoyed the like distinction under the head of Comedy.   As the plays of Sheridan, Goldsmith, and Congreve could claim no higher usefulness than an ability to tickle the sense of amusement, they were rejected, and the Latin Humorists enthroned in their stead.   Chesterfield, in English, and

Sevigné, in French, were admitted under the head of Epistles, and Professor Tucker's *Essays* under the head of Criticism. Bacon, Locke, Selden, Gibbon, Johnson, Berkeley, Blair, and Darwin were represented in their most famous works; Sterne, strange to say, only in a volume of sermons. Pope,— except in his translation of Homer's *Iliad*,— Gray, and other illustrious English poets, were not represented at all.

From the point of view of the ancient classics, the library, in its original selections, was of extraordinary value; its value from a scientific point of view was hardly less; but from the point of view of English belles-lettres, it was so starved and spindling as to be undeserving of praise. There was a moral and a practical explanation for this disproportion: first, Jefferson seems to have relished but little the delights of the classics of his native language; and second,— and this is the more important reason of the two,— the University's means were so narrow that he was compelled to restrict his purchases to the collection of a working library for the professors and students. He, perhaps, thought that the study of the ancient classics would ripen the literary taste of the young men without the need of bringing in the works of the principal English writers. Had there been, at the start, a separate chair of history and literature, it is quite possible that he would have swelled his list with a greater number of books bearing on the authors of his own tongue, for such a school, once created, would have required as many authorities as the School of Latin and Greek A supplementary list removed some of the English deficiencies of the first list, for in it we discover, not only Roscoe's *Leo X*, O'Meara's *Napoleon*, and Wirt's *Patrick Henry*, but also Thomson's *Seasons*, Tasso's *Jerusalem Delivered*, and Butler's *Hudibras*; and in addition, the most famous works of Swift, Molière, Voltaire, and Franklin.

Thoughtfully and precisely as Jefferson's classification had been drawn, it was not employed as a guide in the final arrangement of the library. The one really followed contained several important modifications; instead of the titles being distributed under forty-two heads, they were compressed under twenty-nine,— which was effected by reducing, under a single head, subjects that had, at first, been assigned to several. Law was not subdivided at all, and religious history and ecclesiastical history were united. Medicine, on the other hand, was expanded under half a dozen heads. This new classification, however, was attended with a loss of analytical lucidity.

The books that were purchased before Jefferson's death were obtained through the agency of either Francis Walker Gilmer or William Hilliard, of Boston. A large proportion arrived at the University in time for his personal inspection. These were hauled up from Richmond by wagon under the supervision of W. B. Garth, who, in March, 1826, delivered seven hundred and thirty-three volumes in two boxes, and in July, three additional cases. It is a proof of the closeness of Jefferson's scrutiny, that he descried a defect in the title of one of the books after they had been assorted on the shelves in an apartment of the present Colonnade Club.[1] He had ridden over from Monticello, and so soon as he entered the room, he began to take up and look through one volume after another. After some time thus spent, he called Mr. Wer-

---

[1] Mrs. Sarah Conway has recorded her recollection of seeing Jefferson placing the first books of the library on the shelves in the present Colonnade Club. "I was an inquisitive little girl," she said, "and peeped in the window." This would seem to prove that the books were placed on the ground floor.

tenbaker to his side; pointing to a copy of Gibbon's *Decline and Fall,* he said, "You should not have accepted that copy of that book. It should have been returned at once." "Why, sir?" asked the librarian in surprise. "It is a very handsome edition" "That may be so," replied Jefferson, "but look at the back." An inspection revealed that the title, instead of being Gibbon's *Roman Empire,* as it should have been, was Gibborn's *Roman Empire*

Jefferson had been dead only a week when we discover Hilliard himself in the library busily assisting Wertenbaker in opening the boxes which contained the final instalment of the volumes that had been last bought. They were found to be in perfect condition, and, in number and title, in conformity with the invoices. "The amount furnished for the purchase of the books," Hilliard reported to the Faculty, "was altogether inadequate to the accomplishment of the catalogue made out." The most expensive works, indeed, had to be omitted at first because there was only a sum of ten thousand dollars reserved for the purchase. As the commission on this amount was too small to assure Hilliard a satisfactory compensation for his exertions and loss of time, the Faculty consented to his firm's establishing an agency in Charlottesville, which was to supply the students with text-books, and the library with all future additions to its collection So great, however, was the dissatisfaction caused by the failure of the firm to furnish the German editions needed by some of the classes, and also by its dilatoriness in general, that the Faculty complained to the Board of Visitors and urged that New York booksellers should be employed, as they were in much more regular and frequent communication with Europe than those of Boston. The committee reported in September, 1826, that the present collection was " an excellent foundation for a public library, especially in ancient works," but that " it was deficient in modern publications "; and they earnestly recommended that numerous additions should be made to it in the two departments of literature and science.

By what means was the number of volumes in the library gradually increased? In his will, Jefferson bequeathed to the University all the books that should belong to him at the time of his death. In spite of the sale of the choicest volumes to Congress, the residue still contained works of extraordinary interest and value; but owing to the debts for which his estate was liable, his executor, his grandson, Thomas Jefferson Randolph, was reluctantly compelled to sell this important remainder. " Feelings of the most affectionate devotion to my grandfather's memory," he said to the Faculty, " would induce me as his executor to gratify his wishes upon these points at all risks but that of injustice to his creditors, and the fear that his memory might be stained with the reproach of a failure to comply with any of his engagements. An assurance is, therefore, given that, when his debts are discharged, however much his family may be straitened in their circumstances, no consideration of pecuniary interest in their individual distress will bar immediate compliance."

The only books that had belonged to Jefferson which found their way to the shelves of the library were presented by him during his life-time. These were but four in number, and were not of uncommon interest beyond their association with Monticello. The library also failed to acquire the collection previously the property of Francis Walker Gilmer. At his executors' request, these volumes had been inspected and appraised by a committee of the Faculty, but the Board of Visitors declined to purchase them for the reason that the funds at their disposal would not justify it. It is possible that many of these books were duplicates of some already in the library's possession, and that few of them were modern enough to supply that deficiency in works on science and literature which had already become a ground of complaint.

The first gift of importance was from Bernard Carter, in 1826, which consisted of one hundred volumes. In the course of the next year, Christian Bohn, of Richmond, presented five hundred more; and about the same year, Joseph Coolidge, of Boston, eighty-four of a miscellaneous character. An addition of some value was made by purchase from Dr. Dunglison [1] Dunglison, accustomed to the English university libraries, was acutely impatient over the absence of new books in the library of the University of Virginia. "It is impossible for the professors to keep pace with the advancing state of science," he wrote Cabell, in January, 1829, "unless the necessary materials are furnished them, and none have been received here since the year 1824. For a period, we may retain a respectable footing, but unless we can obtain new materials, the period must arise when our capability of communicating instruction will fall below the existing state of knowledge." Lomax had already expressed the same apprehension. "Certain books," he said to Cocke, "are indispensable to me, and among them are Wharton's *Reports of Cases in the Supreme Court of the United States,* which are not to be found in the library." "Without these reports," he added, "in-

---

[1] We learn from the *Collegian* of 1838 that Peter K. Skinker, a recent student, had presented fifty books to the library, "many of which were extremely valuable for their rarity"

struction upon some of the most important and interesting subjects must fail."

During the session of 1827–28, there was no lack of periodicals at least; all the principal American and English reviews and professional journals were then sent to the library by Hilliard, Gray, and Company, of Boston, at an annual cost of over one hundred dollars; but the subscriptions could not have been renewed, for, in April, 1829, the Faculty adopted a resolution that each member should order one or more periodicals at his own expense, to be retained by him for three weeks, and then deposited in the library for general use. The number to which the library itself subscribed had fallen from forty-two to six. Hilliard gave up his agency, and Wertenbaker suggested that, thereafter, the domestic journals should be taken through a bookseller at the University, and the foreign through one with a shop in a seaport. In 1830, the number of volumes stored in the library was supposed to be eight thousand. It appears that, in July of the preceding year, the Board of Visitors had directed that a large sum standing to the University's credit in the hands of Baring Brothers, of London, should, after deductions to meet existing engagements, be expended in the purchase of new books. The surplus to be devoted to this end could not have amounted to much, for, in 1832, the Faculty endeavored to enlist the powerful influence of Governor Floyd,— who had shown a friendly interest in the institution,— in their effort to persuade the General Assembly to make an annual appropriation for the benefit of the library. The Board of Visitors had begun, in 1829, to apply a small sum to its use. This, in that year, was five hundred dollars; but in 1834–5, it was only three hundred. Money was now very urgently needed for other purposes.

Heavy rains had fallen in 1834, and so excessive was the dampness which had followed in the library-room that it was feared that the entire collection would be irretrievably damaged. When the librarian, Thomas Brockenbrough, was sent for by the Faculty, in their anxiety to stop the progress of the threatened ruin, he was found to be absent from the University, and a temporary substitute had to be appointed to take the measures called for at once. The same dampness had occurred in 1827; and so great was the apprehension then of injury to the books stored in the galleries that they had been removed for the winter.

An addition to the library was made in 1834 by a friend of Jeremy Bentham, who had, for this purpose, discriminately picked out the most interesting volumes among the productions of that philosopher   Two boxes of books were also presented by the English Government. To a committee appointed by the Faculty was now referred the choice of such volumes as the University could afford to purchase.   Bonnycastle was at the head of this committee in 1836, and his keen critical judgment in English belles-lettres was shown in his selections, which comprised such works of established reputation as Selden's *Table Talk*, Sir Thomas More's *Utopia*, De Tocqueville's *America*, and Count Hamilton's *Memoirs*. Jefferson's principle that the shelves of the library should not be lumbered with books that were only intended for amusement, did not appeal to this highly educated English literary and scientific scholar; and on every occasion open to him, he continued to increase the miscellaneous collection by adding to it classical English works that had found their chief reason for a prolonged popularity, not in pedagogic utility, but in the gratification of cultivated tastes.   It became customary in time for each professor to hand in a list of books which he considered desirable, and from the entire number of these lists, a selection was made for actual purchase. By this means, the heavy linguistic, scientific, and professional character of the original assortment was further diminished, to its great improvement for the general and casual reader.

The first endowment fund for the library's benefit had its origin in a provision of Madison's will: he bequeathed it the sum of fifteen hundred dollars; but with the restriction that the interest accruing from that amount should alone be used. He also left it a legacy of about one thousand volumes out of his own collection. The Board of Visitors instructed Wertenbaker to send Mrs. Madison a catalogue, in order that, in picking out these one thousand volumes, she might be able to avoid the selection of duplicate copies; but this spirit of helpfulness fell upon stony ground, for Mrs. Madison not only neglected to comply with the Board's request at once, but, as we shall see, deferred all attention to it so long that it was found necessary to threaten a law suit.

The largest addition to the library made previous to 1842 was embraced in the gift of Christian Bohn, of Richmond The books which comprised it included many volumes that were either duplicate copies or valueless, for we are told that a committee, headed by Gessner Harrison, was, for this reason, appointed by the Board to inspect and assort them with unusual care. Those decided to be suitable for the library were deposited on shelves specially reserved for that purpose, while the rest were packed in boxes and stored away for future disposition. There were discovered many periodicals belonging to complete or broken series, and for the most part unbound. In the course of the following year, Dr. Joseph Togno, the tutor in the School of Modern

Languages, gave the library a portrait of Cosmo di Medici; a large portfolio with a handsome engraving in it; and numerous casts of club-feet,— a present more appropriate to a collection of anatomical specimens than to a collection of books, unless, by a stretch of the imagination, it was supposed to be reminiscent of Byron's deformity.

xx. *Librarians and Rules*

John V. Kean was the first person to be chosen as librarian of the University.   He was the son of Andrew Kean, of Charlottesville, who, in recommending him to the favorable consideration of the Board, said that he possessed a good English education, a tolerable acquaintance with the Latin tongue, and some small knowledge of the Greek.   A portion of this learning had been garnered by him professionally, for, previous to his appointment in 1835, he had been a busy school-master in the adjacent county of Louisa.   He occupied the position of librarian during nine months, at a salary of one hundred and fifty dollars.   His incumbency was concurrent with the first session.   Few functionaries of the institution were ever so little burdened with the duties of an important post as he, for it was not until after the close of his term that the library was really formed.   The only books of which he could have been custodian in 1825, were such as had been purchased abroad by Gilmer; and these must have made up a collection of modest proportions.

The vacancy created by his retirement was filled by William Wertenbaker, who was appointed temporarily by Jefferson as a member of the committee of superintendence, and in April, 1826, permanently by the Board. Thus began this officer's connection with the University, which he was to serve, during more than half a century, with a diligence, fidelity, and integrity that have made him one of the outstanding figures in its history. His selection, while still so young a man, was a signal proof of Jefferson's discernment. Although a mere lad at the time, he had, through his father's influence, obtained a seat in the clerk's office in Charlottesville, then in the charge of Alexander Garrett Garrett was a capable man of business and a highly respected citizen, and under the supervision of this excellent exemplar, young Wertenbaker remained until he arrived at his majority. During the War of 1812–15, he joined the company of Captain Estes, a part of General Cocke's Brigade, and with his musket on his sturdy shoulder, marched on foot to Eastern Virginia to assist in repelling the British. After the close of hostilities, he became deputy sheriff of the county,— a position that called alike for business habits and for personal courage. He seems to have entered the University law school as soon as its lectures began.

Wertenbaker was chosen librarian and secretary of the Faculty simultaneously. Opposition to his appointment to the latter post was expressed by several professors, on the ground that he was not a member of their body; such an appointment, they predicted, would put a sharp curb on the free play of their discussions; and it certainly led to one disclosure,— that of Key angrily kicking Blaettermann's shins under the table,— which has caused the dignity of some of these early proceedings to be doubted by posterity. The librarian's salary now amounted to fifty dollars only; but the position was accompanied by distinct advantages of another sort: it not only took up a small share of his time, but also entitled him to a dormitory free of rent, and to tuition in every school without the payment of a fee. He was at liberty too to use the volumes in his custody without being

liable for the regular charge.   His earliest task, as we
have seen, was to arrange the books on the temporary
shelves in the Central College pavilion; his next was to
remove them to the alcoves and galleries of the great
circular room on the main floor of the Rotunda; and his
third, to catalogue them in the proper shape for printing.
This work was finished in 1828.

It was thought to be such a privilege to have access to
the books without being subject to the rigid restrictions,
which, as we shall soon find, were imposed on their use,
that there was no difficulty in obtaining the services of a
student as junior librarian, although no salary went with
the post.   In 1827, when the senior librarian must have
been busy in his leisure hours with making up the catalogue, his assistant was James C. Bruce, the heir to the
largest fortune in the State, and, subsequently, a planter
of wealth and distinction in Southern Virginia.   Wertenbaker, however, was determined to pursue his original
plan of being called to the bar, and in 1828, a candidate
to succeed him was brought forward by Nicholas P.
Trist in the person of Lewis Randolph, a matriculate of
the University.   But Wertenbaker does not appear to
have resigned at once.   In 1829, he was appointed to the
office of assistant proctor, which, carrying with it police
duties of importance, threw him more than once into
sharp collision with lawless students.[1]   He also undertook the functions of the local postmaster.

During the brief interval of his retirement from the
office of librarian, it was filled by W. H. Brockenbrough,
a kinsman of the proctor of that name, who had been so

[1] "You are too fond of reporting," exclaimed a student with an oath
to Wertenbaker in 1831   "I shall do the same thing to-morrow that I
have done to-day, and if you report me for that, I shall flog you   I suppose you will report me for what I am now saying. If you do, I will
flog you." Minutes of Faculty, July 16, 1831.

intimately associated with Jefferson. He was, at the same time, a student in the School of Law, and in later life, rose to be a judge of some distinction in Florida. The salary had been increased in 1830 to two hundred and fifty dollars per annum Brockenbrough proved to be an unsatisfactory incumbent of the office. We have referred to his absence from the University during the heavy rains of 1834. He seems to have constantly left his post without giving notice; and he did not always take the trouble to engage a substitute during his absence. In a report to the Faculty by a committee appointed in 1834 to investigate his delinquencies, he was charged with selecting incompetent assistants; with putting off the hour for opening the library; with admitting students without tickets, as required by the rules; and with winking at their taking down freely any volume that appealed to their curiosity Very often the library was unlocked by the bell-ringer, a negro servant, without the librarian being present; and not infrequently, the students entered it privately accompanied by strangers. They kept the books in their dormitories as long as they wished, and were never hauled up for any damage which they had caused to the volumes.

Proving incorrigible, Brockenbrough was compelled to resign in July, 1835, and Wertenbaker took his place. Under the rules adopted six months earlier, the latter had the right to select two assistants, at least one of whom was required to reside within the precincts. Of the assistants named, one was his brother; the other, Colonel Ward, who was now in charge of a University hotel. Wertenbaker retained the office of postmaster, and was told to expect a summons at any time to serve as secretary of the Faculty. This duty was reimposed upon him, the following year. In addition to being postmaster, secretary of the Faculty, and librarian, he was, as we have already stated, the local agent of the firm of Street and Sanxey, the Richmond stationers.   The shop was popularly known as " Wertenbaker's book-store," but with his multifarious employments, it must have been left for the most part under the eye of a clerk.   At a later date, he contracted to manage one of the hotels; and in fact, seems to have been ready and competent to fill any position except that of professor, at an hour's call   He was married to the sister-in-law of Warner Minor, the most discreet and sober-minded of the original hotel-keepers, and, during some years, resided in the middle building in the East Range occupied by the proctor after the close of the War of Secession.   It was his custom, when he was advanced in age, to salute the students, even in the late afternoon, with a cheery " good morning "; and when his reason for this was asked, he would reply that he bade them good morning because they were in the morning of life,— a proof of the quaint, but benevolent humor of the man.

The regulations for the government of the library were drafted in March, 1825, just three days before the University was thrown open.   To the members of the Faculty was granted the privilege of an almost unrestricted use of the books; but no student was permitted to carry away a volume unless he could show a request to that effect from one of the professors; and the number which he was allowed to remove was limited to three. The fine imposed for the detention of a book beyond the date assigned for its return was graduated by its physical character: if it was a 12mo, or smaller, and he held it back one week, he was to pay ten cents; if an octavo, twenty cents; if a quarto, thirty; and if a folio, forty. Should he deface a volume only moderately, he was required to pay its full value; should he damage it seriously, double its value; and should he lose it, three times its value.

The librarian was ordered to be on hand in the library once a week, and to remain at least one hour to receive all books returned, and to give out all those that were asked for. A professor had the right to bring back a book at any hour, and on any day, that was convenient to him, except Sunday. No stranger was privileged either to enter the library, or to take down a volume from a shelf, except in the presence of the librarian. In 1825, the day for the latter's attendance was Monday; and in 1826, Tuesday. So anxious were the young men to obtain the volumes that some of them went so far as to forge their professors' names to formal permits. In February, 1826, a box was placed outside of the library door, in which the petitions for books were to be dropped the day before the library opened; and on the latter day, the volumes were handed out like loaves of charity through the iron bars of a monastery. Later in the course of the same year, the library was accessible to students on every day of the week, except Sunday; but no one of them was authorized to enter the room, unless, on the preceding day, he had sent a note to the librarian containing that request. A ticket was then made out with his name, which had the advantage of being transferable. Only twenty such tickets could be issued for a single day. When he had succeeded in getting through the door, the student was not permitted to take down a book of reference without the consent of the librarian in writing. If he was guilty of breaking the silence by speaking aloud, or causing other noises, he was denied the privilege of a second admission.

In 1825, every student was required to make a deposit

of one dollar as a library fee; and this was, in 1826, increased to ten dollars; and should this sum be exhausted at any time during the session by the volume of fines which he had incurred for damaging or losing books, he was compelled to renew the original amount.   In October of this year, the hour of opening the library was shifted to half past three in the afternoon, and of closing to five; and the only days to which this rule did not apply were Saturday and Sunday, on which days the library remained locked   Dr. Blaettermann suggested that each professor should be provided with a key to the door, but the Faculty quietly voted this proposition down.   The members of this body were quite as harsh and conscientious in imposing rules on themselves, in the use of the library, as they were on the students,— fifty cents was to be paid for every day that a book was withheld by one of themselves beyond the time fixed for its return.   If the offender had taken out a periodical, he was to pay four dollars and a half for every day it was held back after the first week of its unlawful detention

In 1831, the regulation was adopted that the library was to be accessible for a definite interval daily except Sunday; but no student was to be permitted to enter the room save to consult a book.   He still had to receive the removable volumes which he asked for, through a hole in the door.   The rules of 1835 required that the library should be open, from the first day of the session down to May 1, between the hours of three and five; and after May 1, between the hours of four and six; but the former regulation that only twenty students should be admitted on any one day was still retained   The librarian was now instructed to furnish, once every two months, a list of all books which were held back without his permission; of all fines that had been imposed, whether paid or unpaid; of all damages to volumes that had been caused by students or professors; and of all recent additions to the collection, whether by gift or by purchase.

An examination of the records of the library during these earlier years brings out the fact that it was used very liberally by the professors Sometimes a member of the Faculty would be credited with the possession of as many as ten volumes. Key was the one who drew most frequently on the resources of the collection; and he very amiably sponsored many students who belonged to classes other than his own. The first year the completed library was open to readers, thirteen hundred and forty-five volumes were taken out,— among them, Shakespeare's *Plays*, sixty-three times; Johnson's works, forty-two; Chesterfield's *Letters*, twenty-one; Cervantes's *Don Quixote*, twenty; and Gibbon's *Decline and Fall*, fourteen. Other books that enjoyed a decided popularity were Thomson's *Seasons*, Sterne's *Sermons*, the works of Voltaire, Locke, Bolingbroke and Robertson, the *Histories* of Smollett and Hume, Middleton's *Cicero*, O'Meara's *Napoleon*, Wirt's *Patrick Henry*, and Plutarch's *Lives*. The number of volumes withdrawn in the following year were thirteen hundred and twenty-four. The favored authors during this session were again Johnson, Gibbon, Chesterfield, Cervantes, and Shakespeare. Among the books which had numerous readers were Erskine's *Speeches*, Robertson's *Histories*, the *Life of Chatham*, Boccaccio's *Decameron*, *Hudibras*, *Old English Plays*, Thomson's *Seasons*, Pope's *Homer*, Swift's works, and the *Columbiad*. Many fines were imposed in the course of 1826,— there were thirty-nine young men delinquent in this way, during that session; and some of them were liable for very respectable sums.

XXI. *The Dormitories and their Regulations*

Having obtained their tickets of admission to the courses of study which they had decided to pursue, the matriculates were next required to choose their rooms and hotels. If the student had brought with him the written authority of his parent or guardian to reside outside the bounds, he was permitted to do so; and he could claim this privilege, without such authority, if he had passed his twentieth year. In both instances, the outboarding house, as it was called, selected by him, must be able to show a notice of the Faculty's approval. During the session of 1832–3, as many as thirty of the young men,— a very large proportion of the entire number then in attendance,— found lodgings and meals in the immediate neighborhood of the University; but this secession was probably due to the indifferent fare at the hotels within the precincts, which, at this time, was causing so much dissatisfaction. In many cases, a single student would be domiciled for the session with a friend of his family who resided in the town; but the majority of these out-boarders were inmates of houses belonging to refined ladies, like Mrs. Brockenbrough and Miss Lucy Terrell, who, by the comforts of their hearths, and the excellence of their food, were able, with more or less success, to compete with the University hotel-keepers.

The far greater number of the students, however, preferred to occupy rooms within the precincts, and to eat their meals at the hotel tables,— a disposition that, naturally, was encouraged by the Faculty, as the prosperity of the institution was largely dependent upon the payment of the rents, and the very existence of the hotels upon the payment of the monthly board bills. In 1829, in order to make the dormitories more homelike, a door-

way was cut through the wall separating each two of
them.   By this device, one of the rooms could be used as
a chamber, and the other as a study, by two young men.
The executive committee, at this time, was also instructed
to hang a Venetian blind on the alternate door so soon
as the funds in hand should be sufficient.   The object of
this ornamental addition was to assure a greater draught
of air in the warm season without diminishing the
privacy.

When the University was completed, it contained, besides the pavilions, one hundred and nine dormitories,
with accommodations for double that number of students.
Some of them must have remained unoccupied throughout the first session, since the attendance of young men,
during this session, was a limited one.   Five years afterwards, many vacancies still existed, although thirteen of
the rooms had, by that time, been assigned to the use of
different professors.   In 1835, ten were in the possession of the hotel-keepers and members of the Faculty.
Of the remainder, twenty were inhabited by one student,
respectively, and seventy-nine by two.   This disproportion, no doubt, had its explanation in motives of economy,
for when two students were tenants of the same apartment, there was an equal division, not only of the rent,
but also of the cost of fagots and candles.   As early as
October, 1826, the name of the occupant of a dormitory
was ordered to be " painted above its door."   This apparently was done on a small adjustable panel furnished
by the regular carpenter of the University,— who, in
1832, was Mr. Vowles,— at the trivial cost of fifty cents
apiece.   Although the signs were so inexpensive, the
young men usually failed to put them up, until formally
warned that the consequence of omission was a fine; and
towards the end of the session, they seemed to derive a

joyous satisfaction from throwing them into the nearest ashheap.

Whatever right the student may have possessed at first to follow his own whim in choosing his dormitory, it was seriously curtailed, if not taken away altogether, by a later enactment, which impowered the proctor to assign the rooms to the students in such manner as to ensure an equality of boarders at the different hotels on the Ranges;[1] and under the operation of the same regulation, no student was permitted to change his room without first obtaining the chairman's approval.   For each hotel-keeper, a definite number of dormitories were reserved, the inmates of which were required to take their meals in his hotel.   This was the first rule that made that functionary of almost as much importance in the young men's lives as the professors under whom they sat.   The second was that the hotel-keeper was to supply each one with the furniture and linen which he would need in his dormitory; with servant's attendance; and with laundry. In the beginning, the student was expected to furnish his own bedding, fagots, lights, and washing, and it was anticipated that he would be able to do this with ease through the hotel-keeper; but in the course of the second year, the duty of obtaining these articles was imposed directly on the hotel-keeper in the first instance, with the provision that his outlay on that account was to be cov-

[1] On October 4, 1826, the following minute was adopted by the Board " The students shall be permitted to diet themselves in any hotel of the University at their choice or elsewhere as shall suit themselves "   But not more than three days later, this arrangement was modified· " Hotels and dormitories are assigned to the students by the proctor under the control of the Faculty, and they shall be so distributed among the different hotels as to preserve equality of numbers at each   In this arrangement, they shall be assigned in accord with the wishes of the student as far as may comport with equality in numbers at the hotels and fitness of residence in the dormitories "   These entries appear in the Minutes of the Board of Visitors for October 7, 1826

ered by a general charge.[1]   The proportionate cost of the several items is stated in a report drawn up by the proctor in 1838,— the total expense, during that session, was one hundred and twenty-five dollars, distributed as follows: one hundred for table board, ten for laundry, ten for service, and five for the use of bedding and furniture.   That officer, at this time, supplied the fuel and candles.   On the other hand, it was the hotel-keeper's function to procure clean sheets, pillow-cases, and towels once a fortnight; once a fortnight also, he was required to have the dormitories thoroughly scoured; and once a week, to make an inspection of each room, either in person, or through a reliable agent, and to receive the complaints of the young men, should their comforts have been neglected by the servant.

This servant was a negro slave who had been hired by the hotel-keeper, with a view to his performing all the menial offices of that set of dormitories.   The list of his duties, in 1835, throws light on a characteristic side of the students' life at that time.   At six o'clock in the morning, he entered the room with a pitcher of water,— which, in winter, was quite often little below the temperature of freezing,— and started the fires and cleaned the shoes.   So soon as the student left the apartment for his hotel to get his breakfast, which was eaten by candle-light, the servant swept the floor, made up the beds, and carried away the ashes.   Once a week, he blackened the andirons and polished the fenders; once a fortnight, he

[1] The Faculty at their meeting, October 1, 1842, prescribed the following articles of furniture for each dormitory:

One table	One pair of shovel and tongs
Two chairs	One bed and suitable bedding
One looking glass	One wash-bowl
One water-pitcher	One candle-stick
One wash-stand	One pair of snuffers
One pair of andirons	One towel

wiped off the " paint work " of the room; twice during the summer, he whitewashed the fireplace; and daily, at that season, brought the ice, and in winter, the wood. At 2 :45 o'clock in the afternoon, he took his stand at some point convenient to his line of dormitories in order to receive specific instructions from such of the occupants as should wish him to run on errands to Charlottesville; but he was not permitted to loiter about the spot after three o'clock.

The state of neglect into which the students' domiciliary conveniences and comforts sometimes fell was full of danger from the modern hygienic point of view. It taxed the chairman's vigilance to the utmost to compel the lessees of the hotels to keep their respective rooms in a wholesome condition of order and cleanliness; and the smallest slackening on his part too often resulted in a return to the slovenliness and untidiness against which the young men so frequently rebelled. The hotel-keepers relied upon the shifty negro servants; and the servants themselves, even when willing, were sometimes unable to maintain the apartments as they should be because they were not provided with the necessary linen. In December, 1830, there was an outcry from the dormitories, and an investigation was begun. It leaked out that many of the students had not been furnished with fresh sheets and pillow-cases for three weeks, while the floors had not been scoured since the first day of the session. One of the hotel-keepers said, in his own defense, that the negro in charge of his rooms had been too sick to attend to them with regularity; another admitted that he never visited those assigned to his boarders; and a third asserted that, as she was a woman, it was not proper for her to inspect hers in person. Some of the students were accused of bad habits, such as spattering the walls with tobacco juice, and even with dragging the sheets and blankets from the beds and sleeping on the floors in front of the fire.[1]

In the beginning, the young men, as we have mentioned, were expected to purchase their own fuel, but as many neglected to do so before cold weather set in, that duty was afterwards assigned to the hotel-keepers; and as this led to bickering, then to the proctor.   During these early sessions, when the vacation occurred in the winter months, it was calculated that each fireplace would consume from four and one-third cords to five and a half.   The proctor, in making up his fuel-book for the season, was authorized to recoup himself for certain incidental costs, and also for the time and trouble in contracting.   The conviction arose among the young men, three years afterwards, that they could fill their boxes themselves at a lower rate than he was willing to grant; and it shows how closely they figured their expenses, that the entire amount which each expected to save by buying without the intervention of this middle-man, was only six dollars.   They claimed that they could purchase a cord of wood at the rate of two dollars and a half,— as it was, they were compelled to pay the proctor at the rate of four dollars.   He asserted, in his own defense, that he was able to obtain a supply for each student more cheaply than the student himself could do, because he secured it in large quantities and at the cheapest season of the year.   The sawyer too asked less for cutting up a very large pile than for cutting up the single load which each inmate of a dormitory would buy.   The proctor was successful in holding on to the right to furnish the fuel; and in his accounts with the

[1] There was a conspicuous improvement in the condition of the dormitories after the disappearance of the first group of hotel-keepers, who, as will be shown in a later chapter, were chosen without any real regard to practical capacity.

students, he continued to charge for the sawing of the wood; for the shrinkage in its weight from drying; and for his commission as before. He seems to have been put to little inconvenience by this duty, as it was performed through an agent. In 1832, this agent, under his agreement with his principal, furnished a sound horse and cart for hauling wood to the dormitories. He was the overseer of the woodyard, managed the hired laborers employed for the sawing, and kept accurate memoranda of the loads that went out. His remuneration was fixed at five per cent. of the amount in payment. The wood was purchased from the owners of forests situated in the vicinity of the University, and it was delivered at the yard by their own teams

At times, the students suffered keenly from nipping weather. In February, 1836, the thermometer sank to zero, and as the yard was then empty, owing to mismanagement, many of them were permitted to leave their dormitories and temporarily engage rooms in the taverns in town. Although fagots could be bought even at this season at three dollars a cord, the unreliability of the yard-master raised the question with the Faculty of experimenting with grates and coal in order to find out whether coal or wood was the cheaper fuel. All the coal then used in Eastern and Piedmont Virginia was procured from the Midlothian mines near Richmond. If a supply was to be obtained from these mines for the University, it would be necessary to transport it by barge up the James and Rivanna rivers to Milton, and thence overland by wagon.

During several sessions, the hotel-keepers were required to furnish the candles used in the dormitories, but in 1832, this duty had been taken over by the proctor. In the course of that year, Davenport, Allen and

Company, of Richmond, supplied as many as fifteen boxes in one shipment, the contents consisting of spermaceti candles, the finest in quality manufactured at that time, and always sold by the pound weight. Oil lamps also were now used by the students. We find J. Hanson Thomas, of Maryland, paying Raphael, of Charlottesville, one dollar and a half for a gallon of oil. But for some years yet candles continued to be the most popular means of illumination; in 1833, twenty boxes arrived by wagon from Richmond; and the like heavy loads were constantly repeated until 1838, when lamps seem to have come into more general use in the dormitories. Some of these cost as much as five dollars, but such were perhaps of metal, for, in 1840, a glass lamp could be purchased for fifty cents. Oil, however, had advanced to one dollar and seventy-five cents a gallon. Spermaceti candles were still in use, for, in the course of the same year, thirty-two boxes were unloaded at the Milton wharf from a barge that had brought them up from Richmond.

The students needed the flame of both lamp and candle, not only after night had fallen, but also at break of day, for the morning bell was heard before the invisible sun had risen near enough to the horizon to scatter the darkness entirely. In 1827, the ordinances required that this bell should be rung at half past six, and in 1828, at dawn, throughout the session. The young men were enjoined to leave their beds at this signal and dress themselves at once. By sunrise, the rooms were to be in order for the day, and the occupants, to use the words of the law, " prepared for business."

The most famous of the early janitors, Doctor Smith, whom we have described elsewhere, seems, in spite of his personal popularity, to have been looked upon along the

Lawn and the Ranges as an intermeddler, whenever — the sound of the bell having died away,— he walked down the arcades to find out whether the rule to ensure early rising had been complied with   He did not perform this duty daily, but somewhat irregularly intentionally in order to take the sleepers unawares, and to confuse any plot that might have been woven to trip him in following his round   If he had been without a sense of humor, his position would have been intolerable, for every device that the most ingenious boyish deviltry could suggest was used without scruple to anger, discourage, and thwart him   Like an army in bivouac, apprehensive of attack, the students set sentinels behind the pillars, and so soon as the janitor was seen approaching through the half darkness, word was quickly passed along, from door to door, in warning to the startled sleepers to rise at once, and jump into their clothes with all the celerity of men frightened by a cry of fire.   Sometimes, the janitor would enter a dormitory too quickly for the toilet of the occupant to be completed.   A jacket and trousers would, by one roommate, be thrown on in haste, without regard to the absence of undergarments, while his companion would bolt under the bed or into a closet.   Doctor Smith would gravely take his seat before the fire beside the one who pretended to be dressed, and remain until exhaustion forced the delinquent to acknowledge that he was caught.   In the meanwhile, his half naked roommate had been shivering in the cold and in darkness. But sometimes the table was turned on the Doctor by placing a basin of water above the door, which discharged its full contents on his head and shoulders as soon as he seized the knob and entered the room.

But neither he, nor the servants, nor the proctor,— who was also required to visit the dormitories at sunrise,

once a week,— could force the students as a body to run
so sharply in the teeth of a natural instinct as to comply
with the ordinance with persistent fidelity.   The observance of this senseless regulation was, in the beginning,
however, more constant and general than would have
been predicted.   The violations, during the early sessions, were, in fact, decidedly moderate in number.   In
November, 1830, ten young men were reported for rising
late.   Some of these had been guilty as often as five
times, and at least one, habitually.   In December of the
same year, there were six delinquents.   One of them offered a rather singular excuse, which, however, was put
forward, not in irony, but in good faith: Archibald Henderson, of North Carolina, asked to be exempted because
early rising, he said, was invariably followed with him by
a pain in the chest; and he had also noticed the same effect on himself while a pupil at Yale.   In May, 1831,
eleven students were summoned before the chairman for
the offense, one of whom had been guilty on seven occasions.   In April, there were seventeen culprits.   At this
time, the earliest class assembled at half past five in the
morning, and some of the young men were required to
attend as often as five times a week at this ghostly hour,
for even in summer the sun had hardly yet risen above
the horizon.

Did the Faculty ever show any disposition to recommend the abolition of the ordinance? " With all its
imperfect execution," remarked the chairman in 1833,
" and with the utter impracticability of a rigid enforcement but by means and with consequences disproportion-
ate to its benefits, I am still of the opinion that the
law is a salutary one.   It makes almost all, even the
most indolent, rise earlier than they otherwise would do,

and the consciousness of having offended in this particular is a check sometimes on other violations "   This last
observation indicates the chairman's delicate insight into
the contradictions of human nature; but it is questionable
whether it was strictly accurate as applied to these young
men, who quite probably agreed with the modern view of
the regulation; namely, that the Board and Faculty were
as open to criticism for adopting it, in the beginning, as
the students were for breaking it while it lasted.   " Before sunrise, this morning," the chairman records in
December, 1835, " I was sent for by Mrs. Gray because
one of her boarders had struck one of her servants whilst
at breakfast."   Was it very heinous that young men,
kept up late at night by their studies, should have been
inclined to be sulky and irascible when they found themselves, after dragging themselves out of bed by five
o'clock, eating the first meal of the day by murky candlelight, and quite probably too in a chilly apartment?

The passage of time only served to make the regulation more grinding and intolerable.   In 1836, ninety-six
of the student body of two hundred and forty-two were
reported in the month of October for leaving their beds
late; in November, thirty-six; in December, seventy; in
the following January, one hundred and nineteen; and in
March, eighty-three.   There were, in 1837, three hundred and fourteen cases in the course of the entire session.
At this time, only two hundred and sixty-three students
were in attendance.

But the effect of the law was not alone to encourage
among the young men a spirit of indifference to all laws
by forcing an unwise one on them,— it unquestionably
tended to lower their health by compelling them to leave
their dormitories before dawn, and to eat their meals, and

to be present at lectures, by candlelight. The rebellions and epidemics of these early years can, in some measure, be hunted down to this ill-advised ordinance.

XXII. *The Hotel-Keepers*

There was no department in the system of his new University which Jefferson was not solicitous to invest with scholastic dignity, even if that dignity should fail to pierce below the shadow to the substance. The janitor himself was at first expected to be a man with skill enough to handle the philosophical apparatus in the most delicate experiments. How was it possible to bring the hotel-keeper,— whose only real duty was presumably to satisfy the appetites of the students,— into the magic circle of that student's purely intellectual interests? He might be a tactful manager of servants, an unerring judge of beef, mutton, and veal, and an expert in all the countless varieties of Virginia breads and desserts; he might be able to discriminate to a nicety between the best shade of cooking and the next best, at a single tasting; he might have an extraordinary aptitude for obtaining the earliest vegetables, the most recently laid eggs, the freshest butter, the plumpest poultry,— in short, he might be the pattern of all that a well-informed, honest, energetic, and bountiful hotel-keeper should be, and yet be unable to contribute one cubit further to the intellectual stature of his boarders.

Jefferson's ingenuity,— which was able to convert the blank ceiling of the Rotunda into a starred and constellated celestial vault, and to change a simple walking stick, by a twist of the fingers, into a comfortable and handy seat,— was quite equal to finding a distinct scholastic use for the hotel-keeper, apart from his daily ministrations to hungry youthful stomachs. His plan, it will be recalled, for the first of the "refectories," as he mediaevally designated the University boarding houses,— under the spell, no doubt, of the cell-like dormitories, and the monastic arcades,— was to use it as a seminary for colloquial French. It was to be rented to a French family, and only the French tongue was to be spoken at its tables. The students were to drop their own vernacular and employ, to the best of their ability, the language of France. The hotel-keeper was to turn the intervals between courses to linguistic account by correcting faulty accents and suggesting more correct grammatical usages.

The plan was not so fantastic as it seemed. Many Americans have picked up an excellent knowledge of the French tongue in private homes in Paris,— the shortest way of learning,— and there was no reason why twenty-five students, taking their meals in a small hotel within the precincts of the University of Virginia, should not have gradually acquired a fair acquaintance with colloquial French at least. If it was possible to set up a French seminary in one hotel, why should not a Spanish seminary be established in another, an Italian in a third, and a German in a fourth? Jefferson undoubtedly canvassed such a plan in his own mind, and was anything impossible with a philosopher, who, standing upon his own academic lawn, could look around and see his native blue sky indented by the tops of those exotic Roman temples and baths which he himself had erected? A man who was able to plant on Virginian soil such an architectural group as that, would not have wanted the power to carry out any other innovation which had received his own approval.

Cocke, who was not as prone as Cabell to be dazzled by Jefferson's original schemes, no doubt joked a little on the score of the novel French seminary that was actually proposed, but he too had formed a very dignified conception of the part that the hotels should play in the University life. " Let us stick to our resolution of reducing their number," he said, " and by giving due notice of it, we shall be able to pick out men of such stuff as will really make our hotel faculty worthy of the other departments."

What did he mean by the expression " hotel faculty "? This is only intelligible when we recall that the hotel-keeper of the University, at that time, was presumed to discharge several important functions besides supplying his boarders with their daily food. We have seen that he was required to visit their dormitories at regular intervals, and in these tours of inspection, he was expected to come into something more than a formal and shallow intercourse with the occupants. The future was to prove that this intercourse,— in some instances, at least,— was to be confined to participation in the drinking and gambling bouts of the students; but this possibility, which was anticipated, made it all the more imperative that the hotel-keepers should themselves be men who would set a good and not a bad example. In the first place, they were in reality health officers of the University,—certainly to the extent of being obligated to maintain a condition of perfect cleanliness in the dormitories, the points from which most of the epidemics of that day started; and in the second, they were the assistants to the proctor in preserving good order throughout the precincts. They could not only be called upon to aid in suppressing a riot and checking every other form of turbulence, but they were also under orders to report all minor violations of the ordinances.

Against this last regulation, they, not unnaturally, were

disposed to revolt. The success of their hotels was largely dependent upon their own popularity with their respective sets of boarders, and they were afraid lest the furtive observation which was expected of them, would arouse the suspicion of their patrons and sour their good-will. In the beginning, before a definite row of dormitories had been assigned to each hotel, this good-will was indispensable to the keepers' success   Jefferson, in 1826, complained to Joseph Coolidge that competition had made them too obsequious to the wishes of the young men.   "We must force them to become auxiliaries towards the preservation of order rather than supporters of irregularities.   We shall continue this evil until the renewal of their leases."   In September, 1827, at least one-half of the students put off matriculating because sanguine of obtaining greater advantages from the several hotel-keepers, who were actively canvassing among them. With such inducement, in these first years, to win the young men's favor, there was small prospect that they would conscientiously discharge their police duties; and even after they were made independent of such good will, they positively declined to testify about delinquencies, unless peremptorily called upon to do so by the Faculty.[1] In short, the hotel-keepers failed to perform the part which was expected of them in the higher administration

[1] " It is with real concern," the hotel-keepers wrote about 1833, " that we see ourselves called upon by you (the Faculty) to give information against the young men   We will, without hesitation, do so so far as relates to our houses   We are anxious and desirous for the good government of the institution, but conceive we should be placed in an extremely disagreeable relation by binding ourselves as required   We wish by no means to screen offenses,— far from it,— neither wish we to be placed in the disagreeable situation of subjecting ourselves to constant insult, which would inevitably be the case   We are tenants at will placed here to board students   If we conduct ourselves well and keep proper order in our houses, we conceive we have fulfilled our part "   Signed by Warner Minor and Edwin Conway   Library Manuscripts

of the University's affairs.   Ordinances had actually to be adopted to bring them under penalties for permitting gaming and drinking beneath their roofs, or for receiving students who had been dismissed or expelled from the precincts.   As we shall soon see, several were compelled to leave the University, owing to this undisguised indifference to their obligations.

When we come to examine the type of person selected, during the period under review, for the position of hotel-keeper, we soon perceive that it was not, as a rule, the one represented by stern upholders of temperance, or by rigid censors of the other popular forms of college dissipation.   It was calculated, at first, that the office would bring in a net income of at least fifteen hundred dollars. " This makes it a post," said Cocke, " that some of the first men of the State, who have been unfortunate in their circumstances, would be glad to accept."   He was right.   There was no period in the history of Virginia, before the War of Secession, in which so many families of good and even distinguished birth, were so down at the heel as at this time.   The hotels were still in the hands of the builders when there began to rise up a large number of candidates of this class, who were not naturally inclined towards careful management, and who possessed no personal sympathy whatever with the austerities of Puritanism.   A taste for cards and for liquor was then very general, and to set half a dozen men with such tastes themselves over a large body of high-spirited and self-indulgent young boarders was not the course that was at all calculated to restrain the latter from imitating the habits of so many of their elders.

These early hotel-keepers were, with one exception, men who keenly relished their toddies and loved to shuffle a pack of cards, either in their own apartments or in the dormitories. At the spring term of the Circuit Court of Albemarle, in 1826, several of them were actually indicted by the grand jury for gaming. It was the loose practice of the times, from which they can be no more absolved than the students themselves.

Without an exception, they belonged to families of high social position in the State. One of the earliest applicants was Major Griffin Stith, of Petersburg, who was warmly recommended by Charles Fenton Mercer; and with equal amiability, Mercer also recommended Mr. Ewell, of Prince William county, who had been forced by the fall in agricultural prices to look to some other calling for a livelihood. Mrs Patton, daughter of W. S. Crawford, of Amherst, found an earnest supporter in Chapman Johnson, who, perhaps, correctly thought that a woman could manage a University hotel more successfully than most of the unfortunate gentlemen whose names had been submitted. Thomas Burwell, a member of Congress, was of the like opinion,— when a vacancy occurred in 1827, he suggested the name of Mrs. Nicholson, a daughter of Carter Wormeley, of Rosegill, and, through him, a scion of the most distinguished social stock in Virginia. She was described as a " woman of great dignity of character and propriety of manner "; but what was more pertinent, Mr. Burwell declared that she was the best housekeeper whom he had ever known. A few days later, Nicholas P. Trist advocated the claims of T. E. Randolph, a kinsman of Jefferson himself. Mr. Randolph was spoken of by Mr. Trist as a " spotless gentleman," and his family " as one of the most virtuous, high-minded, and in every way meritorious families that exist " There was a silence as to Mr Randolph's practical capacity; but his nomination, with that of Mrs. Nicholson, indicates the high social standing of the persons who sought the post.

Both Johnson and Breckinridge urged that the hotels should be carried up to a second story, since, they said, some persons would be influenced to seek their management by the desire to educate a family of sons, for whom there would be but small accommodation so long as the buildings were of one flight only. This forewarning proved to be correct. One of the reasons that led Mrs. Nicholson to apply for the post was that she had four sons whom she was anxious to enter in college; and the same reason governed several of the candidates who were successful in obtaining the office.

There were six hotel-keepers at the start,— John Gray, G. W. Spotswood, Warner Minor, S. B. Chapman, and John D. Richeson. Spotswood was a distant cousin of Washington, and had received the name of his celebrated kinsman. He was, from a personal point of view, the most tempestuous figure in the entire erratic group. He too had been induced to become a candidate by the opportunity which the position opened up to educate his six sons. His family numbered a wife and eight children in all. He occupied the hotel standing at the southeast end of East Range, and from the beginning, cultivated very intimate and jovial relations with the young men, even to the extent of drinking and playing cards with them constantly, though punishable under the ordinances; and this led, on several occasions, to violent altercations, in which he claimed that he was so much the innocent party that the offending students should have been expelled. This brought him into collision with the Faculty, who refused to accept his point of view. Being of an impulsive temper, that brooked no disagreement, he

threw up his lease in 1827, on the ground that he had
been insulted by a student, and that the Faculty had
condoned the outrage.   He declined to discharge further
the duties of his place, although his resignation had not
been acted upon; he refused, when called on, to give evidence about a notorious gambler who had secretly
crawled within the precincts; and he conducted himself
generally in what Dunglison, writing to Cocke, described
" as the most reckless and extravagant manner."   Some
of his boarders complained that he had failed to provide
them with beds; some that there were no pitchers, wash-
basins, or andirons in their rooms, the consequence of
his default.

In spite of his choleric spirit, vehement moods, and
constant neglect of his dormitories, he was patiently retained in his position; but before another year had passed,
he was again heels over head in a characteristic wrangle.
Entering the room of a student named Hove, who occupied one of his apartments, he found him in bed, although
the hour of rising had long gone by.   "Why are you
not up, sir?" Spotswood roughly asked.   "I have no
fire," was the reply.   "Why have you not had one made,
sir?" Spotswood again imperiously inquired.   "If you
were more regular in your habits, sir, then we should be
more regular in making your fire, sir; and your dog, sir,
how can you expect the servant to clean up after a dog,
sir?"   Further hot words were bandied between them.
Spotswood indignantly called Hove "a puppy," and
Hove quite naturally was provoked thereby to strike
Spotswood with the iron shovel snatched up from the
hearth.   Again, Spotswood endeavored to have an
assaulter expelled, and again the Faculty refused to take
so summary a step.   Then he abruptly resigned for the
second time.   Asserting that "his feelings were more

deeply wounded than words could express," he nevertheless exhibited a certain generosity of mind that was characteristic of him in spite of dissipated habits and an
ungovernable temper. "Permit me in my poor way,"
he wrote the chairman, "to return to you and every
member of the Faculty my sincere thanks for the kind
attention I have received from you and them, and if I
ever did feel unfriendly to any one member of your respectable body, reflection, and that magnanimity of soul
which I hope I possess, has done away that feeling, and
I have a hope that it is reciprocated."

In spite of Spotswood's constant violation of the ordinances, and disposition to quarrelsomeness, the Faculty
decided to extend his lease until July 29, six months
longer.   In this interval, he continued to show the habits
which had previously exposed him to censure.   His mind,
however, seemed to dwell only on his own supposititious
wrongs,— he complained, that, when he accepted the position of hotel-keeper, he had in his possession a capital
of three thousand dollars, and that now he was thirteen
hundred dollars in debt; that the rise of water in his
cellar had caused fever in his house, which had carried
off three of his servants; and that he had been knocked
about by so many insults that he could scarcely bottle up
his indignation when he recalled them.   "I deserved
them," he added, bitterly, "for not at first taking in
my own hands the punishment!"   Such were the bellig-
erent emotions with which Spotswood's flurried career as
a University hotel-keeper terminated!

John D. Richeson, like Spotswood, sought the office
for sake of the opportunity which it offered of educating
his sons   He too could not resist the temptation of playing cards and drinking deep with the students, although
he loudly asserted that the card-playing was confined to

innocent whist, and that the entire amount of ardent spirits which he had consumed could, to a nicety, be incompassed in an ordinary quart. Richeson was the son of a Revolutionary soldier, and he seemed to think that, on this account, he had that permanent claim on the position which he would, as the son of a veteran, have possessed, had it been a purely political office. In December, 1827, when the number of students was not great enough to justify the retention of all the hotel-keepers, there was a resolution before the Faculty that Richeson should be one of the three to be dismissed. When he was informed of the intention to get rid of him, his patriotic blood seemed to boil over with indignation. "Was it for this," he exclaimed in a letter to Cocke, "that my father, Colonel Holt Richeson, expended his fortune and toiled so hard all through the Revolutionary War? Was it for this, that, besides being in many other hard-fought battles, he had his horse shot dead under him at the Battle of Brandywine, when he was almost in the very ranks of the enemy, and made his escape without being taken prisoner, with his pistols in his hand? Was it for this that he was at the capture of Lord Cornwallis at Yorktown in 1781? Was it for this that he pledged his life, his fortune, and his sacred honor, to obtain that liberty we are now enjoying? Was it for this that he was a volunteer at Braddock's defeat in 1754, when he was but seventeen or eighteen years of age?"

Cocke, sitting in his library at Bremo, must have found the reading of this letter a delightful morsel to his sense of the ridiculous; but he was sufficiently versed in character to know that Richeson was not the first man who had endeavored to bolster up his own deficiencies, official or personal, by a pathetic or stirring appeal to the military achievements of his ancestors. The Faculty very

properly decided that there was no real connection between the battles of Brandywine and Yorktown and the
management of a University hotel, for Richeson lost his
place. After leaving the precincts, he opened a school at
Rose Hill, near Charlottesville, and on Nicholas P.
Trist's resignation of the secretaryship of the Board of
Visitors, he was an unsuccessful applicant for that position. By 1831, his family had fallen into a state of extreme destitution, and many of the professors generously
subscribed for its relief.

Edwin Conway, like Spotswood and Richeson, was of
a jovial temper, and as early as 1826 was accused of
playing cards and drinking with the students in their
dormitories. Loo was now the favorite game throughout the term, while the eggnog party was the popular
entertainment in December. The genial face of Conway
was often seen shining in the midst of these jolly gath-
erings, but, by the supple exercise of shrewdness, he managed to escape the forfeit of his lease. He was still in
possession of his boarding-house as late as 1837, although, during that year, to evade the consequences of
two protracted sprees, he was forced to join the Temperance Society,— an extraordinary hardship to the hotel-
keeper. It was noticed by the suspicious eyes of the
Faculty that his period of abstemiousness was not to be
indefinite, but was to end on the fourth of July, with the
close of the academic year.

In the opinion of Cocke, a cool and discriminating
judge of men, with a dry, sarcastic insight into their in-
firmities, Warner Minor, "was the only man of the
whole set of the right character for the station." He
alone of all the hotel-keepers was reserved in disposition, and being a man of quiet domestic tastes, found
no pleasure in participating in the gambling and drinking

bouts of the students.   But he was disliked personally.
In 1828, at least nine young men declined to matriculate
because they would be assigned to his hotel.   They criticized his table, his linen, and his servants.   All declared
that he was disagreeable in his manners; and one spoke
feelingly of his " closeness."   Minor would have been
more popular, perhaps, had he been inclined to play loo,
drink juleps, and loan money to his boarders.   He was
careful in his business, and his reputation for parsimony
was probably based on foundations not more solid than
his laudable endeavor to make both ends meet in the management of his house,— a strenuous and perplexing task,
as we shall see.

However great may have been Minor's deficiency in
joviality, it was supplied to a surfeit by John Gray, who
leased the hotel situated at the southwest end of West
Range.   Gray had married the sister of Arthur S.
Brockenbrough, the proctor, who was a member of an
old and distinguished family.   When he obtained the
lease, he had a large family of children; but this did not
deter him from plunging even deeper than Spotswood
and Richeson into the merry dissipations of the students,
and contemning the ordinances which he had sworn to
observe.   By his conduct, he forfeited his lease in December, 1826.   " My heart is full to overflowing," he wrote
Lomax in a lachrymose strain on the 18th of that month,
" but for myself I would ask nothing; but for my wife
and seven children, I must implore your utmost exertions to have us reinstated."   As Lomax was the father
of nine boys and girls, this appeal must have touched his
sensibilities in a very tender spot, although he had already
gone so far as to say that Gray had been guilty of " im-
moralities," by which he meant only drinking and card-
playing.   Mrs. Gray herself, writing to Madison, in

1827, sadly complained that her husband had " always been unfortunate in his progress through life "; and that the " small remaining portion of his property would soon be sold for the benefit of his creditors."

It had been the Visitors' policy up to this time to appoint no woman to the position of hotel-keeper, as it would be impossible for any one of that sex to inspect the dormitories in person, or to serve as the proctor's assistant in the enforcement of the police regulations. But Mrs. Gray had so many strong claims to special consideration that, when her husband's rights were forfeited, John Carter was permitted to lease the vacated hotel nominally, and then practically to sublease it to her. She continued to be what she had previously been,— the most vigorous personality in the circle of the hotel-keepers. She was described by Leiper Patterson, son of Dr. R. M. Patterson, who accompanied his father to the University, as " an elegant and aristocratic lady, who always wore a white turban after the fashion of the famous Dolly Madison." A student, testifying about an altercation that had taken place between her and one of her boarders, affirmed that " she had returned fully as much as she had received." [1] This was her character,— she was prompt, resolute and outspoken. Her husband, after seeking employment as a book agent, in the North, finally removed to Florida; and during his residence there visited his wife and children in Virginia only at long intervals.

S. B. Chapman, the last of the six original hotel-keepers, did not offend as often as most of his associates by furtive indulgences in the rooms of the students; but

---

[1] A student, who, in 1845, was accused of firing a cracker in Mrs. Gray's drawing-room, said, in his testimony before the Faculty, that " he did not choose to make an apology to her because she was very haughty "

he was very hospitable in his own hotel; and on one occasion at least, was summoned before the Faculty for violating the terms of his lease by setting strong waters before his guests. He frankly admitted that he had "introduced wine and brandy, but not until some of his company had asked for it" "Finding that the students made too free with it," he said, "he prudently put it up."

When Spotswood's lease expired in July, 1829, he was succeeded by J. N. Rose, who would have taken the post the previous December, had he then been able to obtain the funds for the purchase of the indispensable outfit for the dormitories. Although a member of a wealthy family residing in Nelson and Amherst counties, he had been reduced to the point of applying for the office of toll collector on the James River and Kanawha Canal, and had even failed to secure this When he resigned in 1834, the two candidates for his berth were Captain Daniel Perrow, who had been the proprietor of the tavern in Rockfish Gap, and Colonel Ward, who was the popular landlord of a hotel in Charlottesville. Their military titles were more probably conferred in a spirit of courtesy by genial guests than won by arduous services even in the militia. It shows the weight given to deportment in selecting an incumbent for the position that the proctor, in writing to Cocke, thought it necessary to say that "Colonel Ward had more dignity of person and manner than his competitor." "Captain Perrow, however," he added, "is wholly free from pecuniary embarrassment, whilst Colonel Ward is involved" The Board wisely preferred solvency to dignity, and Perrow was appointed; but he lost the place in July, 1835. Ward apparently succeeded him. During several years, Wertenbaker leased one of the hotels.

XXIII. *The Hotel Fare*

In the beginning, a vegetable garden was reserved for each hotel. These gardens were actually laid off on the borders of the University grounds, but their area was afterwards re-appropriated by the Board for other purposes. Several acres situated further off were assigned in their stead, but the hotel-keepers found this land so poor that they did not think it worth the expense of enclosing, especially in the light of the fact that the materials for doing so had to be hauled from a remote spot. They all asserted that it was necessary for each one of them to own a horse, and they united in petitioning the Board for stables. These animals were chiefly useful in the search for supplies through the countryside. Captain Perrow testified, in 1829, that nearly all the articles of food consumed by the students,— meat as well as vegetables and fruit,— were procured from the country people, who came at their own convenience, and sold at prices which they themselves had named. He complained that they were irregular in delivering; that no dependence as to the time could be put in them. " One scarcely knew at the close of the day," he said, " what these people might choose to furnish the next." " Sometimes," he added, " I have been compelled to go twenty and even thirty miles for fresh butter." There were no means of transporting meats from a great distance before the construction of the railway; and it is possible that the only fish that ever reached the University were obtained from the Rivanna. In winter, occasional barrels of oysters were brought up from Richmond by wagon.

However inclined to drinking and card-playing they. may have been, Spotswood, Richeson, and Conway knew to a nicety what good food and what good cooking was.

When Spotswood was informed, before he first went up to the University, that the monthly charge for each boarder was to be limited to ten dollars, he openly expressed his indignant and contemptuous surprise. " This," he said, " will only suit a Yankee, who has never been used to anything more than onions, potatoes, and cod-fish, and his coffee sweetened with molasses, and who will mind the abuse of the students no more than a Spanish dog would mind the kicks and cuffs of his master." The Board of Visitors had merely required that the fare should be " plentiful, plain, of good and wholesome viands, neatly served and well dressed," but several of the hotel-keepers, in the beginning, went far beyond this modest restriction. " Some of them," Cabell wrote Cocke, " are producing an infinite deal of mischief by the luxury of their tables and other indulgencies, which they provide to conciliate their boarders and give fame to their hotels." This was in 1826, when there was still room for competition; but after the assignment of an equal number of dormitories to each hotel-keeper, there was not the same stimulating motive for maintaining the excellence of their fare.

The low price of board would not have permitted of a good table even for a short time, whatever the incentive, had not the price of food been also low. In 1827, a pound of ordinary beef was purchasable at the University for three cents; and the best portions could be bought at the rate of five. During this year, thirty-two pounds of mutton were sold for two dollars and sixty-five cents, or eight cents a pound, and four hundred and seven pounds of bacon for thirty-two dollars and twenty-six cents, or seven and three quarter cents a pound.

These reasonable prices, which prevailed until the fifth decade, when the inpouring of Californian gold led to inflation, ought to have assured the continuation of the excellent original fare, but, after 1830, the students had, on many occasions, ground to complain, not only of uncleanly service, but of very indifferent food. In April, 1831, the boarders at Rose's hotel, in protest against the meals of the previous day, went in a body to town and ordered their dinner there. The customary way of proving that the dissatisfaction was fully justified was to send the unfortunate chairman of the Faculty specimens of the bread that had aroused indignation,— thus on the day of the revolt just mentioned, the seceders solemnly handed him, through a formal committee, two rolls, which he, after examining them, had to acknowledge were unfit to be eaten. Under these circumstances, he always felt constrained to direct the proctor to take a meal at the offending hotel and report his opinion of the food. This was an unpleasant duty for that officer to perform, for the hotel-keepers were all on a friendly social footing with him, and in some instances they were his kinsmen. Mr. Gray, for example, was a brother-in-law of Brockenbrough, who was so often called upon to inspect the fare. The proctor's disposition was naturally to be lenient in his judgment; and this only provoked further complaints. Even when he was frank in his condemnation, the supple hotel-keeper had numerous excuses to offer, some of which, unhappily, were rendered only too sound by the occasional uncertainty of the local supplies.

One of the reports sent in by the proctor taken at random will be a good sample of many others which were submitted to the Faculty during these early years. He had been ordered to inspect the table of Edwin Conway's hotel. He found that Conway provided his boarders at least twice a week with turkey; that the roast-beef was ordinarily very badly cooked; that sometimes, at dinner, the dishes were boiled beef and boiled bacon, and that next day, there would be cold beef and cold bacon, without a single hot meat; that the bacon, hot or cold, was always poor in quality; and that it was rare for a pullet to be seen on the table.   Fish was, of course, still rarer. Turnip-tops in season, however, were never missing from day to day; but dessert was only brought on once a week. The tea and the coffee served were very mean to the taste. There was complaint of the constant use of rice as a vegetable; this was easily purchased along with potatoes; and both could always be looked for in the fare throughout the session.

This monotony was one of the principal causes of the students' dissatisfaction with the food; and their discontent on this score finally became so chronic that the Faculty, in 1834, decided to draw up a regular bill of fare, and to hold the hotel-keepers strictly to its observance; and it may be taken for granted that they called for no dish that, in their own combined opinion at least, was not procurable, whether by weekly importation from Richmond, or by daily purchase in the surrounding country.   In our times, when a world war has not only raised prices to an unprecedented height, but cut down the number of articles for consumption, the following varied and appetizing ménu, adopted by the Faculty eighty-six years ago, proves, on its face at least, that the students of that period enjoyed a substantial advantage over the students of our own; but, unfortunately for the former, as we shall see, this ménu was too often a mere scrap of paper: " Breakfast shall consist of hot or cold meat or fish; light and sweet loaf bread or rolls, biscuits, and cornbread; sweet and good butter, good molasses; tea and coffee to be made of good materials; good loaf sugar for the tea, and good brown sugar for the coffee, and cream or rich milk for both; and fresh milk for drink for those who desire it. Dinner shall consist of hot bacon, hot roast fresh meat and poultry; soup well boiled; four kinds of vegetables, from the commencement of the session to the first of January, three kinds from the first of January to the first of May, and four kinds again from the first of May to the end of the session; sweet and good butter for the vegetables; a supply of mustard, pepper, and other proper seasonings for the meats and vegetables, good molasses, wheat and cornbread, and dessert once a week, to consist of pies made of fresh fruit, or mince pies, puddings made of raisins or rice, fritters, with sugar and butter, or tarts, or any two of them occasionally varied. Supper shall consist of hot or cold meat or fish, good molasses, light and sweet loaf bread or rolls, biscuits and cornbread, sweet and good butter, tea and coffee and cream, or fresh milk for drink for those who desire it, from the commencement of the session to the first of March, and from the first of May to the end of the session."[1]

The articles embraced in this bill of fare were to be furnished in abundance; and they were also to be of

[1] The following was the bill of fare prescribed by the Faculty in 1851

BREAKFAST — "Hot or cold meat or fish, cold loaf bread; warm rolls or biscuits; warm corn batter-bread; tea and also coffee of good quality; loaf sugar for tea and good brown sugar for coffee; good butter; milk in the months of October, November, April, May and June, molasses from November 1 to May 1 —

DINNER — "Hot bacon; hot roast or boiled fresh meat in due variety from day to day, or poultry, soup well boiled, rice and potatoes, and other vegetables in their season, properly dressed, a supply of mustard, pepper, and other proper seasonings for the meats and vegetables, wheat and corn bread; dessert twice a week; provided that, on those days poultry is furnished, it shall be considered to be a substitute for the dessert; dessert shall consist of pies to be made of fresh fruit, or of mince pies, rice or other puddings, sponge cake, with sauce or tarts, to be occasionally varied.—

SUPPER — "Same as breakfast, except meat or fish."

wholesome quality, well cooked, and served without slovenliness.   It was not accepted as a valid excuse that they
could not be obtained at the University or in its neighborhood although this was quite probable during the
severest part of winter and during protracted spells of
bad weather in summer.

Only a few months had passed when the students' protests assumed as outraged a tone as formerly.   Rice and
potatoes were dished up with all their previous regularity,
and no attempt was made to lessen this monotony by occasionally obtruding a third vegetable.   So mean became
the food again that, in 1836, the students began to turn
surreptitiously to the kitchens of the professors, whose
cooks were always ready to earn, in this furtive way, a
few dollars by providing a dinner or a supper,— sometimes at their master's expense, but the young men, doubtless, in most cases, supplied the raw materials for these
meals.   Breakfast was smuggled into the dormitories by
means of a shrewd little black boy, who went up and
down the arcades with a covered basket ostensibly selling
apples to the passersby   When the hotel-keepers, during
the same year, told of their inability to purchase the fowls
called for in the prescribed bill of fare, the chairman required them to serve two desserts a week instead   A
committee of students was now appointed, which criticized almost with ferocity the patent deficiencies of Col.
Ward's table.   There were no biscuits furnished for
breakfast; no wheat bread for dinner; and there was a
very small amount of butter allowed for the vegetables.
All the popular dishes were so meagre as to fail to go
around to all.   The middling was too fat to be eaten;
the tea and coffee too watery to be drunk; the desserts
too much restricted to dried apples to be palatable   Very
naturally a spirit of rebellion was aroused by these short-

comings, which were made the more intolerable by the
chilliness and disorder of the dining-room. A student
would sometimes seize a dish of vegetables and pour the
entire contents into his single plate; rolls would be thrown
about the room as in a game of snow-ball; hands would be
loudly clapped; and above all the noise, would rise the
ear-piercing notes of the jewsharp.

The poverty and meanness of the food, the slovenliness of the napery, the crudeness of the table, and the
clumsiness of the attendance, which were only too often
observed, sprang principally from the smallness of the
margin of gain. During the period when there were
as many as six hotel-keepers, this margin was so slim
that it was always trembling upon the vanishing point.
"The profit," said Warner Minor, the most capable
manager among them, "will induce no man who is well
qualified in all respects to keep a hotel. My candid
opinion is, that, admitting to each house its greatest number of thirty-three boarders, the profits are not worth the
attention of any man of business. . . . My house, this
year, with an average of twenty, will feed my family and
clear about three hundred dollars:

Total amount of board	$2,035 00	Hire of cook and two dining room servants . .	$266.00
		Wood	200 00
Lodgings .	158.00	Amount eaten .. .	1,320.00
Servants and washing .	290 00	Keeping two cows	100.00
		Other necessary expenses	200.00
	$2,483 00		$2,086 00 " [1]

[1] In 1847, Addison Maupin computed his annual expenses, as one of
the hotel-keepers, as follows:

"Rent	. .	$200.00	Flour	$175 00
Servants' Hire	. .	450 00	Corn meal	50.00
Fuel		275 00	Salt .. .	10 00
Keeping 2 cows and 1			Vinegar	10 00
horse		150.00	Loaf and Brown sugar .	200.00

Minor, in this estimate, placed no valuation whatever on the services of himself, his very capable wife, and his five robust negroes.   After deducting three hundred dollars for profit, he was left with only ninety-seven dollars to pay his contingent expenses.   He was all the more dissatisfied with this annual upshot because every article of food on his tables, except the meats, was bought at wholesale prices, and most of the meats on the hoof. And to darken still further the outlook for the hotel-keepers, the students were not very prompt in depositing the second and third instalments due for their board As many as thirty-two were delinquent in March, 1831. The chairman stated, the following year, that unless the number of hotels was cut down to three, there would be no room for gain; and Mrs. Gray expressed the same conclusion, in another form, when she said to Cabell, that, unless the hotel-keeper could count thirty mouths in his dining room, he could not expect to possess a satisfactory margin of profit.

XXIV. *Health of the University*

The University precincts were unable to show that they were proof against those alarming epidemics of disease which were so common in those times, even when the precautions then considered sufficient had been taken to prevent their occurrence.   It was an age when the true laws of hygiene had not yet been intelligently

Coffee and Tea . ..	$100 00	Pickles ... . $	25 00
Condiments, Spices, etc	20 00		
Fresh Meat . .	270 00	Total cost $2,740.00	
Fowls	30 00	Return from Boarders.	2,800 00
Bacon and Lard . ..	300 00	Less 2 per cent. paid the	
Molasses .. .	30.00	University	56 00
Vegetables . .	150 00		
Butter and Eggs .	250 00		$2,744 00
Lights	50.00	Net profit $4 00 "	

grasped.   The necessity for constant vigilance in maintaining systematically the highest degree of cleanliness on
private and public premises, was not, in actual practice
at least, owing to the slipshod slave service, always ener-
getically complied with.   The climate of the mountain
region,— which was so loudly trumpeted for its salubrity,
and in the main, deservedly so,— was subject to recur-
rences of a malignant type of typhoid fever; and it was
this distemper which broke out at the University again
and again during the first half century of its existence.
That, in these early years, it should do so was a fact to
be expected in the light thrown on the causes of this fever
by modern research and observation.   The water, which
was undefiled enough in its origin on the roofs, or on the
watershed of the academic mountain, was drawn, not
directly from one open central receptacle for immediate
distribution in the pavilions and dormitories, but from
scattered closed cisterns, to which it had been first
allowed to flow.   These petty reservoirs depended upon
a periodical cleaning out for their purity; and even with
frequent drawing off of their water with this purpose in
view, deleterious substances must have often percolated
in through the interstices of natural drainage.

Moreover, the dormitories were, to a certain extent,
shut off from untainted and invigorating draughts of
fresh air.   The Lawn, though open to the south, the
direction of the prevailing wind, was often close in its
atmosphere in comparison with the high and breezy tops
of the neighboring ridges.   The two Ranges faced respectively east and west, and the bitter cold and the torrid
heat which their situation exposed them to at certain
seasons of the year, may have caused something more
than discomfort to the occupants of those rooms.   As
early as 1825, there was an impression that East Range

especially was liable to the recurrence of typhoid fever. Major Spotswood, who had leased the hotel at the southern end of this Range, lost, as we have already mentioned, three of his servants by this disease, and for a time was forced, with his family, to find refuge in a vacant pavilion.   The inefficient services of that day furnished by lazy, untrained slaves, who had been hired out only too often because their characters were bad, was an additional cause of these outbursts of distemper.   There were perpetual complaints of the state of neglect in which so many of the dormitories were suffered to remain, and the word " filthy " was frequently on the lips of the chairman when constrained to inspect them in person.   Not a quarter of a session passed that he was not compelled to remonstrate with some of the hotel-keepers for their inattention to this dangerous condition, and he again and again, in words of sharp impatience, reported them to the Faculty for this reason.

Perhaps, a partial cause at least of the sickness that so often occurred was the one we have already censured; namely, the ill-judged regulation which required the young men to leave their rooms before the sun had dissipated the cold humidity of the mountain air, to attend classes, frequently before breakfast, to bolt that meal by candlelight, and to go back to the same ill-heated and ill-ventilated lecture-room, out of which they had groped their way half an hour earlier.

There was no real provision for the sick among the students; no hospital to which they could be carried where their needs would be met by constant and skilful nursing. When stricken, they remained in their comfortless and lonely dormitories, without any attendance beyond that afforded by the visiting physician and one untrained, unsympathetic servant   It is far from improbable that the natural depression caused by their forlorn situation in illness had its influence in aggravating the epidemics that so often occurred. Occasionally, a hotel-keeper would provide a room in his own house for a sick boarder; this, Colonel Richeson, a kindly man, did in 1827; but it was an act of benevolence too risky for the keeper's family to have been frequently repeated. Richeson's unselfish conduct suggested to the proctor, Brockenbrough, the advisability of erecting another story on the top of each hotel for use as a private hospital for the exclusive benefit of the young men occupying the dormitories assigned to that hotel; but although this plan was submitted to the rector, Madison, it does not appear to have won the Board's approval,— quite probably because they anticitpated that it would put the families of the keepers in jeopardy, and also diminish the privacy of their homes.

When the epidemic of typhoid began in the winter of 1829, there were no ameliorations of this character whatever for the afflicted students. The first announcement of that outbreak was made by the chairman on January 22, and at the same time, he gave warning that the disease might be contagious There were already fifteen young men down in bed with it. He was constrained to report that most of the dormitories were in a very unclean state, in consequence of their not having been scoured since the beginning of the session. The Faculty, at their meeting on the same day, decided to convert a vacant hotel into an infirmary, but the space open to use was too contracted for the comfortable accommodation of so many patients. At the start, Dr. Dunglison was sanguine of soon stamping out the disease, for he found the cases to be of a mild character, though the debility seemed to linger for an unusual length of time. But the outlook did not long continue so propitious, and on the

31st, the Faculty were hastily called together again, and decided that it was imperative that the intermediate examinations should be suspended   Forty-four of the students had already left the University, and eighteen were busily packing up in expectation of an early departure.   Hardly a week had gone by when the Faculty were again hurriedly in session.   Two additional cases of fever had developed; one of them in a very aggravated form; and there was now good reason for thinking that the distemper was highly infectious.   Already one of the students had died, and it was doubtful whether several others would survive.   There was an alarming turn for the worse in the complexion of all the new cases, and in consequence, the Faculty determined to stop all lectures until the first of March, which would enable every student, not already infected, to leave.   At the same time, the professors let it be known that they were willing to continue to teach, however few members of their original classes might stay on to listen.   Sixty-two of the students had already withdrawn, while twenty of the remaining fifty-five were victims of the distemper.

There being no improvement by February 1, the University was then closed, with the announcement that the return of the young men was to be postponed beyond March 1 for an indefinite time.   As a change for the better began to manifest itself after that date, the first of April was appointed as the day of the re-opening, but the absent students were advised to engage rooms and board,— for a time at least,— without the precincts. This would seem to indicate that the epidemic had not spread from the dormitories into the country roundabout.   Seventy young men had, by April 10, resumed their studies.   Only one case of sickness was then reported as present within the limits, and this belonged to a disease which was not of a contagious or infectious nature. It will be recalled that, when the institution was first opened, one reason given for prolonging the session through the summer was that this would tend to enlarge the patronage from Eastern Virginia and the States further South, owing to the proverbial healthfulness of Piedmont Virginia at that season. Regret was now felt by some that the original arrangement had been altered. Two students, who had hastened to their homes in the Tidewater region, had died after their arrival, and it was correctly presumed that they had carried the infection with them in a form that had quickly developed after they had begun to breathe the warmer atmosphere of the lower country. "If summer vacations continue from July to September," remarked the proctor, Brockenbrough, warningly, "I think it probable we shall not have many students from that quarter."

The explanations of the cause of this typhoid outbreak which were heard differed in character. The proctor, Brockenbrough, a man of excellent practical sense, thought that it was due to the following condition: "Few of these young men," he said, "were accustomed to sleep in rooms with the outdoor opening immediately upon them, which are thrown open by daylight of a cold morning, after a hot fire the night before. This led to colds, the first symptoms of the disease." Dr. Somervail of Essex county, whose two wards had been students at the University, but had escaped the disease, remarked that it could not spring from the air, "for this was common to that and the adjoining county, but must come from something in the place itself, though undiscovered. I am told some of the dormitories have cellars under them, and others are near the ground, and here the fever began, and most of the sick were. It is said the rooms near the ground were floored over shavings.   Chips, which may be now in a state of decay and lacking air, may have caused the sickness."

Dunglison himself was of the opinion that the distemper rose and sank with the alterations in the state of the atmosphere; but nevertheless he was careful to have all the infected rooms fumigated, and the uninfected thoroughly scoured.   Mr. Madison also thought that the disease had its origin in the air.   "The fever, whatever its cause," he said, "is well understood to have no respect for places as ordinarily distinguished by healthiness or the contrary.   It prevailed in my family a few years ago in a very mortal degree, notwithstanding the salubrity of the situation, without any visible circumstance that could account for it, and without prevailing in situations adjoining of a like character   It is a fact, I believe, that it visited a solitary family dwelling on the summit of Peter's Mountain, the Chimburazo of our Lilliputian Andes, where all the known atmospherical and local causes, instead of explaining the phenomenon, ought to have been safeguarded against it.   As the radical cause must be referred to some mutable condition of the atmosphere, we must hope that a favorable change, if not already commenced, will soon take place."   Tucker, like his colleagues, the other members of the Faculty, declared that he had no explanation to offer.   "I can hear of nothing," he said, "which is common to those attacked, either as to situation, diet, or habit of life."   The Board were forced to content themselves with the statement that "it was one of those epidemics to which the most salubrious situations were subject"; and that it raised "no reasonable ground for apprehension in looking to the future." It is quite probable that the real cause of the fever lay in the contaminated water of the University cisterns, or in the contents of the milk pitchers placed on the tables of the several hotels. The distemper was, perhaps, aggravated after it began, by the unwise exposure of the young men to the chill and dampness before sunrise.

The University's enemies seized upon the occurrence of the epidemic as a means of blackening its prospects and damaging its reputation. An onslaught on that ground, full of sly malevolence, was published in one of the Richmond journals,— to which Dr. Dunglison made a pointed and dignified reply. The fever was also brought up by persons who attributed a strong irreligious leaning to the institution; it was a proof, they said, that Providence inflicts punishment on atheism, whether hospitably entertained by men or by seats of learning. A clergyman, who was later to become a distinguished bishop, did not entirely cloak his approval of this explanation when, not long afterwards, he delivered a sermon under the roof of the Rotunda, and in the presence of the professors and students. The injustice of the hinted slur, as well as the inappropriate hour and spot for utterance, aroused, as we shall see, lively indignation among the listeners.

One natural result of this epidemic,— the first to befall the University,— was to create a feeling of nervousness during the years that immediately followed. In 1832, the whole country was menaced with an invasion of cholera. Tucker, then the chairman, ordered the proctor to cleanse the precincts thoroughly without delay. " It is generally admitted," he wrote in August, " that the cholera will find its way into all the inhabited parts of the United States, villages as well as towns, and that its malignancy can be partly mitigated by timely precautions." The precautions upon which he insisted were: (1) the whitewashing of all cellars and dormitory

walls, and the scrubbing of the woodwork; (2) the cleaning up of the outside closets; and (3) the removal of all
kitchen slops to a distance. Thomas Jefferson Randolph, a member of the Board, acknowledged, in a letter
to Cocke, that the " whole establishment " was now in a
most menacing condition. A large drain was at once
dug between the pavilions of Professors Davis and Emmet on West Lawn, and all stagnant water about the
buildings and under the arcades was drawn off in the
endeavor to purify the grounds. Dr Dunglison proposed that a large barn standing on the University's
land should be so altered as to afford room for fifteen to
twenty negro patients. The hay which it contained was
carted away and the roof and frame-work repaired.

In the course of the ensuing spring, a panic was caused
by the discovery in the pond from which the ice for the
pavilions and hotels was obtained, of an anatomical
cadaver that had been dropped into its waters for preservation, or mischief's sake, at an unknown date, by medical
students. It had, when brought to the surface, wasted
away to a skeleton.

The young men who were sick were still forced to be
physicked and nursed in their dormitories   Although it
was planned, in 1836, to allow a separate apartment for
them, yet no step, owing to the contracted income, seems
to have been taken at that time to carry this out. The
University doctors who professionally called on indisposed students charged, like regular practitioners, for
their services: thus, in 1840, Cabell received, for six
visits, fees at the rate of one dollar a visit; and he added
one dollar and a half for medicines furnished, and two
dollars and a half for office prescriptions. Dr Johnson's stipend for five calls, in 1831, was four dollars and
a half altogether. He also performed dental work, for

which his surgical education had perhaps very well fitted him; nor was this confined to mere tooth pulling; for in 1832, he demanded five dollars for filling three teeth with fine gold. The gold had quite probably been supplied by the patient. The like work of Dr. Porter, of Charlottesville, was much more costly, as demonstrated by a bill presented to a student named Pickett, which amounted to thirty dollars.

xxv. *The Uniform Law*

It would be presumed that the Board of Visitors, with so many grave causes for irritation and rebellion already rankling in the students' breasts, would have been slow to adopt any new ordinance that was quite certain to increase the existing discontent. Now, a uniform law was as nicely calculated as the rule requiring early rising to create perpetual friction with the Faculty, for it too could only be enforced by espionage, and by an espionage that would be frequently constrained to descend to a pettiness that was as exasperating as it was undignified. This law was in operation as early as 1827. The proctor, Brockenbrough, once spoke of it as "the favorite measure" of the Visitors. Why was it of such preeminent importance in their view? As we have previously stated, the University, during these formative years, was looked upon by many persons with a censorious eye as the institution of the wealthy alone,[1] and this popular impression was to be particularly deprecated in its case, since it had to rely upon the General Assembly principally for its support The accusation seemed to be

---

[1] Not by all, for R H Alexander, guardian of Archibald Henderson, of Salisbury, N C, wrote that he had been influenced, in sending his ward to the University of Virginia, by its reputation for reasonable expenses Letter dated December 5, 1828, Proctor's Papers.

confirmed by the spirit of profusion which pervaded Southern life at that time, and which, naturally enough, was reflected in the behaviour of young men turned practically at large, before they were of age, upon the free arena of the University.

The reasons for the passage of the ordinance were set forth succinctly in a circular issued in 1828,— they were the enforcement of economical habits among the students, the prevention of invidious distinctions, and the discouragement of frivolous tastes.   The law was primarily a fulmination against extravagance in dress, and its general purpose was to preserve the University's reputation for sobriety, on which its ability to retain popular favor depended; and also to maintain, as far as feasible, an equality of expenditure among the young men, so that those of small means would not be made to feel the disparity in fortune   The ordinance had in view, not only the cultivation of the public good-will, but also an increase in the attendance, for the lower the general expenses could be cut down, the more students would be led to matriculate.

It is possible that the idea lurked furtively in the minds of the Visitors that the University of Virginia, like all its great prototypes, should have an academic costume, but that the adoption of the English cap and gown would appear imitative, if not pretentious, in a Republican seat of learning   In their judgment, the uniform agreed upon accomplished the same sentimental and ornamental purpose, accompanied by an equal, if not higher, degree of practical utility in the spirit of economy which it would foster.   Madison did not assent to this view.   He declared that the peculiar organization of the University made such a law inconvenient   " I am of the opinion," he said, " that a cheap black gown, such as is used in other like institutions, would answer all purposes better."

It was thought that the law would strengthen the hand of discipline, but time failed to prove that this forecasting was correct. The expectation probably had its origin in the stern associations of a uniform. The Faculty, as a body, showed a conscientious determination to enforce the law; but it is questionable whether they considered it a wise one, apart from those public aspects which had led the Board to adopt it. It was only natural that they should look at it chiefly in its practical working within the University; and as that working only caused inconvenience, annoyance, and resentment, their judgment may well, on the whole, have been biassed against the ordinance. Two of the most sensible men connected with the government of the institution were the first proctor, Brockenbrough, and the first chairman, George Tucker, both of whom held the regulation in very small esteem.[1]   " I have no doubt that the uniform law was adopted for economy," wrote the former to Cocke, who was its ardent advocate, " but, in many cases, to persons in moderate circumstances, it is otherwise. There are hundreds of Virginians who can clothe their sons decently at home in order to send them to the University, but would find it inconvenient to raise forty or fifty dollars, in addition to the other charges, to purchase clothing at the University, for the kind and cut of the cloth can't always be known in every section of the State. Some might think it proper to clothe them in Virginia cloth. I have known students to come here with clothes sufficient for the session that have been obliged to procure the uniform dress, and some of them

[1] A writer in the *Jefferson Monument Magazine* says, " George Tucker was, as chairman, a model of what that officer should be. He executed the law in its spirit, but was not too strict   Bonnycastle was immoderately rigid in enforcing the laws, either because his disposition was severer, or because the Board of Visitors required it   There was discontent under this strictness, and not any more order."

have found great difficulty in getting it. The objection is so great that I consider it rather a preventive than an inducement to students to come here."

This was the opinion of a man who considered the law on its practical side alone, and whose ability to judge that side correctly had been ripened by his long participation in the administrative affairs of the institution. Prof. Tucker, as chairman, looked at the law on its sentimental side "He has not only made up his mind not to execute it because he deems it unreasonable," wrote Trist to Cocke, in 1828, "but he goes so far as to express himself to that effect to the students themselves. In relation to the proscription of boots, he observed to one or more of the students that he was not going to examine whether they had on boots or shoes, and although Dr. Dunglison made repeated reports to him concerning the violation of the uniform law, they were never noticed " Trist had been asked by Cocke to report as to how far the ordinance was enforced, and it is clear from his words that he sympathized with Cocke's feeling in favor of its being carried out unfalteringly. Tucker's sense of dignity was probably ruffled by the suggestion that it was the chairman's duty to lower his eyes to the feet of every student who passed him; or it is possible that he scornfully regarded such a regulation as puerile in an institution that was founded on the broadest principles of personal liberty. Indeed, to such an absurd point was this opposition to boots pushed that, at a later date, a student who had been reported for wearing a pair, earnestly asserted that, in doing so, he had not intended to "bid defiance to the Faculty."

What was the character of the uniform? It consisted of a coat, waistcoat, and pantaloons, manufactured from cloth of a dark mixture. The coat was cut high in the neck, with a braided standing collar, and skirts of moderate length, with pocket flaps; the waistcoat was single-breasted, and the pantaloons were marked by a conspicuous stripe. The buttons were flat in shape and covered with cloth of the same dye as the suit. One of the students of this period, in recalling the uniform in after-life, said that it was of the color popularly known as pepper and salt, while another speaks of it as having been of an invisible gray tint. The cloth was usually designated as " Oxford mixed," and it was, from year to year, imported in large quantities by the merchants of Charlottesville. The shoes in use were labeled in the stores as "cotton" and "union" In the beginning, gaiters were required in winter and white stockings in summer. Boots were, as we have seen, strictly forbidden. In winter, the stock was made of black cloth, and in summer, of white. The hat was black in color and round in shape; but at a later date, a cheap cap was also permitted to be worn The entire details of the summer costume were not fully agreed on until after 1827. The choice, at first, lay between bombazine, bombazet, and silk. Silk was preferred by the students; they objected to bombazet as too heavy; but it was the least costly of the three. As finally prescribed, the pantaloons for the warm season were-to be of a light brown, inexpensive cotton stuff, while the waistcoat was to be of some white material. An embroidered vest was at first connived at, but was afterwards prohibited.

How unsteady even as late as 1830 was the rule governing the proper materials for the uniform was shown by what Cocke then noticed in the shop of Henry Price, the principal tailor. " I found on the shelves," he told Brockenbrough, " so great a variety of cloths — all of which seemed to be considered to be within the meaning of the regulation for uniforms,— as to explain at once, at least in part, the difficulties we have heard of in this branch of police.   Would it not be best in you to adhere strictly to the enactments in selecting some specific shade of dark mixed cloth, and apprise Mr. Price that no other can be received in compliance with the regulations?"

By the terms of the ordinance, each student's outlay for clothing was not to run beyond one hundred dollars during a single session.   What proportion of this sum was used up in the purchase of the uniform?   In 1832, the cost of a full suit of the best quality, embracing the coat, waistcoat, and pantaloons, was thirty-eight dollars. In such case, the tailor furnished the material.   The charge often ran down to thirty-three, twenty-nine, and twenty-seven dollars.   The cost of the most expensive coat did not exceed eighteen, while the average price ranged somewhat lower.   The students whose incomes were small procured the cloth from the local stores, and then had it converted into a full suit,— under these circumstances, the charge for the uncut material, including the trimmings, was fourteen dollars and fifty cents; the charge of the tailor for making the coat, four and a half to six and a half, for the waistcoat, one dollar and seventy-five cents, and for the pantaloons, one dollar and fifty. The total expense at the shop was rarely in excess of ten dollars   The buttons cost about twenty-five cents the dozen; the cloth cap, two dollars and a half   Every student was called upon to purchase two suits in the course of each session,— one for the frigid season, the other for the warm, which fortunately for him, was less expensive. Some of the young men were compelled to buy at least three suits, if not four, during a single session as their only means of keeping up an appearance of neatness. With one hundred dollars as the limit of their expenditures for clothes, it would not require many suits to trench so closely on the margin as to leave but little for the purchase of under-garments.

When was the uniform to be put on? In 1829, the Board announced that it was to be worn on the Sabbath, during examinations, at public exhibitions,— including balls and parties,— and whenever the student left the University precincts. In the interval, at this time, a plain black frock-coat was permissible in winter, and a light gown or coat in summer. In 1836, the occasions for the use of the uniform were stated to be public balls, private parties, church services, public celebrations, public addresses, visits to private houses, and excursions to Charlottesville. The uniform was also to be worn on Sunday whenever the students were absent from their dormitories. Apparently, it was not required at this time while they were attending lectures

The extreme strictness of the regulation was, from the beginning, subject, during short intervals, to relaxations. In April, 1833, for instance, the young men were permitted to wear round-abouts. They had already obtained leave to put on the summer pantaloons and waistcoats which they had procured from home. So many of them, during the autumn of 1835, asserted that it was necessary to send their uniforms to the tailor that no objection was offered for the time being to their appearing outside of their rooms in ordinary clothes, provided that they were not seen in that dress at a private ball. When, in 1840, Dr Tyng, of New York, preached in the Rotunda, the chairman feared lest the students should remain away because their uniforms were shabby; and as he was anxious for the congregation to be a large one, he posted a notice that the uniform could, if desired, be doffed in anticipation of the services.

At first, there was no relaxation of the ordinance in the case of single individuals   Melville Gillies, a naval officer, was a student at the University in 1834, and having, before he left home, purchased all the clothing he would need, he asked to be relieved from the operation of the uniform law.   " The change of seasons," he wrote Cocke, " required a constant change of dress, but as I have been advised to hold myself in readiness for sea service this summer, I feel very unwilling to subject myself to expense for clothing, which I shall be compelled to lay aside in the course of a few weeks, and I request I may be permitted to wear those in my possession." Reasonable as this application was in substance and in spirit, it was, in obedience to the supposed requirements of the ordinance, denied.   But in the following year, the good sense of this action was questioned; John Rodgers, George Wickham, and George W. Randolph,— all of whom were young naval officers like Gillies,— were now granted the right to wear their professional uniforms J. H. Bryant was also excepted on the ground that he was a married man, and had reached the age when exemption was always allowed.   That age was twenty-three.   Professor Garland, formerly of Hampden-Sidney College, was excepted too; but John B Young, who had lost both parents, was refused permission to wear an ordinary mourning suit

Although the uniform was, as a rule, becoming to the young men, and although too it was noticed that they showed no dislike to wearing it voluntarily when passing the summer in the mountain resorts, yet, within the precincts, they always exhibited a sharp distaste for its use As early as 1828, the hostility to the law was so acute that the Faculty had to seek the assistance of the parents by asking them to curtail their sons' supply of pocket money, with which they had been buying civilian clothing. At a private ball held in Mr. Rose's hotel, a few years afterwards, nineteen of those present were dressed without any regard to the ordinance; and at another ball, given at Mrs. Gray's, there were eleven in the same irregular costume. In 1831, the students held a tumultuous public meeting, and after violently condemning the uniform law, announced that they would not observe it. The resolution was withdrawn when it was suggested that more could be accomplished for its recall by a riot; and this was at once precipitated.

There were, after this date, frequent dismissals and suspensions for defying the ordinance; but this only served to fan the exasperation. In 1833, thirty-seven young men were, on a single occasion, summoned for violating it; the proctor, in fact, acknowledged that, at this time, only one-fourth of the students observed the law; and as spring had now set in, and the hot season was approaching, he predicted that there would be an ever increasing number disposed to ignore contemptuously its hateful provisions. At a ball given in one of the hotels in April, 1835, the members of the Faculty present, we are told, were shocked by the extravagant costumes which were flaunted in their eyes. Many of the pantaloons had been made especially for that festive hour, and in cut and color, bore no resemblance whatever to the sober model which the Board had enjoined; indeed, some of the young men had even had the audacity to discard the plain trousers and to substitute the courtly velvet knee-breeches for them. From this time, the violations of the ordinance continued to grow in number, and the culprits included some of the steadiest and ablest collegians then in the precincts. William J. Robertson, perhaps the most distinguished lawyer and judge of the

State in his day, and James A. Seddon, afterwards a conspicuous member of Congress and Confederate Secretary of War, both very quiet in their general demeanor and successful in their classes, revolted against the irksome inconvenience of the law; and their example was imitated by many others equally temperate and studious in their habits.   Robertson went so far as to prefer rustication at Bowcock's tavern, where so many suspended students, in those times, in supposed seclusion, chewed the cud of defiance of unpopular ordinances. Some, when summoned, boldly said in the presence of the Faculty that they considered themselves fully justified in disobeying the law, as its only effect was to impose offensive restrictions without proportionate advantages in economy or discipline.

The reasons offered for assuming civilian dress were numerous, but, in most instances, bear the stamp of honesty and sincerity.   In the autumn of 1830, a party was given at one of the hotels, and one-third of the young men present were observed to have left off their uniforms, though required to wear them on an occasion of that nature.   The plea of each one was that his coat was too thread-bare to be worn at such entertainments.   The chairman's reply was concise and pointed.   " If your suits are so shabby," he said, " then stay away."   Another popular excuse was that the coat, trousers, or waistcoat had been sent to the shop for repairs; and this was quite probable, for as long as the expenditure for clothing was limited to one hundred dollars, there must have been many students whose wardrobes did not contain a single surplus garment of the approved model   The venerable age of the coats was frequently brought up in defense; so was the monstrous dilatoriness of the tailors in fulfilling their commissions.   Some asserted that no gentleman would be willing to dance in such a plebeian suit as the uniform; one at least justified himself on the score that his coat had been spattered with mud and torn by briars in an " anatomical expedition "; another, charged with wearing a white hat, said that his head was so diminutive that the cap prescribed would not fit it; and still another, who had appeared in white pantaloons, swore that they had been originally brown, but had been worn white. The chairman candidly admitted that, by the end of the session, the excuse of shabbiness was one that it was not possible to rebut.

Although the existence and practical enforcement of the uniform law would seem to have been sufficient to shut out the possibility of the students spending much money in the purchase of other clothing, yet the records for this period show that large sums were often wasted in this manner by those among them of extravagant tastes or handsome fortunes   A single bill sent in by Henry Price to Richard Morris, in 1833, amounted to sixty-three dollars and twenty-six cents; and among the articles that had been bought by him were white silk handkerchiefs, white waistcoats, satin stocks, gloves, and flesh brushes   Robert C. Stanard's haberdasher's account was even larger; and hardly smaller were the accounts of Robert H Tomlin and S Posey,— all men of distinction afterwards in professional or political life.

Pumps seem to have been a very popular footwear in those times, and their variety gave room for a wide latitude of choice. There were prunella, morocco, and buck calf pumps. The shoe most often called for was known by the name of " nullifier,"— in honor presumably of Calhoun   There were several kinds of hats in use,— two of which, the silk and the fur, were very costly. The silk, as it was always associated with a London hat-box, was, doubtless, imported from England. The cap, which was inexpensive, was of cotton and the cloak, of blue camlet. The overcoat was dubbed the " Petersham "; and this, too, was probably from a British factory. There was a rich profusion of satin scarfs and stocks, and also of Pongee handkerchiefs. The gloves were made of white silk or buck-skin; the shirts of linen or cotton; the waistcoats, of figured silk, or of pure white or black stuffs of different sorts; the stocks of silk or nankeen. A handsome pair of trousers was often of checkered pattern, and the dress coat, of dark blue cloth, with brass buttons. Very costly umbrellas are frequently noted; so also are embossed snuff-boxes, elaborated cigar-cases, clouded canes, and the other elegant paraphernalia of fops. These expensive articles of clothing or ornamental service could only, for the most part, have been used at long intervals, and perhaps then surreptitiously; and they were too costly to be in the possession of the average student, who, very probably, continued to wear his more or less shabby uniform even during the hours when he was not required to do so.[1]

[1] Henry Price, whose name has been frequently mentioned in the text, enjoyed the largest patronage among the students, but there were other tailors who shared their custom Such were Peter Fox, G H Savage, George Toole, and J B Walker Price was an Englishman by birth The most prominent merchant among those who supplied these tailors with materials was John Cochran, formerly of Augusta county, but afterwards a successful and highly esteemed citizen of Charlottesville J Raphael sold flannels, gloves, and trunks to the students, R Edwards sold cravats and underclothing Andrew McKee was the popular hatter Other merchants who furnished the different goods called for by the young men were Isaac Marshall, W L Dunkum, A Benson, Andrew Leitch, Twyman Wayt, B Ficklin, John Bishop, Hornsey and Goss, Bragg and Kelley, and Sampson and Gooch Mr Timberlake, whose name appears so often in the students' accounts, was a near kinsman of the first husband of the famous Peggy O'Neal, who, as the wife of General Eaton, Secretary of War in President Jackson's cabinet, broke up that body, and caused an explosion in Washington society

XXVI. *First Code of Discipline*

In a previous chapter, we quoted Jefferson's remarkable opinion as to the best method of governing the young men who were expected to enter the then newly completed University. It will be recalled particularly that he questioned the wisdom of raising the emotion of fear in order to enforce discipline among them; and that he earnestly advised that their pride, ambition, and moral susceptibilities alone should be appealed to, as the most certain means, not only of controlling them, but also of nurturing in them that general combination of qualities which he designated as " erect character." The relation of tutor and pupil should, in his judgment, be the counterpart,— at least in spirit,— of those of father and son, at once benign and affectionate, firm and inflexible. It was not congruous with the genius of American institutions, he said, that the college youth should " be hardened to disgrace, to corporal punishment, and to servile humiliations." The statutes of the country· laid down the penalty for crime, whether committed by student or citizen; academic authority, on the other hand, had only to consider the irregularities that were too small for the statutes to notice,— they, and they alone, were the offenses which that authority had to restrain and to correct.

Before the first session had begun, the Board of Visitors, under his supreme direction, adopted the comprehensive principle that too much government of the students should be avoided; that there should be slowness in multiplying occasions of coercing them by converting trivial actions into actions to be punished; and that ample room should be left to each one of them to exercise habitually his own discretion. In short, it was the University of Adolescent Freedom which Jefferson had in view, and not the College of Juvenile Discipline. The young men were to stand upon a platform of equality in all things,— in the choice of studies; in personal association unhampered by the social ties that accompanied subdivision into classes; in absolute self-domination Public sentiment was to play the same repressive part within the precincts that it played in the great communities without; but at the very time that it curbed the spirit of license, it was expected to give full rein to the spirit of liberty.

The University was constructed in such a manner as to limit the scope of a peeping eye,— each dormitory was a separate house in itself, a legal castle, a monastic cell, that could be securely shut by the occupant against the prying intrusion of his fellow-students, and the suspicious scrutiny of the professors It is doubtful whether a third of the young men, who, in these secluded rooms, violated the ordinances by playing cards, guzzling eggnog and mint sling, or eating surreptitious chicken suppers, ever fell under the Faculty's displeasure through the accident of being detected

The system, not so much of discipline as of lack of discipline, which Jefferson wished to put in force in this academic village, was, on its face, as idealistic as a code of laws adopted by the sublimated Parliament of Utopia; but it becomes perfectly intelligible, whether practicable or not, if we bear in mind his point of view In the first place, he expected the University founded by him to be patronized, not by raw boys, shirking their studies and running after irregular pleasures, but by sedate young men, who were to engage in graduate work in general preparation for some active pursuit in life. Were not persons with such a solid purpose in their minds certain to be animated by a steady and sober spirit, that would reject with scorn the mere thought of indulgence in boyish pranks or wild profligacy? So he unquestionably presumed. In the second place, as he knew that the youthful matriculates would, as a body, belong to the oldest, wealthiest, and most cultured families of the South, he took it for granted that their instincts would be gentle; that they would disdain to violate those precepts of upright conduct which they had learned at home; and that if there were to be found among them, as in the whitest flock, a small number of black sheep, these degenerates would be shamed into decent behavior by the compelling example of the great majority. The plan only demonstrated in another form Jefferson's noble faith in the abstract rights and the ultimate perfectibility of humanity. It was, in reality, an extreme expression of his fundamental principle that that is the best government which governs the least; and that they are the happiest people who are most able to dispense with a constabulary. It is doubtful whether such an administrative conception as this could ever have had the smallest chance of practical success except in the old widely dispersed colonial communities of America, or in those Southern plantation communities, equally scattered over a broad surface, that existed before the abolition of slavery.

Even if Jefferson's expectation of establishing a genuine university had come to fruition in his own life time, it is doubtful whether his system of self-government could have been carried out by the mature body of students whom he so sanguinely counted upon. There would, under these circumstances, have been one fact at least to bring about an unhappy issue for it; namely, the young men would have been pent up within narrow local hedges, a condition in itself provocative of frictions that were

sure to call for restraint and repression.   Jefferson
always held towns in detestation, largely because every
great aggregation of human beings, however civilized,
confused that principle of the least government the
best, which he so earnestly advocated.   This principle
could not work smoothly in a packed community; nor
could it have done so at the University of Virginia and
for the same reason.   Instead of that noble band of
young men visualized by him as too buried in their studies
to indulge the natural wildness of their age, numerous
youths, as heady as greyhounds and as fractious as colts,
matriculated in 1825.   The disorder and insurrection
that followed before many months had passed, appear
logical enough when we remember that these boys were
brought together with little restraint upon their actions
beyond that created by their intermittent consciousness
of the existence of sheriffs, judges, and juries   It was not
because the proper ordinances had not been adopted before the University opened, but because they were to be
enforced, not by the Visitors or the professors, but by a
Board of Censors selected by the Faculty from among the
students of the highest reputation for discretion.   This
was to be the principal judicial body, although their de-
cisions were to be subject to the approval of the collegiate
authorities.   The young men were expected to be meth-
odical and peaceable in their conduct, but should they
slide into irregularities, they were to be punished by a
court of their fellows   This was a novel plan of scholastic government, which almost at once caused much rub-
bing of eyes without the precincts.   " As to our friend,
Mr Jefferson's notion of jury trial by school boys,"
wrote John Patterson, of Maryland, in surprise to Cocke
at the time, " I can't hear of any institution for the education of youth where such a mode of keeping order

among the scholars is in practice, and I have made diligent inquiry about the matter."

The term "school-boys" was not altogether impertinent as applied to the students of the first session. Jefferson, speaking of the matriculates in March, said that only six of their number were twenty-one years of age or more; only nine, twenty; while twenty-three were nineteen years of age; ten, eighteen; ten, seventeen, and three, sixteen. Two-thirds of the entire number were either nineteen years of age or under that age. It was not simply that they were as youthful as these figures would indicate, but that they had been reared under a system tending to nourish in them unusual independence of character in spite of their immaturity. There is no reason to think that, during that period, parental control was less strict in the Southern States than in the Northern; there was certainly as much authority brought to bear upon the actions of the young in the homes of the South as in the homes of the same class in other parts of the Union; but the free life of the plantation and the presence of slaves created an unconscious dislike of restrictions not imposed by parental right; and it is also fostered a haughtiness of spirit that chafed against the supervision which became necessary so soon as these young men gathered in a large but compact community. The majority of them were the sons of affluent parents, and expecting to be wealthy in turn by inheritance themselves, had never acquired habits of extreme self-denial and self-repression. Removal from the vigilant eyes of their natural guardians, with purses more or less lined with money, with bodies tingling with health, and with no need to consider the future, was it to be wondered at that so many kicked up their youthful heels so wantonly when first turned loose in the University pasture?

We learn from a letter written by Cocke to Cabell that, previous to September 20, in the session of 1825, not a single class-roll had been called; not a single examination had been held.   Mr. Wertenbaker also informs us that, during the greater part of this session, no discipline at all was enforced because the Faculty were waiting for the students composing the Board of Censors to carry out the functions of their office   These students either openly or silently declined to do so   Indeed, it was but natural that they should have shrunk from the rôle which had, without their consent, been thus imposed on them. Had they taken it up, it would have put them in the position, not only of judges, but of spies on the conduct of their fellows.   The unpopularity certain to follow would have poisoned their intercourse with the young men in general, and perhaps jeopardized their ability to remain within the precincts with any personal comfort   As they failed to sit, and as the Faculty, in their respect for Jefferson's plans, were reluctant to assume the neglected duties,— indeed, had no power to do so without the Board's specific authorization,— the University, as we shall see, gradually fell, as Mr. Wertenbaker expressed it, into a state of "insubordination, lawlessness, and riot."

It was charged by those who disliked the foreign professors that this unhappy condition was directly traceable to their influence.   Long earnestly and justly resented the accusation.   "I believe," said he, "that they did as well as native professors would have done and even better.   Whatever people thought of our discipline,— and I believe that even those excellent men, the Visitors, thought that we were sometimes too severe,— yet I have not the least reason to regret anything I did."   The English professors, while they regarded with indignant aversion the licentious conduct of the students, were heartily in sympathy with the spirit of freedom which distinguished the University, for it was to this untrammeled spirit that they had been accustomed in the English seats of learning. The disorder that broke out was not due to any abnormal depravity in the constitution of these first students Who had a more complete opportunity of judging their real character than the thoughtful Long, a discerning foreigner without any reason whatever to be biassed for or against them? " I believe and still believe," he wrote Henry Tutwiler, after a host of English pupils had passed through his lecture-hall, " that I never had more youths of good abilities under me, nor more youths more capable of being made good and useful men."

Perhaps, in the whole course of his protracted and diversified life, Jefferson was never so keenly chagrined by an unexpected turn of events as he was by the ungovernable temper which the students manifested during this initial session. Not only was the success of the institution thrown in jeopardy, but his favorite theory was exploded, — certainly so far as it could be made to apply to youths. Consternation and depression must have filled his mind for the moment. " If you regard the future happiness and well-being of our State," Cocke wrote Cabell in September, 1825, " prepare yourself to make an effort at the next meeting of the Visitors to correct these evils. The old sachem is well prepared, from what I learned, as I passed through Charlottesville, to adopt measures calculated to reform the symptoms of irregularity, that, if not corrected, will soon grow into enormities." About two weeks after the date of this letter, Jefferson himself publicly acknowledged that the " experience of six months had proved that stricter provisions were neces-

sary for the preservation of order,— that coercion must
be resorted to, where confidence had been disappointed."
" We are not certain," he added, " that the farther aid
of the Legislature will not be necessary to enable the authorities of the institution to interfere in some cases with
more promptitude, energy, and effect than are permitted
by the laws as they stand at present " It must have been
with a sense of poignant mortification that he made this
admission   He started out with the serene conviction
that these young men should possess the right to govern themselves without any interference of any sort by
the Visitors or the Faculty, and yet before the first half
of the session had terminated, he was compelled to avow,
in the report of the Board, that additional laws would
have to be enacted by the General Assembly before the
authority of either the Faculty or the Visitors could be
successfully enforced.   His disillusionment could hardly
have taken a more dismayed form.

His original plan having been discarded, and the cen-
sorship abolished, the duty was imposed on the Faculty
to pass upon all offenses, and to inflict such punishments
for them as the ordinances had laid down.   " We shall
tighten or relax the reins of government," said Jefferson
himself, " as experience shall instruct us."   But, during
many years, the reins were held so stiffly as to err on the
side of sternness and rigidity, where mildness and relaxation would have been more effective   The code of regulations grew too plethoric; it went down too deeply and
too intimately into the social life of the students; it encouraged an espionage too petty and too unremitting to
be consonant with the spirit of a seat of learning that
justly claimed to be modeled on the standards of a great
university.   The system now adopted was the system
of the strait-jacket.   " Offenses, often trivial in them-

selves," says Frank G. Ruffin, a distinguished alumnus of that period, " were made prohibitive because matters of discipline, whilst multiplying and irritating rules increased the trouble they were meant to correct." Such rules were those which at one time required the young men to retire to their rooms at the sound of the college bell at nine o'clock at night, and to rise at dawn; to wear a uniform which they detested; and to be confined to the precincts and bound down to their studies during the Christmas holidays, when even the slaves were tacitly granted all those privileges of freedom and indulgence which enlivened that season in every Virginian home. These causes of irritation did not justify the turbulence that so often prevailed, but they largely explain it. We have now entered upon the only dark side of the early history of the University, which has to be described in a spirit of candor, if that history, during this formative interval, is to be correctly and comprehensively presented. Fortunately for the permanent reputation of the institution, the very violence of this period led to its own reformation by the creation of a reactionary influence which, in the course of the following period, found its highest expression in the adoption of the Honor System and the establishment of the Young Men's Christian Association.

XXVII. *Minor Offenses: Noisy Disturbances*

The most primitive form of the disorder which so often exhilarated the lives of the students was loud noise created by a variety of instruments. They raised a hubbub, — sometimes for the purpose of giving vent to youthful spirits; sometimes, and perhaps most often, for racking the nerves of unpopular professors. The shrillest sound was that of the split-quill, which must have penetrated far down the Lawn and under the arcades in the silence of night; the young men, after attending a public meeting of protest, would frequently join in a rebellious concert of this piercing character as they marched back in ranks to their dormitories. The raucous blare of the tin-horn was sometimes blended with that of the split-quill; but more often yet, the entire performance was confined to a mighty fanfare of horns.

On the night of April 17, 1832, the precincts were startled by an extraordinary outburst of this hoarse music, which continued, during several hours, to increase in volume. The proctor was quickly aroused by the din, and precipitately leaving his house to find out the reason for it, ran into a large mob of students disguised with masks, who were parading up and down the Lawn with horns at their lips, which they were blowing at the top of their vigorous lungs. When he earnestly remonstrated, they threatened to seize him by the collar; and as he prudently retreated, hurled stones at his back One of their number, who was recognized and summoned before the Faculty, stated, in his testimony, that the " demonstration " was entirely free from resentful spirit, and that it was intended simply as a " frolic " to dispel the " long dull quiet " of college life, which had become fatiguing and depressing. But this was not always its purpose In 1831, William Wertenbaker, then a young man, was serving as assistant proctor. Not only was he conspicuously resolute and energetic in ferreting out offenders, but his age was so near the age of many of the culprits that his activity seemed to them too presumptuous to be allowed to go unrebuked, and, in consequence, the peace of his home was constantly disturbed by inharmonious concerts with tin horns under his window. It must be stated, however, that these concerts sometimes took a legitimate turn, for, occasionally, the performers were invited to give a serenade before a professor's pavilion to gratify the curiosity of young ladies who were his interested guests from a distance.

As a concert with split-quills was apt to be accompanied by the bellowing of horns, so the confusion was often further heightened by the ringing of the college bell. Knowing that the bell gave out a very loud and alarming sound, the mischievous students were always itching to seize its dangling rope and pull it with all the strength of their youthful arms. The Faculty, aware of the allurement, endeavored to keep the belfry closed to every one except the janitor But not always with success. In April, 1831, four young men raised a ladder to one of the windows of the library, and breaking into that apartment, made their way up to the bell by a very dark and precipitous passageway, and tying a second rope to the one already attached, dragged this doubled rope behind them to the Lawn, where they continued to ring the bell with great violence until the janitor came running from under the arcades and frightened them away.   On one occasion, the bell was carried off and was only found after a protracted search and inquiry.

The most obstreperous students amused themselves at night, as they passed under the arcades, with singing what were described at that day as corn-songs.   These songs, which had been learned from the slaves, who sang them with pagan gusto at the corn shuckings in the autumn, were remarkable, not for their musical quality, but for their coarse and sometimes very obscene humor.   The young men having heard them sung on their native plantations, from season to season, could roll them out with as much spirit as the negroes themselves; and after a champagne supper at Keller's, or in a friend's dormitory, they as often vented their hilarity in the corn-song as in a performance on split-quill or tin-horn. Each verse as trolled out ended with a very loud but simple chorus, in which the most untrained voices could join with resounding success. Whenever the students were particularly eager to shock the public proprieties, they always sang the most indecent corn-song in their repertory; and they were sometimes guilty of this form of indecorum when passing in front of a church in Charlottesville on Sunday morning while the services were going on.

Another but more innocent way of making a noise was to drag iron fenders over the brick pavements under the arcades Still another was to explode crackers there, as the echoes redoubled the sound. So reckless was their use, in 1831, that the Faculty prohibited their firing even on the Fourth of July. A popular manner of causing annoyance with a cracker was to light it and hurl it at the study door of a professor, and then to hurry on and hurl another at the study door of a second professor, and so forward repeating the outrage, until half a dozen members of the Faculty had been startled and aroused.

But a far more serious instrument for the creation of noise within the precincts at night was the pistol or gun Although there was a very stern regulation forbidding the carrying of firearms, it was found impracticable to suppress this annoying and dangerous habit. The young men had been accustomed to the use of such weapons in their life on the plantation, and refused to give them up after their matriculation, although compelled to keep them out of sight of the officers, whose eyes were always watchful for their detection. The loudest noise that broke the nocturnal stillness of the Lawn was a fusillade of guns and pistols, and no single explosion was ever heard that it was not promptly, and in a spirit of some alarm, followed up by the proctor. But not invariably with success, for when more than one student was implicated in the firing, a guard was always set at every corner. So soon as the proctor was seen hurriedly approaching, the cry would be passed on: "Look out, fellows," and the culprits would dive into the dormitories or behind the Ranges. "I firmly believe," reported the chairman very sadly in October, 1831, "that nothing can enable us to detect offenses of this kind committed by a combination of students but a system of espionage, to which no gentleman can submit." The minutes for this year are full of entries like these: "Last night, there were several pistol shots on the Lawn;" "Last night about eleven o'clock two guns were fired off on the Eastern Range;" "Last night, a pistol was fired out of a dormitory window." Similar entries without comment are found in the records for later years. So frequent was the explosion of guns and pistols within the precincts in 1836, that the attention of the public at large was called to it with emphatic disapproval; and very properly so. On the night of November 7, between the hours of nine and ten o'clock, the reports of as many as eight muskets were simultaneously heard coming from the Lawn, and when the chairman hastened to the spot to identify the guilty parties, they retired like skirmishers to another position, firing as they withdrew, the sound being repeated from East Range by imitators of the main body. The Faculty always declined to accept any excuse for a disturbance of this kind, great or small. A student, on a different occasion, represented himself as shooting at a mark in anticipation of going to sea; but although his statement was an honest one, he was punished like a wanton offender. If the practising, however, took place beyond the precincts, it seems to have been liable to no interference, provided that the pistols were not brought back to the dormitories.   The popular shooting ground was situated on the south side of the University.

The noises which we have enumerated were raised by the young men either to pinprick the professors, or to afford themselves an hour of idle amusement.   There were other offenses of a different and more serious nature which were wantonly intended deeply to anger the authorities.   One of these was gassing, or " fuming," as it was described in those times.   A student was dismissed in December, 1832, because he had furtively endeavored to fill the chairman's office with the suffocating odour of assafoetida, and when he had seen that his design was frustrated, he had entered the room with a stick in his hand and threatened that officer with a personal assault. A few months afterwards, an effort to smoke the apartments in which the Visitors were supposed to be sleeping was detected barely soon enough to prevent it.   The method used was to thrust paper matches into the key holes, and then to light them from outside   About the same time, a somewhat similar attempt was made on the chairman: the bell in his office rang, and on his going to the door and opening it, he found his feet entangled in a rope, which had been fastened to the knocker.   A paper funnel was lying on the pavement nearby, and when examined, it was found to contain brimstone and tobacco for fumigation.   It had been the student's purpose to keep the door open by pulling the rope while the mixture in the funnel, burning on the sill, would fill the room with acrid smoke.

Another impish act that was sometimes committed occurred at Dr Patterson's expense in 1831 : his stable door was smashed in, and the tail of his horse clipped to the skin.   Dr. Davis's horse was similiarly mutilated during the following year. Another perverted act that sometimes occurred was the removal of the University wagons to the public roads; or the gates in the highway to Charlottesville would be wrenched from their hinges, and with a laborious energy worthy of Samson at Gaza borne away to a great distance. In 1832, a band of students scaled the walls of the proctor's garden late at night, pulled up the young shoots, and turned several cows into the enclosure. A cherry tree was cut down in the garden of Mrs. Gray the same night, and the shrubs there were also destroyed. A fine tree in the chairman's grounds was also felled, and the chicken coops in the other professors' backyards broken open and the poultry quietly strangled and carried off.

An instance occurred in the course of the same year which disclosed the extraordinary persistence with which the students often sought to carry out a mischievous purpose. It was known that Professors Davis and Bonnycastle would leave their pavilions after dark to catch the stage coach for Richmond. It was anticipated that they would mount to their seats near the precincts, as the vehicle passed on its way from Staunton, and in this expectation the young men piled up a great mass of stones and planks in the road between the University and the town. Owing to the delay thus caused, the stage did not set out from Charlottesville until after midnight. About two o'clock in the morning, when it had got some distance beyond the town, the horses came to a stop, and the driver descending found the highway again blocked by a heavy barricade. He was received with a triumphant shout from a band of students who had hidden themselves in the bushes at the roadside; they had run on ahead of the coach, and hurriedly built this barrier in its way in order to delay again the journey of the two professors, and also, perhaps, to break up rudely their uneasy slumbers. This occurred early in the month of February, when the air, four or five hours before dawn, must have been raw and piercing to the marrow.

It was noticed that an illumination of the Lawn by the students was always premonitory of a disturbance. This lighting up was produced by several means. In January, 1833, a small stack of straw was erected on one of the terraces about ten o'clock at night, and a torch applied to the inflammable material. Crackers had previously been thrown into it, and as the heat reached them there was a rapid succession of explosions. At once, the cry was raised all along the arcades that the University was afire, which called out the entire population to the scene. This exciting exploit was repeated the following evening in a more flagrant form. A crowd of students gathered around the burning pile, danced like Indian warriors in a circle about it, and sang corn-songs. The proctor was unable to put a stop to the commotion, and as the young men wore masks, he was prevented from reporting the names of the culprits. The offense to peace and order was made the more objectionable by the selection of Sunday evening for so discreditable an escapade.

In September, 1835, the storage basements of the University were broken open at night and several barrels, full of tar, rolled away to the Lawn, where the torch was applied to them. The great roaring flame that leaped up immediately gave rise at once to the fear that the safety of the buildings was in jeopardy; and the creators of this spectacular scene must have known this to be so, for they were prudent enough to hide themselves within the shadow of the arcades. But the most ordinary way to provide an illumination was to stick candles, separately or in groups, to the pillars, and to light the wicks. So.

smeared with grease, in consequence, had the pillars become by April, 1834, that the Faculty ordered them to be whitewashed; and a charge of five cents was imposed upon each student to defray the expense. An illumination was always accompanied by disorderly noises. One that occurred on the night of Sunday, November 12, 1837, was enlivened by successive fusillades of pistols and guns, and by hallooing so loud that they echoed throughout the precincts. It was repeated, on the following night, with the customary shouting and pistol-firing, rendered all the more deafening and confusing by the ringing of the big college bell in the belfry of the Rotunda. In all this lawlessness, there appears to have been no evil intention beyond raising a delightful uproar.

There were several minor offenses which were not accompanied by alarming or annoying outbreaks in the public eye. One of these was a very mild form of hazing consisting simply of sitting up with a newly arrived student and wrapping him about with a cloud of smoke so thick that the figures of those present were hardly perceptible even in a small room   The tyranny of class to class, so often noticeable in curriculum colleges, never prevailed in the University of Virginia. Profane swearing was a vice which the Faculty endeavored to suppress, but with little success. The Cyprian evil also was an elusive one. In 1828, there was a house of ill repute situated at the foot of the hill on the southeast side of the precincts; this was in charge of a sinister free negro from Philadelphia, associated with a white woman of a still more abandoned stripe.

The University authorities found it impracticable to put an end to the students' patronage of the hostelries in Charlottesville, which was reprobated even when the young men's only purpose was to procure an ordinary meal.   The most popular tables with them were those of the Fitch and Midway hotels, and of Brown's and Vowles's taverns.   The most frequented confectioneries were Garner's, Grady's, and above all, Keller's.   These houses also furnished accommodation in the form of lodging, but were prepared at all hours of day and night to serve a transient customer who wished a beef-steak, mutton-chop, ice cream, or sweetmeats.   No student could lawfully spread a supper in his room for his friends' enjoyment without first obtaining the chairman's permission, and this was always refused if " vinous or spirituous liquors " were also to be provided for the guests.   The meagerest proof that what was described as a " festive entertainment " was going on was seized upon at once and reported, whether or not an investigation had confirmed it.   On the night of November 22, 1831, the chairman, at a late hour, strolled very quietly from one end of the Lawn to the other, and announced to his colleagues afterwards that he had heard a sound that " seemed like the breaking up of a festive party."   The suspicion which he voiced in such cautious language was undoubtedly very well founded, for a student had testified only recently that the dormitories at that very time were very frequently the scene of cozy and friendly little suppers.   Most of them, he said with ingenuous frankness, were restricted to a dish of broiled or stewed chickens, washed down with cups of very cold water.

In enumerating, with great minuteness, the minor offenses that were subject to penalties, the Faculty apparently forgot to include cock-fighting.[1]   When Mr. Winfree was summoned, in 1832, to answer for his having

1 " The Faculty having been informed that the practice of cock-fighting is frequently indulged in by students of the University, resolved that it be forbidden, and the students be informed that those engaging in it will be punished " Minutes of Faculty April 6, 1832.

taken part in this sport, he pointed out that the ordinances had passed over the cocking main in silence,— doubtless, he said, with sly humor, because it was a harmless pastime; but even if they should think differently now, there was, he asserted, no need of punishment, for the day for this amusement had gone by, and there was no prospect of its revival.   But he was mistaken.   Thirteen days after his testimony was received, a cock fight came off on the· Lawn in the shadow of Dunglison's pavilion.   This was on Sunday.   Another occurred a week later; and a third in the following April.   We learn from the records of 1834 that one of the students of sporting tastes was granted a leave of absence, but that instead of blithely going on his way, he remained in concealment within the precincts, and occupied his unlettered leisure in pitting his game-cocks the one against the other.   The scene of battle chosen by him lay just behind the University stables.

XXVIII. *Major Offenses: Dissipation*

A minor delinquency repeated once or twice became a major offense; but there were certain offenses which were designated as major in their first committal.   These were acts that went further than annoying misconduct or petty misdemeanor; indeed, not infrequently, they fell just short of actual crime, or even leaped beyond the border to crime itself; but for the most part, they were social vices rather than flagrant violations of law.   The most common of these vices were gambling and drinking.   Unfortunately, drinking was universal, and gambling not rare, outside the precincts, in that age of hearty geniality and profuse living, and the University was a small mirror that reflected the general condition elsewhere.   The vigilant Faculty, fully aware that habits of this nature would be certain to loosen the reins of discipline, were unyielding in their determination to punish the guilty student, although they were so often thwarted that they had, from time to time, to acknowledge a feeling of profound discouragement.

The playing of cards in the dormitories was constantly detected, but where one instance was dragged into publicity, it is quite probable that one hundred eluded detection. We have already mentioned that one of the duties imposed on the hotel-keepers was to report every case of gambling among the young men that fell under their eye; so far from doing this, they were repeatedly implicated in the practice of this vice by their boarders. Even those who kept aloof declined to testify. " If we do so," said Warner Minor, in 1826, " we will be viewed in the light of informers, and as such treated, and as things are now, it would expose a man who respected himself, and was determined to fulfill his engagements, to constant insult and a certain loss of business." Loo was the most popular game with students and hotel-keepers alike. In a game occurring during that year, one of the young men lost the sum of two hundred and fifty dollars at a sitting; this happened in a dormitory that had the reputation of being a gambling-hell, and it was even suspected that the cards had been packed. At this period, it was the custom to play on Saturday, Sunday and Monday nights.

In 1830, Dr. Johnson, confident, from certain shuffling noises overheard by him, that students were playing cards in the neighborhood of his pavilion, cautiously left his house, and gently knocked on the door of the suspected room. It was furtively opened a little way and then slammed violently in his face; but he had had time to note the identity of those who had been taking part in the pastime, as they leapt recklessly from the back-window. One of the players was dismissed. This incident illustrates the delicate sensitiveness of the professorial ear of that period to the mysterious sound of chips or coin, and also the danger that accompanied even a quiet game i nthe dormitories. Harassed by this unresting pursuit, many of the players retired in dudgeon to Fitch's hotel in Charlottesville for their next bout. In 1831, West Range, which, at that time, was the congenial seat of all sorts of wild spirits, harbored the most inveterate patrons of this sport. The chairman was informed this year that at least one of its denizens had lost two thousand dollars at a sitting. A large gambling-hell now flaunted itself near the precincts; and this was a popular resort with the dissolute students, in spite of the vigilance of the Faculty, who endeavored to find out the habitués by sending the janitor and the assistant proctor to spy upon them. In April of this year, one of the young men was called up to answer the charge of having lost a thousand dollars in one of these disreputable establishments. He testified that the bankers who managed them always refused to play except for cash. He denied that there was a professional gambling apartment within the University boundaries.

The hotels in town, in 1833, were sometimes the scenes of gambling, in which blacklegs from Richmond and Washington took part. In several instances, at that time, young men were prevented from matriculating by the loss at the tables in the local taverns of the money brought by them from home for that purpose On one occasion, a newly-arrived student was thus fleeced of one hundred and twenty dollars in a game into which he had been allured by a sly fellow-student in his second year, who was acting as a stool pigeon for a notorious foreign sharper. So rigid were the regulations that even a game of backgammon was forbidden, although the delinquents forgot this important fact.   In November, 1836, the proctor, while passing the door of a dormitory after dark, heard the tell-tale words " Hearts are trumps.   Play on, friend, I hold low."   When the bolt was turned at his knock, the occupants of the room looked confused, but asserted they had only been playing an innocent round of draughts   Two of the players were, nevertheless, suspended for the remainder of the session.   Sometimes, a game went on in the grounds of a University hotel, but always there at a late hour.   A supper would be given in the dining-room after midnight, and if the weather was warm, the whole party would go out to the secluded backyard and play cards by candlelight.

Drinking was much more general than card playing, since it required no previous scientific training for its indulgence.   The bars of the taverns were open on Sunday, and as the young men were entirely at liberty on that day, many of them were encouraged by idleness to visit these spots.   Drunken collegians were a constant annoyance to the professors, both inside and outside the precincts; and this began almost as soon as the University opened. In 1826, two typical instances of this occurred.   A student, very much under the influence of apple toddy, while driving in a hack from Charlottesville, saw a member of the Faculty passing along the side-walk with one of the ladies of his family.   He poked his head out of the window and reviled the professor in the foulest language. Another, in the same condition of extreme inebriety, insulted Bonnycastle on the steps of the Episcopal church in town after the service   One of these rowdies was expelled, and the other simply reprimanded in the presence of his classmates.

The military company during this period never neglected the social side of their organization. In April, 1828, " a treat," as it was called in those times, was given by the officers, which consisted altogether of ex- hilarating beverages. A large quantity of apple-toddy, among the other brews, was provided for the fifty mem- bers, and they, with some view possibly to mild dilution, ground their arms at one of the University pumps to drink it. The assembling of the company seems to have been frequently only an occasion for this sort of imbibing. A member testified that, at one of these meetings, he had consumed, at a single sitting, about five glasses of brandy julep. Two pitchers of julep and one of sangaree had been provided as a " starter," he said, and in the course of the meeting had been often replenished. A general drinking party occurred on the 18th of January, 1831, and another on March 14 of the same year, which were long remembered for the uproariousness which at- tended their dispersion at a late hour. Bonnycastle, on the latter occasion, went out on the Lawn and barely escaped a serious injury when a bottle was thrown at him, which, missing him by a hair's breadth, was smashed against one of the pillars of the arcade behind him. It was said that this party of young men was composed of the most prominent, and curiously enough, of the most " exemplary " students then enrolled at the University. Perhaps, it was one of this superior band who very po- litely asked the chairman whether he would be permitted to drink in his dormitory a little claret mixed with a large quantity of water,— which very moderate request was very positively and promptly refused.

The smallest clue was now followed up. In the course of 1831, the assistant proctor, Mr. Wertenbaker, re- ported that, in visiting one of the rooms, he had dis- covered an empty glass that was faintly, but still perceptibly, tainted with the fumes of liquor. The two occupants admitted the truth of the charge; but they said, in their own defense, that they had been suffering from colds, and that a young friend in the medical school,— for whose professional knowledge they had the highest respect,— had advised them to drink a mixture of spirits and ginger before retiring to bed at night. They had very cheerfully and trustfully followed this prescription. The chairman drily replied that this recipe was entirely without virtue, but the two students, guided by their own experience, did not agree with him. Perhaps his judgment was somewhat warped by the number of bottles marked " medicine " which were now reported to him to be on the shelves in the dormitories.

Although Wertenbaker was so active in detecting any suspicious odor which might linger about a glass, yet he too, following the long established custom of the hotel-keepers, gave social parties at which the guests were bountifully supplied with toddy, brandy, and wine   The mixer of the bowl at one of his entertainments was accused of showing some " excitement before the end," which was hardly remarkable in a person engaged in performing a duty that called for such constant sampling. Mint-sling was now the popular beverage, and again we notice that it was the habit of many of the young men inclined to this indulgence, to seek the spring situated near the janitor's house, as the proper place for its enjoyment. There was a conspicuous return about this time to the custom of holding drinking-parties in the dormitories; at one meeting of the Faculty in 1835, three such parties were reported for their flagrant violation of the ordinances. The beginning of this session (1835–6) was marred by many instances of drunkenness, which occurred because the delay in opening the lecture-rooms had left the students in a state of idleness. The dissipation again broke out during the following Christmas, when it assumed the form of numerous parties to drink egg-nog; one that was held on December 22, led to fifteen students being summoned before the Faculty and the suspension of the host. These boisterous entertainments took place, not only in the dormitories, but in a vacant hotel. Even the proctor disregarded the ordinances in his own residence,— in 1836, Colonel Woodley was charged with supplying his guests with brandy with which to brew a large mint-julep.

The students, as time advanced, lost none of their ingenuity in evading the charge of violating the law against drinking. One who was called up in 1837 asserted that the julep found in his room had been left by a friend on his table while he was asleep, and that when he awoke, being only human, he had been unable to resist the temptation of emptying the glass. The presence of mint was always accepted by the Faculty as unrebuttable proof of guilt; unfortunately for its possessor, that sweet smelling plant had but one practical use; and the janitor was ordered with sternness to report every instance of its discovery. The same conclusion could not so irresistibly be drawn from the presence of champagne bottles; three espied in a dormitory, in 1837, were boldly declared by their owner to be simply innocent receptacles for his milk, molasses, and lamp oil.

The secrecy accompanying some of these champagne parties was often incredible Having reason to suspect that such an entertainment was going on, the proctor and chairman, on the night of March 4, 1837, spent two hours heroically walking up and down the arcades in the cold and darkness seeking in vain to detect a sound, —the popping of a cork, an outburst of hilarity,— that would indicate the room in which it was in progress.   In general, however, the culprits revealed their merriment in a very blatant manner.   In the following April, a party that had been drinking heavily were not satisfied until they had broken into the courthouse in town and alarmed the awakened population by the violent ringing of the bell and prolonged shouts and war-whoops.   In July, a similar party took possession of a vacant dormitory and kept up their carouse long after midnight, when they dispersed with a wild concert of yells.   A less boisterous demonstration occurred the ensuing Christmas eve   The scene was a dormitory in West Range, and although the noise was restrained, the proctor was sent to suppress it.   He tried to push his way into the room, but the door was finally slammed in his face.   In their defense before the Faculty, the students who were summoned claimed that the proctor had stated, before the entertainment came off, that no objection would be offered to it provided that it was conducted with decorum. He, however, asserted that what he had really said was that, while the Faculty would give no specific permission to drink spirits of any sort at Christmas, he felt confident that there would be no interference if the indulgence was free from excess and the hour unmarred by turbulence.   "It was the general custom of the country," the Colonel had sympathetically remarked, "and to be maintained on condition that the bounds of reason were not crossed."   "Let there be decency and order," he added expansively, "and all would certainly go well." This comfortable doctrine, so much in harmony with the social bent of the times, was promptly repudiated by the Faculty.   They acquitted the culprits in this instance, but announced that such leniency would not be repeated. Few months went by, before the close of the period under review, that the members of drinking parties were not summoned before that body for punishment; and not even severe penalties, ranging all the way from admonition to expulsion, were able to scotch the evil.[1]

XXIX. *Major Offenses: Tavern Haunts*

How were all these liquors obtained? Not infrequently in a very furtive and roundabout way. As early as 1825, a lame free negro named Ben was caught by the proctor in the twilight of the cellar of pavilion I selling fermented spirits to the students. This man was, doubtless, in collusion with the cook of the professor's family. Three years afterwards, a similar dark cellar in one of the houses situated not far from the precincts was also turned into a bar-room, and owing to its proximity, it was very liberally patronized by the young men. It was from dens like this that a great quantity of liquor was smuggled into the University in harmless looking baskets. The chairman, on one occasion, suspecting a servant of Conway's, stopped him on the walkway, and removing the cover of his basket, found snugly hidden away inside a bottle of rum and a bottle of whisky. The proctor, about the same time, discovered a bottle of rum and a bottle of wine in a basket which one of Mrs. Gray's servants was carrying on his arm. But it was to the taverns of Charlottesville that the young men went for their principal supply of stimulants. One of the most convenient of these was Mosby's, which stood apparently close to the road leading down to the town.

---

[1] "Drinking, I believe," said Warner Minor, "it is impossible to prevent or totally suppress It is an unavoidable evil that must in a measure be overlooked" Minor, as we have seen, was a man of perfect sobriety, and this pessimistic opinion expressed by him to General Cocke, shows how discouraged the supporters of the cause of temperance at the University were at this time.

Spotswood testified before the Faculty, in 1826, that the students were in the habit of stopping here to enjoy a glass, and he confessed that he never passed it that he did not treat or was not treated by them.   Other popular taverns for drinking parties were Vowles's, Ward's and Fitch's; and Boyd's also possessed a wide reputation for the insinuating mixtures of its bar.   Heiskell's was a disreputable retail liquor dive situated very near the precincts.   The Faculty endeavored,— apparently in vain, — to influence the court to refuse to reissue its license.

More censurable than even the taverns and the retail shops were the confectioneries, all of which had obscure backrooms for the accommodation of thirsty habitués; and, indeed, they relied for profit more upon sales of liquor to such patrons than upon sales of ice-cream, sweetmeats, and fruits, or upon the income from their eating tables.   Among the earliest was Weidemeyer's, where many scenes of drunkenness occurred.   Garner's, Toole's, Brown's and Miller's also enjoyed a profitable share of the same bibulous and half subterranean custom. But the most frequently mentioned in the records of the University, at this stage of its history, was Keller's. Keller was by trade a baker.   Alexander Garrett, who knew him personally, spoke of him as an " honest and good-hearted man."   " Mrs. Keller," he said, " was a fine, neat, and industrious woman," and she also had some claim to social consideration, for she was related to the family of Dr. Foushee, a distinguished physician of foreign extraction, long a highly respected citizen of Richmond.   The Faculty had numerous reasons for holding this confectionery in low esteem, however meritorious in character Garrett may have justly looked upon its owners to be.   As early as 1830, the students were warned to be shy of the place, not only because all such shops were

banned by the ordinances, but also because this shop,
which stood not far beyond the precincts, was burningly
obnoxious as a chronic scene of disorder caused by the
sale of liquor in copious quantities. The chairman did
not mince his words in speaking of it: he denounced it
openly as a " dangerous den."

In the very first glimpse that we have of Keller's, eight
or ten students are discovered in a group near its door,
one of whom was so intoxicated, that, when a professor
was seen approaching in the distance, they were compelled
to pick up their helpless comrade, and carry him off at a
run to escape detection. The excuses offered by some
of the young men, when summoned for entering its por-
tal, were remarkable for variety, if not for veracity; one
had simply stepped in to get his cane before mounting his
horse; another to purchase candy and fruit; another to
drink a glass of soda-water; and another to eat oysters.
In 1834, rollicking champagne parties assembled here
and caroused to a late hour; and these scenes occurred
most frequently on Sunday night. Wine, whisky, and
brandy mixed with honey were all to be bought here at all
hours; and so flagrant grew the evil in time that the chairman set a permanent watchman opposite the door, with
instructions to report the name of every student who
should enter. The scandal finally reached such a height
that Keller was threatened with indictment by the grand
jury, and in his apprehension, he offered to give bond
that, during the remainder of the session, he would decline to sell liquor and would only sell soda-water, ice-
cream, and sweetmeats. Six members of the Faculty
favored acceptance of this overture, while three,— who
were doubtful of his good faith,— were opposed to it.
In the following year, this agreement was renewed, on

condition that Keller would consent to the examination of his store accounts at short notice.

By the autumn of 1835, the former attitude of suspicion must have returned, for again every student who was known to have visited the premises, was reported and punished; and an attempt was also made to prevent the issuance of a new license to the proprietor.   His old license apparently was not revoked, but his trade with the young men was so much hampered at this shadowed place of business, that he leased the Midway Hotel, and retired from the immediate vicinity of the University.   But, if possible, this hostelry, under his management, became more objectionable to the University authorities than the shop had been.   It was popularly known as Keller's tavern   Students patronized it throughout the day and night, and the drinking was unrestrained in spite of the fact that every collegian seen there was reported to the Faculty.   It was said to have been less difficult to detect them in the hotel than in the confectionery.   The discreditable use so often made of the place was illustrated in an instance that occurred there in 1837, and which involved a student, who, in after life, won a position of national distinction.   A combination was formed by several of his friends to make him drunk, and they set out with him for Keller's   There the former absorbed, with the utmost liberality, weak claret punch and whisky punch, while the victim was confined to raw whisky. The party were able to return to their dormitories,— probably with the   assistance of a town hack,— and on their arrival, one of its members, while flourishing a pistol, accidentally shot another, but happily not fatally.   It was stated in the inquiry which followed that the young men from the University never visited Charlottesville without carrying arms in order to defend themselves against the assaults of a class designated by them as "mechanics." There was a patrol on the streets at this time at night, perhaps for the purpose of watching the slaves who had slunk abroad; and these men were chronically in collision with the students.

In 1837, Keller, having become a bankrupt, expressed an intention of returning to his original trade of baker. We have seen that, during the existence of his covenant with the Faculty, his accounts were open to their examination at any time. This was to prevent the extension of credit to the young men, especially for the purchase of stimulants. An ordinance, adopted in 1837, prohibited the patron from paying any bill drawn on him by a student in favor of a tradesman whom he had reason to know or believe "to be a retailer of vinous, spirituous, or fermented liquors." This ordinance had a rather notable consequence. It appears from the statement of Colonel Woodley, the proctor, that, in 1838, there were several important merchants in Charlottesville whose business would have been sensibly contracted by it, and they were so much irritated by its passage that they joined in an underhanded agreement with the students, by the terms of which the latter were to make the greater number of their necessary purchases before they should matriculate, and the merchants, by a discount, were to recoup their youthful patrons for the two per cent. additional commission, which they, in case the bargains were detected, would be required by the regulations to pay the patron. This furtive stipulation led many of the young men to place in these tradesmen's hands all the money remaining in their possession after their settlement for tuition fees. The deposits with the patron, in 1838, owing to this cause, fell off one-half of the average amount, resulting in a loss to him of three or four hundred dollars.

So anxious were the Faculty to take away from the students all excuse for visiting Charlottesville, that, in 1833, they gave a free mulatto, Jack Kennedy, permission to use a cellar within the precincts as a barber shop; but this primitive apartment was not to be kept open after dark.

The determined effort to discourage drinking habits among the young men was not confined to the strict enforcement of formal ordinances. As early as June, 1830, a temperance society had been organized at the University, but with the odd provision that the members should be allowed to retain the right to drink wine. In the following October, not long after the beginning of a new session, the students met in the Rotunda, and reestablished the society, with the Faculty's full consent. In April, 1832, seventy members were enrolled. For the time being, its influence was very perceptible. "The drunkenness and yells by which our peace used to be disturbed, night after night," said the chairman, "are no longer heard." Cocke, as was to be expected of a man who favored universal prohibition, took a burning interest in the society, and presented it, through Alexander Garrett, with many bulky packages of pertinent documents. But they seem to have had little influence, for, by the session of 1835, the organization had begun to languish. Colonel Pendleton, the proctor at this time,— who, like Colonel Woodley afterwards, was probably without sympathy with the movement,— was frankly discouraging in his reports to Cocke. He very correctly said that the cause of temperance at the University was one hedged about with all sorts of thorny difficulties, and that only the rarest practical wisdom and patience shown there could crown it with success. The methods to be adopted with that view were left by him in the dark, except that he advised that some famous advocate of total abstinence should be invited to deliver an address to the students. A meeting among themselves,— as warmly urged by Cocke,— would, in his opinion, only barb and reenergize the opposition. Professor Davis's report was couched in words in harmony with Pendleton's. "Young men," he said, "accustomed to indulge in the use of ardent spirits at home, and to see them used in their families, as most of our students unfortunately are, can hardly be expected to entertain proper views on the subject."

William Wertenbaker, who, after giving up his hotel, became such a stout and fanatical friend of the Cause, that, in his letters to Cocke, he always signed himself, " In the bonds of temperance brotherhood," was compelled, in 1841, to write in the same disheartened vein: " I have but little hope," he said, " of seeing the professors engage in temperance with anything like unanimity. There are perhaps two who agree with us in principle; namely, Professors Howard and Rogers; and others may be influenced to unite in the usual pledge of abstinence from intoxicants, under the persuasion that their example might influence many students to do the same. The professors friendly to the Cause, do not wish to appear to take the lead, but are waiting the action of some of the students, who have promised that, in a few weeks, they will make an effort to organize a society. . . . Several of the students have united themselves with a temperance society formed in Charlottesville." Cocke firmly refused to give away to depression. " I shall never cease," he said, " while my connection with this University lasts, to urge upon the Faculty, and all connected with it, the vast importance of bringing the temperance reform to operate on the students."

xxx. *Major Offenses: Assaults*

The drinking habit, which was so general among the students at this time, was the principal cause of the reckless violence that was so often exhibited by them.   A furtive device employed in several instances,— at long intervals, fortunately,— was to fill a bottle with powder, insert a quill in the cork, pack this quill with a slow-burning fuse, fire the fuse, and set the bottle on the window-sill of a pavilion occupied by an unpopular professor. If this little infernal machine was not soon detected by a passerby, or an inmate of the house, the explosion that followed was certain to disrupt the window frame and shutters and shatter every pane of glass.   But flights of stones were the means ordinarily employed in such malicious enterprises.   " Last night," records Professor Davis in October, 1835, " the glass and sash of a window of the hotel in which the proctor had his office was broken by a party of students," and this outrage was repeated at a later date in the smashing of the front windows of the same building, and of the front windows of Colonel Ward's hotel.   But the attacks were not confined to windows and doors.   Servants, for real or supposed impertinence, were sometimes viciously assaulted.   In 1828, a student struck a negro who was taking his order in Minor's dining-room   Minor was justly indignant and complained to the Faculty.   The student, hearing this, threatened to flog Minor; and his friends loudly backed him up in the menace: " I was anxious," was the cool testimony of one of them, " that Minor should be whipped, for he had acted in an ungentlemanly way in not suffering Boyd to lead the servant outside to chastise him."

Another scene with a servant characteristic of the intemperate spirit of the age, occurred near the entrance to the precincts in 1839. Several negroes began to fight in the street, and when two students sprang forward to stop them, Bonnycastle's servant interfered. "These men," he shouted, as he waved his stick, "are free, and they shall fight as much as they choose." The students promptly turned on the intermeddler, and while one hit him repeatedly with a cane, the other pommeled him with his fists. They ordered him to leave the ground and as he slunk away, he picked up a stone. This was a signal for one of the students to strike him again with the cane, and for the other again to beat him about the head with his fists. Bonnycastle now came up in a state of excitement, but when he endeavored to defend his servant, he was seized by the collar, roughly shaken, and threatened with further violence, in the midst of a shower of oaths.

The collegians never failed to rush to the rescue of any one of their number, who, whether wantonly or unwittingly, had become mixed up in a quarrel with strangers. In 1832, three students were passing down the road in front of Keller's shop on their way to Charlottesville, and their boisterous singing, broken by drunken hallooing, aroused the dogs belonging to a couple of wagons that had halted by the roadside. One of the wagon boys, in the ignorance and irresponsibility of youth, set the barking dogs on the noisy students without being aware that he was throwing a stone squarely into a hornets' nest. Within a few minutes, thirty or forty young men, hearing the uproar, ran up, and attacking the wagoners with fists, stones, and sticks, forced them to fly for safety, like so many rats, to Keller's cellar. When the frightened

and battered teamsters ventured out again, they found
that all their harness had been cut to pieces and their vehicles damaged.   But it was not simply insolent slaves
and incautious country folk who knew how heavy was the
hand of the angry student.   During a lecture in 1838,
Blaettermann ordered one of his class, who had been impertinent, to leave the room.   The young man quietly
arose from his seat, put his hat on his head, and walked
in front of the professor's chair on his way to the door.
As he passed by, probably with an air of bravado, Blaettermann made a pass at the hat and knocked it to the
floor.   The student quickly turned upon him, and in the
midst of a scene of extraordinary confusion, struck him
repeatedly.

Professor Harrison, who bore himself always with dignity, though sometimes impulsively, did not escape.
There were two reasons for this: (1) he served many
terms as chairman, and as such was an inflexible custodian of order, which made him very unpopular with the
lawless students; and (2) he was, in the beginning, very
young, even for the position of teacher.   Indeed, he was,
previous to 1830, of the same age as many of the members of his own or other classes; and he was also then,
as afterwards, very candid and emphatic in the expression of his condemnation of all forms of evil doing.
Sometime during that year, he happened to overhear
loud and indecent talking at his door, and in a state of
indignation, he went out to put a stop to it.   He chided
one of the young men with vehement severity for his conduct; nothing was said by the latter at the moment; but
after lecture on the following day, he walked up to the
professor, told him that he would not tolerate a rebuke
from him, his former fellow-student, and struck him.
The student was promptly expelled, and a few hours

later, his friends assembled in the Rotunda in a body and passed a resolution justifying the assault and reflecting upon Harrison.   But they were too prudent to send a copy to the Faculty.

This assault, indefensible as it was, was not so aggravated as the one which occurred in 1839, when Harrison was serving as chairman.   He had left his lecture-room only a few minutes when he was confronted by two students, one of whom had been recently expelled and the other suspended.   One of the couple was very much larger and stronger than the professor.   While this one roughly seized him and held him tightly in his arms, the other laid on vigorously with a stout horsewhip.   At least an hundred students rushed from all sides to the spot, but only two or three offered to interfere, and these so timidly and half-heartedly as to be brushed aside. Finally released, Harrison vehemently denounced the outrage of which he had been the victim as the assault of two cowards, whereupon the attack was violently renewed.   Interrupted, the desperadoes immediately took horse and fled towards Lynchburg.   Pursued, they were overtaken, and one was shot in the shoulder.   Both, who had been aiming to escape to Mississippi, were captured and brought back.   The following day, the friends of the wounded man endeavored to arouse sympathy for him and excite hatred against the Faculty by exhibiting in the dormitories the coat which he had been wearing when he was struck by the bullet, now stained with his blood.

The young men who declined to hold the persons of their teachers as sacred were not likely to refrain from equally violent assaults on each other.   The pistol, dirk, bowie knife, and cowhide were properties very much valued by members of this reckless class.   The use of the cowhide was ordinarily provocative of the use of the pis- '

tol.   Many quarrels arose over games of cards, which led to the flourishing of more than one of these weapons. One young man testified, in 1836, that he always carried a dirk because he might have good reason at any moment for whipping it out.   The fact that a dirk had been seen hidden under a student's coat was sometimes reported to the Faculty.   Sometimes, too, as in a rencontre which took place on May 20, 1836, a collegian was shown to have been carrying concealed about his person both a dirk and a pistol.   Should the pistol snap, he could snatch out the dirk   In the following year, one prominent student received a wound in the leg from this weapon in the hand of another, who probably had been thrown to the ground.   A dangerous stab was inflicted with a dirk in a fight in a dormitory in 1838.   A student, summoned before the Faculty a few months afterwards for carrying a bowie knife, explained his action with the remark that it was necessary to take precautions against all contingencies. When asked to define the contingency that would justify the use of such a weapon, he replied, " If a man insults me and refuses to give me honorable satisfaction "

This was probably an extreme method of closing a violent dispute, for there was as strong a sentiment in the University in favor of the more orderly duello, as the proper way of settling an altercation between gentlemen, as there was, at this time, in the society of the Southern States at large   Nothing but the strict regulations for its repression prevented its more frequent recurrence.   As early as 1826, a meeting between Henry Dixon and Livingston Lindsay was arranged to take place beyond the jurisdiction of Virginia.   The seconds advised that it should be put off until the session was ended; but the Faculty got wind of the challenge, and stopped the impending fight by the interposition of the sheriff.

Slyly aware of the nervous apprehension felt by the chairman, the students at this time amused themselves with mock-duels.   One such came off in 1831, and another in 1832.   The latter was reported by Professor Blaettermann, and when the supposed principals were called before the Faculty, they declared somewhat oddly that it was a hoax devised to reconcile the seconds, who, it appears, had been quarrelling.   The chairman was as much shocked by the boyish adventure as if it had been in mockery of a religious ceremony.   He sternly rebuked the thoughtless participants, on the ground that their travesty had brought down ridicule on the most solemn of all the enactments.

In 1834, T. J. Pretlow and Daniel C. Johnson were put under bond to keep the peace, since information had been received that they had arranged to fight a duel; and in the course of the following year, two students, McHenry and Matthews by name, left the University to meet on ground in the District of Columbia which had been made famous by the hostile shots so often exchanged there by quarrelsome Congressmen.

A duel that was brewing between Hamer and Wigfall in 1835 seems to have aroused the chairman to an extraordinary state of perturbation   So soon as the news of their purpose leaked out, he hurried off word to the sheriff in Charlottesville to be on the watch to seize the principals and seconds, for the quartet had got away unobserved before they could be stopped.   Hamer's room, when visited, had been found empty, and Wigfall had contrived to escape after being arrested.   Warrants for their capture were issued, and while the proctor boarded the stage for Washington, the janitor and constable mounted that for Staunton; but before the coaches could leave, Professor Davis, coming up in a hurry, announced that the duellists had gone in the direction of Lynchburg. He also reported that the weapons to be used were rifles, which were to be placed on rests at ten paces. The chairman had hastened after Davis, and finding out when he arrived in Charlottesville that two of the blood-thirsty students had turned their faces towards Scottsville, he sued out additional warrants, and accompanied by Davis, galloped off down the road that led to that village. After they had gone five miles from town, they overtook Wigfall and Cheves, his second, who promptly disputed the validity of the papers for their arrest thrust into their hands; but when threatened with an uprising of the county, Wigfall reluctantly consented to return, on condition that the Faculty would defer the question of the penalty to the county court. He and Cheves asked permission to withdraw at once from the University, but this was refused. Hamer and his second turned up again a few days afterwards

The Faculty's inflexibility in punishing the offense of duelling was illustrated in the case of B. F. Magill. Magill, a student, was absent in Staunton on leave, and while there, went to a ball as the escort of a young lady There being a drunken fellow present, he advised his companion to decline to dance with him, should he ask her to do so. The man approached her, was refused, and hearing that she was acting on a warning from Magill, he called the latter to the door, and being the strongest, there gave him a severe beating. Magill challenged him on the following day, but being informed upon, was arrested. The Faculty, apprised of the challenge and arrest, expelled him from the University.

A challenge passed between W. H. Armistead and H. C. Chambers in January, 1840. Although their purpose was suspected, they were permitted to leave the Uni-

versity on another excuse. When their real object became fully known, warrants were issued for their capture, but Chambers alone was taken   It seems that the
weapons chosen by the challenged party were sticks, but
as the challenger refused to fight with such contemptible
weapons, rifles were substituted.   Chambers and Armistead, and their seconds also, were expelled.   This severity failed to put down the evil, for, in the course of the
following month, Walke and Bell, two students, were
said to have actually fought a duel in the District of
Columbia.

xxxi. *Major Offenses: Riots*

The students, during 1825, being free of all personal
control,— the Board of Censors having declined to act
and the Faculty possessing no real power,— a spirit of
insubordination soon boiled up to the surface. Premonitory symptoms of this rebellious mood cropped out
as early as the night of June 22.   A similar outburst took
place on the night of August 5, and again on the night
of September 19.   These " vicious irregularities," as
Jefferson himself described them, came to a furious head
about ten days later.   After dark, a great crowd of
students collected on the Lawn disguised with masks,
and the cry arose, " Down with the European professors."   A large bottle, filled with a foul liquid, had been
tossed through a window of Long's pavilion into his
sitting room, the night before, and the violent feeling
which broke out twenty-four hours afterwards was chiefly
directed   against   Key   and   himself.   One   student,
wrapped in a counterpane, was the most conspicuous of
all.   Dr. Emmet, who, with Professor Tucker, had
boldly gone among the rioters, seized him by this flow-
ing garment.   " The rascal," cried the youthful outlaw,

"has torn my shirt!"   Immediately, one of his friends
threw a brick at Emmet, while Tucker was assailed with
a cane.   The vulgarest words of abuse were hurled at
both, and they were determinedly resisted by the entire
band, amid the tumult of derisive shouts and howls.
The ensuing day, instead of showing contrition for their
violent conduct, they sent a committee to the Faculty
with a resolution that sharply criticized Emmet and
Tucker because they had both ventured to lay their
hands at the same moment on the person of the same
student.   About sixty-five young men had joined in this
resolution, which was so extraordinary in its assertions
that it was taken to be a sly device to shift the burden of
responsibility from their own shoulders to those of the
two stout-hearted professors

Key and Long, as the direct upshot of these lawless
events, gave up their respective chairs.   "We have lost
all confidence in the signers of this remonstrance," they
said, "and we cannot and will not meet them again."
This spirit of disgust was not confined to them   The
Faculty, as a whole, adopted a resolution that, unless
an effective system of police was established at once by
the Board, they would send in their resignations in a
body.   The Visitors were now in session at Monticello;
and after their arrival at the University on the following
morning, they were indignant eye-witnesses to the state
of extreme disorganization into which the institution
had been thrown.   They assembled in one of the apartments of the Rotunda.   Professor Tutwiler, who was a
student during the first session, has left a record of his
vivid recollection of that memorable scene.   "At a long
table near the centre of the room," he says, "sat the
most august body of men I had ever seen,— Jefferson,
Madison, and Monroe, who had administered the Gov-

ernment, twenty-four out of thirty-six years of its existence under the Constitution; by their side, Chapman Johnson, the head of the Virginian bar; J. C. Cabell, statesman and patriot, and John H. Cocke, generosity and philanthropy unbounded. Jefferson rose to address the students. He began by declaring that it was one of the most painful events of his life, but he had not gone far before his feelings overcame him, and he sat down, saying that he would leave to abler hands the task of saying what he wished to say. Johnson arose and made a very eloquent and touching speech. He did not spare the offenders, and ended by calling upon every one who had been concerned in the riotous conduct to come forward and give in his name."

This appeal went straight to its mark; the numerous culprits crowded forward to have their names set down by the secretary of the Board; and among them was a nephew of Jefferson, whose appearance in such a discreditable position aroused an indignation in the agitated sage which he found it impossible to disguise. The young men most seriously implicated in these disorders were expelled. Jefferson now drafted a resolution, addressed, through the Faculty, to the students, who were told of the necessity for establishing at once an inflexible system of discipline, to be applicable as well to those who were conscious of their own rectitude as to those who had committed notorious breaches of the peace. He was very sharp in his reflection on the general disposition to shelter the guilty by declining to testify against them. He urged the innocent to throw off with disdain " all communion of character " with offenders by exposing their identity, and by co-operating with the Faculty in their repression. " Let the good and the virtuous of the alumni of the University do this," he exclaimed, " and the disorderly will then be singled out for observation, and deterred by punishment, or disabled by expulsion, from infecting with their inconsideration the institution itself, and the soundness of those it is preparing for virtue and usefulness."

The next riot of importance occurred on the night of May 18, 1831. The night before, there had been an intermittent firing of pistols within the precincts. While the Faculty was in session, the students began to assemble on the Lawn; at once a pandemonium of discordant and alarming noises broke out; pistols were fired off; shrieks and yells were raised; split-quills and tin-horns were blown; and the college bell rung with unexampled violence. Slowly the collegians withdrew to one of the gymnasiums fronting the Rotunda. Leaving the Faculty-room, Emmet, Davis, and the chairman started towards the spot, and as they drew near, several students hurried forward and warmly counselled them to go back, as the mood of the rioters was such that there would certainly be personal violence if the professors endeavored to remonstrate face to face. A shower of stones began to fall about them, and they decided that it would be discreet to retire The tumult, it seems, was designed as a protest against the Uniform Law. At a late hour, the crowd dispersed, with a final outburst of noise, but without having done any damage to property.

In 1833, an ordinance was passed which provided that, in case of a riot at night, all students were to retire to their rooms so soon as the signal was sounded on the college bell. The young men seem to have strongly resented this regulation. A mass meeting was called to take place at Hotel C, the present hall of the Jefferson Society, for the purpose of resisting " the late tyrannical movements of the Faculty." The chairman, observing

302 HISTORY OF THE UNIVERSITY OF VIRGINIA

this notice on the college boards, incorrectly supposed that it was directed against a new rule touching the Uniform Law, and he gave an order that the hotel door should be closed. The students, when they assembled, finding the door locked, smashed in the panels and entered. A resolution was promptly adopted condemning the passage of the retiring ordinance as an *ex post facto* one, and advising that it should be ignored. The proctor now came in and wrote down the names of forty-four of the seventy students present; and three of these, at his instance, were summoned before the Faculty as having broken down the door. Before action could be taken in their case, Rev. Mr. Hammett, the chaplain, in person warned the Faculty that, if these three students were dismissed for their supposed offense, the entire body of their fellow students would withdraw from the University. He entreated the Faculty to put off their decision until the excitement had subsided. That body concluded to take no action at all against the three, as they were apparently no more culpable than the rest of their companions   They announced explicitly that they had no wish to curtail the students' right to hold public deliberations, provided that permission had been obtained to assemble in a room previously approved, and that the spirit shown was an orderly one.

XXXII. *Major Offenses: Riots, Continued*

The riotous humor which had been so often displayed before 1836, swelled to the proportions of a small rebellion in the course of that year. In September, on the threshold of a new session, the military company had been formed as usual, but had intentionally neglected to ask for the Faculty's approval. The captain, when summoned by the chairman to explain this omission, coolly said that he was not aware that the Faculty's consent was required either for the organization or for the use of the muskets   He was informed that he must obtain this consent at the Faculty's next meeting, but, in the meanwhile, the drills would be permitted to continue.   When application was finally made (October 29), the conditions that had been always imposed on the company were renewed,— these were, that the University uniform should be worn; that no musket was to be fired on the Lawn or in the Ranges; that this weapon was only to be handled in the course of military exercises; that the company was to be dissolved if it violated any of these regulations; and that the muskets were then to be returned to the armory in Charlottesville,— which, it appears was the common jail.

Early in November, the chairman was told that the company had not accepted the conditions imposed: and when the Faculty assembled the same day, they sent for Captain Morris, who, when questioned, replied nonchalantly that, while the company had not actually rejected the conditions, it had taken no action on them simply because the Faculty's right to prescribe them was disputed.   Indeed, the company went so far as to claim that it existed as a State military body independently of the University, and even in opposition to it   The Faculty emphatically denied this, and ordered the company to return the muskets at once to their place of safe-keeping in Charlottesville.   Those who should hold back the firearms were to be summoned, on the ground that they had violated the ordinance which expressly prohibited such retention.

As the military company had not accepted the conditions so plainly laid down, it was, in reality, not a legal organization at all, and, therefore, there was no reason why it should be formally broken up. The only step necessary to be taken was to deprive its members of the muskets. To disband it was to recognize its legality. The members of the company met, and no patriotic association in the War of the Revolution ever breathed forth more burning sentiments of defiance to tyranny than they did in their speeches and resolutions. It was the spirit of 1776 in a perverted form, and in a very small teapot. They pledged themselves by a solemn oath to stand together. A committee of six, with Captain Morris at their head, was appointed to lay an ultimatum before the Faculty. This ultimatum consisted of three clauses: (1) the company would not disband; (2) it would attend the drill as usual without the least regard to the Faculty's command to the contrary; (3) every member having bound himself to remain faithful to his comrades, the action of the Faculty against one would be accepted as action against all.

When the committee called on the chairman to submit this ultimatum, the firing of muskets had again started on the Lawn, and the sound of the explosions was so loud and continuous that the indignant protest of that officer was drowned in the uproar. The firing was prolonged for two hours, and was finally only stopped by the rain that began to fall The proctor was ordered to search the dormitories to find out whether the muskets were still held back, and he discovered that the very first member of the company whom he visited still retained one in his possession. The proctor's purpose of ferreting out others becoming known, Captain Morris sent to the chairman a full roster of his men, with the announcement that, if one gun was to be removed, all must be removed. The Faculty convened on November 11 to examine this roster, which they found to comprise seventy names,— among them, some of the most prominent in the contemporary social and political life of the State. It was determined to call upon each in turn for an explanation of his use of a musket at an unlawful hour. The first on the roster was Thomas S. Walker, and the janitor was dispatched to summon him to the Faculty's presence. " He cannot come. He is on parade," was Captain Morris's curt reply.

The Faculty then decided to ascertain who were the students participating in the drill, and to institute action against them all in a body. The proctor, with the roster in his hand, went to the spot where the drill was taking place; Morris, with studied politeness, called out the names from this roster; and then quietly offered the following brief and emphatic·resolution, which was adopted with unanimous voice: " We have our arms and intend to keep them." The proctor having returned to the Faculty a list of the sixty-six members present at the drill, that body at once recorded the statement that these young men had, without lawful authority, brought firearms into the University grounds, and had since announced their intention of retaining them there without permission. The organization had thus become a combination that illegally defied the valid commands of the University's officers. The entire company was then formally expelled.

On the ensuing Saturday, the drill was held as usual, and when the company halted, the proctor informed its members of the Faculty's decision, which was received with groans and shouts of defiance. They then marched to the Rotunda, raised their flag to its top, and deliberately shot it to shreds. A large number of other students now joined them, and while one party remained to ring the bell without any cessation, another hastened to Charlottesville, and taking the bell from the belfry of the Episcopal church, carried it away. That night was marked by ungovernable disorder. The students broke the glass in the windows of the pavilions, battered the blinds with volleys of stones, beat violently on the front-doors with heavy sticks, and fired fusillades of musketry under the arcades. In several instances, the professors and their families, in a state of very justifiable alarm, withdrew to their upper stories for personal safety. They were threatened, reviled, and hooted. The following night, which was Sunday, the rioting again grew furious. The bell had been tolling all day long, and as darkness fell, the fusillades were renewed and all the terrifying incidents of the previous night repeated.

The professors now began to arm themselves, in the expectation that they would be called upon to defend their families,— not from mere personal assault as before, but from attacks with deliberate intention to kill. Two students, well informed as to the spirit of the rioters, privately told the chairman that the outrages so far committed were much less heinous than those which were designed for the future. So soon as he thus heard that the violent disorders of Sunday and Monday were to begin again in a more aggravated form, he adopted the course that should have been followed on the preceding day: he summoned the civil authority to the Faculty's assistance. On the morning of the 15th (Tuesday), two magistrates and the sheriff appeared on the ground; the grand jury was called; and a military guard was placed in control of the Rotunda. The students who had been most deeply implicated in the riot, now, in a state of consternation, started to scuttle away from the University precincts. The grand jury convened on the 16th, examined the professors, and brought in indictments. By the 19th, under the salutary influence of this firm and sensible action, order was fully restored.

It shows the perverted spirit of the students who remained that they had the boldness to assemble and pass a resolution that the " unhappy difficulty,"— which had really been precipitated by their own indefensible conduct alone,— should be "calmly and deliberately reviewed by the Board of Visitors, and by an enlightened and impartial public opinion." They magnanimously promised that, should the Faculty's order disbanding the military company be confirmed as within the power of that body to adopt, they would "cheerfully acquiesce in the decision." They gave their word of honor that no firearms would, in the interval, be brought by them within the precincts. Emmet sternly urged that not a man should be readmitted who was unable to swear that he had had no part in the disorders. Davis, on the other hand, advised, in a conciliatory spirit, that none should be shut out who were willing to make the proper atonements; and this course was, in the end, followed by the Faculty. The public journals, as a rule, condemned the weakness shown by that body in not calling in the assistance of the civil authority at an earlier hour, and in inflicting so mild a punishment on the bulk of the culprits. Smarting under the whip of popular criticism, Davis, as the spokesman of the Faculty, issued an exculpatory reply, in which he stated that all the muskets had been handed in; the company disbanded; and only those young men readmitted, who had been the least responsible for the riots, and who had expressed regret for whatever share they had taken in them   At least thirty of the dismissed members of the company failed to return, and their action indicated that they looked upon themselves as too much discredited to be acceptable to the University again as students.

A serious riot occurred in the course of 1838 because the Faculty declined to permit the students to celebrate Jefferson's birthday with a ball. This refusal was based on the information that the drunkenness which had disgraced the similar ball on the previous February 22 was to be repeated. It was known that one of the young men who had taken part in that entertainment had had so severe an attack of *mania a potu* that he was, with difficulty, rescued from the grasp of death. In retaliation for their disappointment, the college bell on April 13, was rung throughout the night; tar barrels, taken from the cellar of the proctor's house, were rolled upon the Lawn and ignited, thus causing a conflagration that the wind at one time threatened to spread to the roofs of the pavilions and dormitories; there were processions up and down in masks; pistols and guns were fired off in volleys; the arcades rang with shouts and corn-songs; and the houses of the professors who had opposed the ball were attacked. " Most insulting ribaldry was used," writes Professor Rogers, who was the most obnoxious of all for this reason, " and neither I nor my family considered their persons safe. Hence we got firearms for defense."

The disorder continued until midnight. The chairman was threatened in his office next day by one of the offenders The third night a large body of students made an assault on Professor Rogers's house again. The front-door was battered in, and a great number of missiles of all sorts hurled against the four outer walls. Most of the glass in the windows was broken. The work of destruction at the back was done by a single student, who had crept up to the rear of the pavilion,

and hidden himself in the shadow   In vain the sturdy
Rogers watched for him to show his body, for, with his
pistol loaded and cocked, the outraged professor was determined to shoot the marauder on sight.   "Our police
is worthless," he wrote with bitterness afterwards.
"Two or three rowdies can, with impunity, stone our
dwellings, destroy our property, jeopard our lives, and
take away from us that quiet without which the situation
is worthless to a man of science."   The Faculty had
learned from experience a practical lesson of importance:
so soon as order was restored, civil process was obtained
against six of the ringleaders in the riot.   One of these
took to his heels when he received the summons to court,
while another hurried to the chairman's office and made
him the target of foul abuse.

The spirit of the rebellion of 1836 always flared up
on its anniversary; that event was celebrated by the
students as another Declaration of Independence; and it
was held in as much honor in their college annals as the
glorious Fourth of July, 1776, was in national   This
perverted and intemperate attitude culminated in November 12, 1840, in the murder of Professor Davis, a
man who had shown a forbearing, though firm, spirit
in his relations with the young men, and who, of all the
professors, the least deserved such a fate at the hands
of one of them.   Aware of their custom of celebrating
every return of this date, he was always anxious to suppress the demonstrations that accompanied it, because
he correctly thought that it fostered a hostile and insurrectionary spirit.   Hearing a great noise under the arcade in front of his pavilion, which was situated on East
Lawn, he went to the door to find out the immediate
cause.   Stepping down to the pavement, he attempted
to remove the mask from the face of one of the rioters,

who had taken refuge behind a pillar, and as he did so, he was fired upon and fatally wounded. After lingering several days, he expired, amid the grief, horror, and indignation of the entire community.

So soon as the shooting was known, the young men as a body showed the most ardent determination to run down the assassin, and it was through their assistance that he was detected and arrested. The principal was proved to be Joseph E. Semmes, a student from the far South, and the accessory, William A. Kincaid, of South Carolina. Semmes had remained quietly at the University the day following the crime. The bullet, when cut out of Davis's body, was recognized to be one of those which, on the morning of the fatality, had been given to the murderer by a friend, who promptly came forward and testified to this fact. It seems that Semmes had no reason to nurse a grudge against Davis, but he had been heard to say that he intended to shoot the first member of the Faculty who should attempt to tear off his mask during a riot.

Very able counsel were employed to defend him, and when the Circuit Court convened, they urged that he should be released on bail on the ground that his health was likely to be undermined by close imprisonment, and that his life even might be put in jeopardy by it. Judge Lucas P. Thompson, a man of learning and experience, and remarkable for his common sense, declined to acknowledge the pertinency of this line of reasoning; he refused to admit Semmes to bail; and very pointedly intimated that if his health was really poor, it was due to his own excesses The Court of Appeals, unfortunately for the credit of the judiciary, showed itself to be more amenable to the sentimental plea of the lawyers, and liberated the criminal on his giving bond with the penalty of twenty-five thousand dollars.   Semmes failed to appear, as might have been anticipated; his bond, in consequence, was forfeited; and he himself afterwards perished miserably in Texas.   Kincaid returned from South Carolina to Charlottesville to testify at Semmes's trial, and when that was postponed, decided to remain until the following October, the time set for the second trial. He was placed under bond and became an inmate in his surety's family.   He seems to have attended lectures at the University during several years after the murder, and apparently he was not again brought up in Court.

XXXIII. *Punishments*

Unless an offense took place directly under the eye of a professor, or one of the officers, it was very difficult to detect the culprit to an extent that would justify an open charge of misconduct against him.   The authorities of the University, under the influence of Jefferson's principles of freedom, had voluntarily deprived themselves of all power of finding out the facts in each case by forcing the young men to depose as in a court of law. When the rules were adopted in 1824, it was announced that, should a student be unwilling to testify, when summoned as a witness, the moral obligation which rested upon him to speak out should alone be held up before him, in the hope that he would perceive it to be his duty to relate whatever he knew respecting the offense under investigation.   The regulation that went into operation in March 1825, and continued apparently throughout the period now under review, was that a student, when asked to make a statement in such a case, was to be informed that he was altogether at liberty to refuse if compliance was repugnant to his sense of right. Under no circumstances was he to be required to take an oath. The upshot of this system of voluntary testimony might have been predicted. When Dr. Patterson's stable was broken into at night, in 1831, and his horse's tail mutilated, the chairman, after inquiring into the incident, remarked with asperity: " All the students whom I have seen, or whose sentiments I have heard, speak with indignation of the outrage, yet I doubt whether there is one who would not screen the offender from punishment were he known to him." " The discovery of offenses," he added regretfully, " is the greatest difficulty in governing the institution, and with the existing feeling of honor among the students, insuperable."

In the annual report for 1832, the Board of Visitors dolefully acknowledged that the false sentiment which deterred one collegian from testifying against another was the real cause of their lack of ability to combat disorder successfully when it had got well underway, or to put it down so soon as it started. That body was finally compelled, with palpable reluctance, to adopt an ordinance which provided that, when an offense falling within the supervision of the civil courts, had been committed, every student who was likely to have had any personal knowledge of it was to be summoned before the grand jury to give testimony under oath. It was natural that the professors should shrink from such a confession of failure in enforcing discipline as this enactment would seem to indicate, and, in consequence, they urged that the process should be sought with extraordinary caution, and only in a case in which there had been a most flagrant violation of law. Even under these extreme circumstances, the Faculty thought that they should have the right to decide whether the process should or should not be asked for.

We have seen that, in his petition for the incorporation of Central College, Jefferson endeavored to clothe the proctor with all the powers of a justice of the peace; and this was probably a wiser measure than the very elaborate judicial one proposed by the Board of Visitors at a subsequent date.   Under the provisions of the latter scheme, a court was to be erected at the University, in which the professor of law,— who was to receive an addition to his salary for his supplementary services,— was to sit as the sole judge.   The jurisdiction of this court was to run on all fours with that of the Albemarle county court, with the single exception that it was not to reach out to felonies committed within the precincts; it was, however, to extend to all the smaller offenses of which the students should be guilty within the county at large.   The judge was to be a conservator of the peace in the county as well as in the University, with the right to arrest any one charged with a breach of the law, to issue warrants, to take recognizances, and to exercise all the other powers of the office.

The terms of the court were to be held quarterly in November, March, May, and July, and monthly in October, December, January, February and June.   A grand jury was to be summoned from Albemarle county to sit at every quarterly court.   Students above nineteen years of age were to be qualified to become members of this jury, and a certain number of them were to be impaneled at each session.   Petit juries, with the same proportion of students, were also to be called together. The proctor was to act as the sergeant of the court, with all the customary functions of that office; and was, as conservator of the peace also, to possess the right to call a *posse comitatus* to enable him to enforce his legitimate authority. The University court was to be empowered to issue process beyond its jurisdiction, and like the county court, could compel obedience to its summons. The University jail was to be identical with the county jail. The attorneys who practised in the county court were to be admitted to the University court, and they were to have the same right of appeal in the one tribunal as in the other.

The real object of this elaborate scheme was to employ the enginery of the grand jury in ferreting out students who had committed separate offenses, or participated in general disturbances, within the precincts. There is no reason to doubt that, had the Legislature approved of it, it would have made impossible most of the discreditable events that darkened the history of the institution throughout this formative period. The young men seemed always to contemn the Faculty's authority, but they never failed to exhibit a very lively apprehension when dragged across the threshold of a civil court. The General Assembly, in refusing to grant the right to establish the University judgeship, was probably afraid that it would conflict in jurisdiction with the county court of Albemarle; and they would, doubtless, have declined a second time on that ground, had the same plan,— which was again broached in 1832,— come up for decision once more.

It is possible, as Professor John B. Minor has suggested, that the erection of this court would have been looked upon by the students as a threat, and on that account, would have caused still greater friction in their relations with the Faculty. But this friction could hardly have been more exasperating than it was, and if it had been mingled with a little of that fear which Jefferson deprecated so earnestly,— and as the upshot proved, so unwisely,— perhaps the harassed professors would have loomed up more formidably to them, and thus appeared more entitled to their respect.   There was no sound reason why the proctor should not have been invested with the powers of a justice of the peace as Jefferson himself had proposed.   This would have given the Faculty almost as direct and immediate means of suppressing disorder as if the University court had been in existence, for this officer would, in that character, have been able, not only to arrest offending students, but also to summon outsiders to his assistance to put down disorder in its very incipiency.   And this power would not have been in conflict with the jurisdiction of the local courts.

We have seen that there were four different forms of punishment,— reprimand, suspension, dismissal, and expulsion.   A student who was suspended might be ordered to return to his home for a definite period; or he might be rusticated in one of the numerous taverns standing within the boundaries of Albemarle county, or even in private houses in that county which were willing to receive such a guest.   The inns usually selected for this purpose were Cocke's, Bowcock's, and Clarke's.   The Cocke hostelry was situated near Greenwood, on the well-trodden stage highway running from Charlottesville across the mountains to Staunton   It was under the skilful management, first of Colonel Charles Yancey, and then of Colonel Cocke, and the reputation of its excellent fare was carried far by the numerous patrons who halted here for a meal while journeying to and from the summer mountain resorts in Western Virginia   Colonel Cocke was a useful and respected citizen; occupied for a time a seat on the bench of magistrates; and survived to a period as late as 1879. Clarke's tavern was situated on the stage-road leading from Charlottesville to Gordonville. There was a large stable maintained here for the exchange of coach horses, and there were so many other houses also that the place resembled a village. Bowcock's tavern was a less animated centre, but its landlord was a man of high repute for integrity and public spirit.[1] This inn was rather remote in its situation. A student, who was rusticating there in 1837, left before his term of suspension had expired, and when charged with the delinquency, defended himself by saying that the house was so solitary and dull that it was impossible for any one to remain there.

Occasionally, however, the number of young men under ban stopping in these taverns was so large that they must have formed a congenial group of their own, to whom, not only was a public bar accessible, but also, in season, the pleasures of the hunting field and the fishing stream. The period of rustication was sometimes protracted for three months, and it rarely terminated under

[1] The most respectable of all the taverns was Bowcock's. This house of entertainment belonged to John J Bowcock, and was under his management. His father had kept an inn on the same spot,—which was not far from Earlysville,—and had died in 1825 The son, we learn from Woods's *History of Albemarle County*, "occupied a large place in the hearts of the people of the county His early advantages in the point of education were slender, yet few people exercised a wider or more beneficent influence in the community. His powers of perception were clear, his judgment sound, and his integrity without spot. He inherited his father's farm and followed him in the conduct of a public house. He adopted the temperance views, and turned his house into a house of entertainment The disputes of the surrounding country were referred to his arbitration, and his decision was accepted as the end of the strife. His neighbors often desired him to be the guardian of their children, and settle their estates He was the presiding magistrate of the county court, and also Colonel of the 88th Regiment. He was a member of the House of Delegates No competitor could stand before him, and he might have been re-elected as often as he wished." He died as late as 1892. His wife was a daughter of Nelson Barksdale, the second proctor of the University of Virginia.

one week. Among the private houses that received suspended students were Mr. Howell Lewis's and Mr. James Duke's; and they were certainly brought under far more refining and restraining influences in these very respectable homes than in the county ordinaries, which were either crowded with travellers, often vulgar and dissipated, or almost empty of guests, with no amusements, during most of the year, beyond tippling in the public room It is true that there was a law that inflicted a heavy penalty on tavern-keepers who permitted students to become intoxicated on their premises; but incidents of this kind occurring in country inns were not likely to be reported to the authorities for punishment.

XXXIV. *Diversions*

The " vicious irregularities,"— to use Jeffersons' indignant phrase,— of the students, during this formative period, unquestionably made up the most exciting, and, perhaps, the most enjoyable, part of their diversions. These, however, did not consist altogether of ringing the college bell, firing off pistols and muskets, blowing tin-horns and split-quills, shouting at the top of their vigorous young voices, playing games of loo and whist for stakes, or drinking an uncountable number of glasses of wine, whiskey-toddy, and mint-sling. There were other and more legitimate recreations; but as the University was remote from the large centres of population, the social life of the students, on the whole, moved along in a rather sluggish fashion. Its current, in fact, was rarely enlivened by any pastime except what they themselves had created for their own entertainment. They derived but little from the professorial circle within which their own revolved because there was only an occasional point of social contact between them; but they owed much to Jefferson during the sixteen months that he survived after the institution opened. Indeed, the social life of the young men, like their intellectual life, harkens back to the philosopher of Monticello. It was a beautiful and touching habit of his to invite them in turn to dine with him on Sunday, the day chosen because they were then exempt from attendance on lectures. On each occasion, at least a dozen were asked, and in the course of the session,— as the number of students, during the first and second years, was small,— each of them was present under his roof more than once; and gross and obtuse, indeed, must have been he who failed to value the privilege!

One of the many remarkable characteristics of the great Virginians of the Revolutionary Age was the polished politeness of their manners. It was accompanied in Washington, as we know, with sternness, and perhaps, with stiffness, and in Madison, with stateliness, in spite of his diminutive size. Jefferson impressed Long at first, as we have seen, as cold in his deportment, but this was probably due to his transitory disappointment over the too youthful appearance of this English professor. No one could unbend with more grace and dignity than he, or could put forth, without affectation or pretense, a greater personal charm. Not only was he, through his mother, sprung from a family that possessed all the social culture of Colonial Virginia,— the ripest that has been noted in the long history of the same community,— but he had been thrown, at the most susceptible era of his life, with the most accomplished gentleman of those times, Governor Fauquier, and with the members of the hardly less courtly circle who passed the fashionable season in the capital of Williamsburg. It was a school of manners

as well as a school of politics, a school of gentlemen as
well as of statesmen; and in neither particular has it been
since surpassed on the American Continent.

So simple, unassuming, and cordial was Jefferson's
bearing towards his youthful guests, so patently sincere
were his warm words of welcome, so sympathetic and re-
sponsive was his interest in their welfare, that they almost
at once forgot his age and great personal distinction, and
were as much at ease in his presence as if they were dining under the roof of a near kinsman or an intimate
friend   He knew well the histories of the old families
from which most of them were descended; a grandfather,
a father, or an uncle, perhaps, had been a contemporary
and disciple of his own in the political struggles of the
past; he was familiar with the counties from which they
came, and with the people and varied interests of their
native localities; he was also apprised of the standing of
the most prominent students in their several classes; and
upon all these topics, he would comment in so sprightly a
manner, would intersperse his conversation with so many
of the entertaining experiences of his own career, that
his hearers listened to him with delight and engrossing attention.   " His hospitality and sociability," says Burwell
Stark, recalling one of these visits nearly seventy years
after it occurred, " made us free in his company and endeared him to all our hearts "   It was the memory of
these charming hours under his roof that caused so many
of the young men to step out of their way to receive his
kind salutation as he walked or rode through the University grounds.

Previous to 1827, lessons in dancing could, with the
Faculty's consent, be taken within the precincts; but the
pupils were not permitted to attend the cotillions which
the teacher gave, at intervals, in Charlottesville.   Mon-

sieur Ferron, the instructor in fencing, applied for the place of instructor in dancing also. He had been suspected of using the opportunity created by his connection with the University to draw off to his private French school many of the members of Blaettermann's classes; and on this ground, the Faculty declined to allow him the use of a dormitory for his dancing pupils; but as there was reason to think that he would, in consequence, establish a dancing academy at Charlottesville, which would afford many students an excuse to visit town, the executive committee revoked the refusal, and approved the petition   But, apparently, he did not act on it, for, when, in 1830, Mr. Bigelow asked permission to teach dancing, Ferron, fearing a dangerous rival, made haste to say that he would instruct a class at once.   Bigelow was now giving lessons in music, and wished, in addition, to give dancing lessons.   Ferron seems to have been successful in his protest, for we learn that, previous to July 2, 1831, Bigelow confined his instructions within the precincts to the young ladies of the professors' and officers' families. He had, however, been engaged in teaching the same art to such students as were willing to learn in his home without the bounds.

At the beginning of the session of 1831–2, Ferron was authorized again to accept pupils in dancing. Its most popular branch at this time was waltzing, and for three months' instruction in it, he was paid a fee of six dollars.   A rival of Ferron arose, in 1833, in the person of Louis Carusi, who asked to be granted the use of a dormitory in giving his lessons.   His charge for an entire course was the modest sum of twelve dollars.   Subsequently, Carusi met his classes in the middle hotel on West Range, the modern Jefferson Hall.   His instructions, unlike those of Ferron, were confined to dancing.

Ferron derived an income, not only from teaching the combined arts of dancing, fencing, and boxing, but also, through his wife, from needlework, since Madame Ferron, probably a Frenchwoman, was a skillful and industrious seamstress, and as such was constantly patronized by the students when supplying themselves with underclothing.   Carusi failed to give full satisfaction, for, in 1834, many of his pupils, disappointed with his lessons, applied to the Faculty for permission to engage a teacher who would furnish the necessary music as well as correct their movements at the weekly assembly which they were then planning to hold.   This permission was granted on condition that each set of lessons should terminate at the end of two hours.

In September, 1835, at the beginning of a new session, three persons,—Xaupi, Carusi and Enoch C. Breeden,— sent in their several petitions for the position of dancing-master within the precincts.   Carusi's was denied because it was thought that his engagements in Charlottesville were incompatible with the full performance of his duties at the University.   Breeden was appointed to the place; but two years afterwards, Carusi came forward again as a candidate, and the Faculty decided to license them both, provided that they would consent to give lessons beyond the bounds in private houses approved by the chairman. Every student was left at liberty to attend the class of whichever of the two he should prefer.   Carusi was authorized to give twenty-four lessons for the sum of ten dollars.   Breeden's term lasted eight weeks.   A third instructor also was licensed to teach at a private house at this time.   His fee was ten dollars for thirty-six lessons. In 1840, Robert Williams was added to the number of the dancing-masters at the University.   All these instructors gave, each session, what were known as practising balls, which resembled the ordinary party, with the exception that the young men present were all members of the class of a particular teacher, and were unquestionably less expert in the art of dancing than persons who had enjoyed a longer experience on the floor. Each member was privileged to invite a young lady, and there was the usual provision for an abundant supply of spirits. Occasionally too an obstreperous drunken student was present. In 1833, such a one was guilty of uttering grossly profane language in the hearing of the ladies who were taking part in a ball of Carusi's pupils, and when Carusi interposed, he received a blow which led to a scene of great confusion.

The practising balls were not, in all their details, on an equal footing with the balls so frequently given by the boarders of the several University hotels. As early as 1828, these hotel balls had begun, and so heavy was the expense entailed in supplying the wine, supper, and musicians, that the chairman counseled the Faculty to impose rules that would limit their cost, and this advice was promptly adopted by that body. When, in October of this year, permission was asked by the students who took their meals at Mrs Gray's to issue invitations to a party, it was granted only on condition that the dancers should disperse before midnight, and that the expense to each student participating should not exceed one dollar and a half. We obtain a glimpse of the scene at this ball through a letter written, a few days after it occurred, by Robert Hubard, of the distinguished family of that name so long and so honorably associated with Buckingham county. "The party," he says, "was given in one of the hotels which was unoccupied. Mrs. Gray assisted the committee of arrangements, and we had a very nice supper for the ladies and gentlemen; music by Jesse

Scott and son. A great many ladies were invited, and it was said that there were more ladies at our party than ever were at any University party. I suppose that there were thirty or thirty-five ladies, perhaps forty. Each boarder invited one friend, and we had forty-five or fifty men. There were two or three pretty girls present,— Miss Miller, Miss Tucker, (the oldest of the three), and Miss Eliza Gray. The great beauty, with her red head, Mrs. Bonnycastle, was there, and Mrs. Blaettermann; likewise, Mary Byrd Emmet . . . Nearly all the professors were there,— Mr. Lomax, Mr. Bonnycastle, Dr. Blaettermann, Dr. Patterson, the new professor, Dr. Johnson, and Dr. Harrison; so you see we had the collected wisdom of the institution The party was highly agreeable, all appearing to be enjoying themselves, either in dancing or in conversation. The students were under no restraint because the Faculty were present, as they, the Faculty, gave themselves no airs. Dr. Emmet was the only one of them who danced; he danced once or twice and tolerably well to boot. Mary Byrd was dressed elegantly and danced a good deal with the students. I was introduced to her as I took it for granted she had forgotten me As we were standing up in a reel, I had no opportunity to have any chat. I appeared that night in my new olive coat and looked tolerable decent for once in my life. Whatever you may say against the colour, it is very much admired at this place. I will have you understand that my own personal beauty is sufficient to make my coat look well."

There were several details of particular interest comprised in this letter: (1) during the first years at least, the professors and their wives were present at the hotel balls, although they seem to have, as a body, taken only a conversational part in them; (2) the reel as well as the waltz was danced; (3) the students were now permitted to wear their most elegant suits in order to increase their attractiveness in the eyes of the belles; and (4) the musicians were two colored men, who continued to enjoy for many years the patronage of local fashion.

xxxv. *Diversions, continued*

The Faculty must have decided that the party at Mrs. Gray's was sufficient for thirty days, for on December 2 of the same year, they refused to permit the boarders of Minor's hotel to repeat it. The entire body of students united in giving a large ball on Christmas Eve of the same year. It is not stated where this took place. Apparently, the custom had not yet been introduced of holding the University, as distinguished from the hotel, balls in the noble circular room of the library,—an apartment that would have lent splendor to any entertainment, however imposing in itself. The middle hotels, as they were called,— the two houses on West Range and East Range, the one now used as the Jefferson Hall, and the other formerly as the home of the proctor,— were hardly large enough to allow free movement to so great throng as two hundred and fifty or three hundred people, the number quite certain to have attended a University ball in those times. From January 1, 1829, down to 1842, not a year went by that a dance was not given by the boarders of each hotel, and in some instances, it took place in the vacant middle building on West Range. Such a party was given on October 14, 1829, by the young men assigned to Mrs. Gray's tables, and on November 13, of the following year, by those assigned to Colonel Rose's. The latter was held at Rose's hotel. Only four days later, the boarders of Spotswood's hotel obtained permission to invite their friends to a ball in their turn.   There were sixty students present on this occasion, and as each was granted the privilege of inviting a young lady, there was, with the escorts and members of the professors' families, a large company in attendance.   Only one student appeared on the floor without his uniform, and the entertainment was marked by perfect decorum [1]

Professor Harrison and his wife, just after their marriage, were guests of honor at a ball at Conway's hotel given by the members of the School of Ancient Languages, a proof of the good will in which he was held by those who attended his lectures.   In the following October, a ball was given at Wertenbaker's hotel.   There were ninety students present, with a proportionate number of young ladies.   Wertenbaker, as we have seen, had become unpopular with many of the young men in consequence of the vigilance and firmness which he had shown as assistant to the proctor in the enforcement of the police regulations; but this did not prevent them from gathering under his roof in a great throng when an opportunity for amusement was offered.   A subscription ball was held in this hotel twelve months afterwards The fee that was paid by each participant was four dollars.   When the chairman objected to this amount as too large, the managers brought forward as an excuse the fact that at least sixty students belonging to other hotels had

[1] One of these hotel balls has found an amusing niche in the *Recollections* of Colonel Charles C Wertenbaker   "My mother, Mrs William Wertenbaker," he writes, "attended a dance at Mrs Conway's once, and when she became tired, she slipped away and went to bed   As there were a good many guests, a lot of pallets had been prepared on the basement floor for the ladies, so she went down and found the baby and his nurse there fast asleep   After going to her pallet and putting out the light she heard something moving about the room, so she awakened the half-grown negro nurse and told her what she heard   The girl said, " I speck it a frog.   I seed one just now on Billy's head."

been present, and as the whole of the University was thus really represented, it was as if one ball had been given by the boarders of three hotels; or to describe it in their own words, as if three balls had been given for a single subscription.   It was perhaps on the same ground that the fee for a party at Conway's hotel was not long afterwards put at a figure as high as five dollars.   When this was mentioned as a precedent for the ball at Mrs. Gray's a few days later, the chairman refused to assent to its propriety, and only with great reluctance finally agreed to the amount being fixed at four dollars.   By 1835, the sum to be paid was ordered to be reduced to two.   The boarders at Colonel Ward's hotel complained of this regulation because it would limit the liquid refreshments to a weak sangaree, while a four dollar subscription would enable them to buy at least sixteen gallons of wine. It was the misuse of spirits, on these occasions, that aroused the Faculty's opposition, and led them to debar it in a measure by cutting down the sum to be expended in its purchase.   So much drunkenness disgraced the ball given on the night of February 22, 1838, that the students were refused permission to give a second one on the night of April 13 of the same year.

The medical class invited Doctor Cabell to a large party in honor of his appointment to his chair, and in his turn, he, at the beginning of the next session, reciprocated by feasting all its members.   But it was not often that the Faculty contributed to the students' recreation by the like entertainments.   This was perhaps to be explained by those relations of friction which existed between them as a body and the students, through so many years.   Had the professors been less aloof in their bearing, the strain would have been less perceptible.   They must have sometimes acknowledged the truth of this in

their own breasts, for, in 1831, there seems to have been
at least a temporary disposition on their part to enter into
a more cordial personal intercourse with their pupils.
There were two balls given by them in the month of
March of that year, and two, in addition, in October.
At one of the latter, several of the young men appeared
without uniform, an act so patently in the teeth of the
regulations that it had the aspect of an intentional af-
front to their hosts.   There was a fourth party in one of
the pavilions in November   Few records exist of other
entertainments by members of the Faculty in the years
that immediately followed; but it is probable that the
chairman gave an occasional party or reception.

It was only rarely that the students could obtain permission either to give balls in the taverns of Charlottesville or to accept invitations to balls given there by towns-
men.   The reason for this refusal was, in general, a
sound one; liquor, owing to the existence of bar-rooms
in these inns, was so conveniently at hand that few of
the young men could resist the temptation to drink to
excess.   In 1831, there were uncommonly deep potations
at a ball given at the Midway hotel, and in the same year,
at another given at the Central.   It was their knowledge
of this discreditable indulgence that caused the Faculty
to decline to allow the boarders of Gray's and Conway's
hotels to hold a ball at the Midway in the following October, and again in December.   Many students, however,
attended a party given at Fitch's in January, 1832, and
it was so cold a night that some of them were detained
until next morning   There was a public ball given at
Midway's on the night of February 22; and on March 4,
a subscription ball at Fitch's to the young ladies of
Charlottesville.   To the latter about fifteen students had
been invited to subscribe.

Fitch's hotel seems to have remained under a permanent ban with the Faculty. Permission was usually refused the students to hold balls there. The chairman, however, consented to one at the Midway when told by the pleading young men that it was to be "very genteel and proper." "I thought," he said, "that it would not be right to withhold my consent." "Indeed," he added, "these parties at which ladies are present are the least objectionable of all the indulgences that can be granted to the students." The records reveal that the collegians were sometimes very sly in their methods of twisting around the Faculty's refusal to permit them to hold a ball in an inn of Charlottesville. In January, 1833, the boarders of Col. Rose's hotel persuaded their friends in town to become the patrons of an entertainment at Ward's tavern, the cost of which the young men promised to defray; they justified this furtiveness by asserting that the dimensions of the University hotels were too small to accommodate with comfort all the persons whom they wished to invite. A very large public ball was held at Boyd's tavern on April 12, 1833, and no obstruction for once was placed in the way of the students' attendance. The corresponding ball in 1835 was also celebrated with extraordinary distinction; on this occasion the Faculty was scandalized by the arrival of many of the young men in knee breeches and velvet coats, ordered specially for the occasion; and these fine clothes, by comparison, made the gray uniform worn by the others appear drab and shabby. In the following November, the students were permitted to give a dancing party at the Mudwall boarding house [1] provided that the

---

[1] We learn from Woods's *History of Albemarle County* "that Cocke built a large hotel on the southside of the University street near the present Union Station He named it the Delavan, after his friend and coadjutor (in prohibition) in Albany The hotel had a wall in front

only liquor to be served was a weak sangaree. Having once obtained such permission in any case, they were often disposed to push the privilege rather far. A ball in celebration of Washington's birthday was held by them at the Midway on the night of February 22, 1836. On the ensuing day, the committee of eleven managers returned to the hotel to settle the account, but before doing so, summoned a number of their friends among the young ladies of Charlottesville, and beginning at two o'clock in the afternoon danced until nightfall. In explaining their action to the chairman, they asserted that the night before they had been so busy superintending the course of the ball that they had been unable to take part in it on the floor. They escaped with a reprimand.

Not all the balls attended by the collegians at this time were given at the University or in Charlottesville. On December 23, 1837, an entertainment of this kind took place at Standardsville, in Orange county; and again on December 27. Numerous students who had obtained leave to visit their homes during the Christmas vacations participated in these balls, which seem to have been given by subscription One of the party testified that it had cost him six dollars; another, ten; and a third, fifteen.

XXXVI. *Diversions, continued*

The popular dinner of those times was the public dinner. The anniversary of no supreme political event was then ever allowed to pass without its celebration with a banquet, when many quarts of spirits were drunk, and many patriotic toasts offered and responded to The

flanked with heavy pillars, and covered with stucco stained with the hue of the Albemarle clay; and from this peculiarity, acquired the name of Mudwall The site of this hotel is now occupied by the Delavan colored church " The hotel seems to have been used as a Confederate military hospital.

first great public dinner that took place at the University occurred before all its buildings were completed and even before a single student had matriculated; this was given in honor of Lafayette's visit in 1824,— an incident to be referred to here because it forms a very interesting part of the social history of the institution. The distinguished Frenchman arrived in Albemarle on November 4, about four months before the lectures began. After a public reception in entering the county, he went straight to Monticello, accompanied by thousands of enthusiastic people, who had assembled from the neighboring valleys and mountains   The meeting of the two venerable patriots has been often described,— how the one greeted the other with, " God bless you, General," and the other the one with " God bless you, Jefferson," and how the two embraced each other, amid audible sobs from the spectators of that moving scene.

On the 15th, Jefferson, Lafayette, and Madison set out from Monticello in a landau for Charlottesville, with a numerous escort of cavalrymen and citizens on horseback. A reception was held in the town, and then the procession started for the University; and only came to a halt when it reached the foot of the Lawn. On the verdant terraces, rising one above the other, had gathered groups of gayly dressed ladies, who waved their handkerchiefs when the French hero appeared, and then rushed forward and formed a lane, along which he and his companions, with many polite bows, passed from their carriage to the Rotunda steps. William F. Gordon there received them with an eloquent address of welcome. A short interval of rest ensued, and then Lafayette, with Jefferson and Madison on either side, returned to the Lawn, and, with kindly urbanity, mingled with the assembled people. The dinner was held in the great circular

room of the Rotunda, and there could not have been
found in America another apartment more imposing for
the purpose   The hour chosen was three o'clock in the
afternoon.   The tables were arranged in three concen-
tric circles; Valentine W. Southall presided, with Lafayette on his right, and beyond him, on the same side,
Jefferson and Madison; and with George Washington
Lafayette, a son of the General, with his suite, on the
left   The first toast was to the " American Revolution "; the second, to the " Father of his Country "; and
the third, to Lafayette himself.   When he had responded, he gave four toasts: " Charlottesville and the
University," " the Sages and Heroes of the Revolution,"
" the President of the United States," and " Jefferson
and the Declaration of Independence "

Jefferson's reply was read by Southall, and it contained
a pathetic allusion to the new seat of learning, and his
paternal hopes for its future career.   " If, with the aid
of my younger and abler coadjutors," he said, " I can
still contribute anything to advance this institution, within
whose walls we are now mingling manifestations of affection to this, our guest, it will be, as it has been, cheerfully and zealously bestowed.   And if I could see it
once enjoying the patronage and cherishment of our
public authorities with undivided voice, I should die
without a doubt of the future fortunes of my native
State, and in the consoling contemplation of the happy
influence of this institution on its character, its virtue, its
prosperity, and its safety."   Seven regular toasts followed, and many voluntary ones   Among the latter was
a toast by John Coles: " To the Future Students of the
University of Virginia,— may they equal General Lafayette in love of Liberty and Political Consistency."
The day, according to the graphic report of the *Cen-*

tral Gazette which has survived, was characterized by unbroken dignity and orderliness, universal enthusiasm, and profound emotion.

The first public dinner given by the students was held on the Fourth of July, 1826, and it was followed by an oration in harmony with the patriotic nature of the occasion; but it must have been accompanied by some dissipation, for when the request for permission to give a public dinner on the next anniversary of the same date was sent in by them, it was, at first, refused, although they obtained at once the arid privilege of listening to an address and to the reading of the Declaration. So persistently, however, did they urge a reconsideration of this decision that the Faculty reluctantly reversed it upon receiving their promise that all present would conduct themselves with "unexceptional propriety." As the 22nd of February, 1828, approached, they sought permission to celebrate that day also with a public dinner; and this was granted, doubtless because the pledge for the preceding Fourth of July had been strictly observed. But as if they feared that the occasion would be marred by frivolous toasts, the Faculty proposed a number that were of a highly suggestive historical flavor, but not very appealing to the heated patriotism of the youthful orators; such, for instance, as the " Effect of Climate on National Character," the " Influence of Art on Painting," the " Study of the Classics," and the " Influence of General History in Instructing by Example." To young fellows fully charged to explode on the subjects of the " Crossing of the Delaware " and the " Surrender of Cornwallis at Yorktown," these utilitarian and didactic themes, submitted probably in a sly spirit of humor, must have appeared extraordinarily dull and inopportune.

From year to year, public dinners were given in town

to celebrate the 13th of April, and these were popular occasions with the students.   The transfer of the intermediate examinations to February seemed to have discouraged their celebration of the 22nd of that month, for they were too much absorbed in the work of preparation to amuse themselves with public dinners at that time.

In 1831, one of the buildings of Charlottesville was converted into a public theatre, and we first learn of its existence through the drunkenness which it encouraged among the students.   A Thespian society had already been organized in the town; and it was perhaps due to the influence of its members that a theatre was opened. This establishment was under the management of a strolling player named Richardson.   Several students were accused of joining the society, but they denied all personal connection with it   At least one, however, John Leitch, was known to have participated in a theatrical performance that took place in the town; but this may have been a drama staged by an obscure company in the course of a tour.   Such actors were frequent visitors to Charlottesville.   In 1834, Meredith Jones, the proprietor of a University boarding house situated without the precincts, asked permission of the Faculty to rent one of his rooms for a few nights to such a band, but was refused.   Fairs were also held in town; and in 1835,— and, no doubt, in other years,— there was a show of wild beasts.

Many of the students cultivated a taste for music. In 1825, a teacher was licensed to give lessons on the violin.   Perhaps, this was the citizen of Staunton, who, crossing the Ridge, distributed many prospectuses among the hotels with the view of obtaining a sufficient number of pupils to make up a class.   He offered to give three or four lessons each day in the week.   That the use of musical instruments within the precincts was now constant is disclosed by their interdiction by the Faculty during the hours of lecture, and throughout Sunday. Bonnycastle and Key declined to unite with their colleagues in the adoption of this ordinance. The prohibition was carried even further in 1831, for, in the code of that year, all musical instruments were to be laid aside also after two o'clock at night. It shows the determination of the authorities, that, when, in the course of this year, a student insisted upon his right to play on his violin during the forbidden hours, he was promptly dismissed for his obstinacy.

In 1832, the echoes of the arcades were awakened by the music of a band composed entirely of students, and the chairman was very pleasantly impressed by their skill. This band, so long as it existed, always played during the intervals of the exercises on the 13th of April and the 4th of July. A serenade with stringed instruments, accompanied by a drum, which took place in March, 1833, called forth only delighted approval; but when repeated, a short time afterwards, was condemned, — doubtless because it had changed to an offensive character; thus, in 1835, a disorderly party of performers playing on fiddles and other instruments, and singing very obscene corn-songs, raised a very discordant hubbub in front of Mr. Wertenbaker's house, which was only discontinued when the proctor came upon the ground. So many flutes and violins were, during the following year, in use in Mrs. Gray's district, and so often, and at such inopportune hours, did their owners employ them, that several of the young men asked the Faculty's permission to remove their domicile to Mr. Conway's. It was reported, indeed, that some of these concerts in the dormitories were kept up until two o'clock in the morning;

and the effect finally grew to be so distracting that the Faculty restricted all playing to the intervals between two and three o'clock in the afternoon, and four in the afternoon and eight in the evening. It was prohibited altogether now, as formerly, on Sunday. Both rules were constantly broken.

There were only a few amusements besides those already mentioned to enliven the leisure moments of the students. One of these was skating. The pond afforded an excellent surface for this sport in the course of the winter, while skates were easily procurable from among the miscellaneous contents of the University shops. The price of a pair, however, was not very low, for four dollars seems to have been the figure Pitching quoits was also a frequent form of recreation; and in this both the proctor and the professors sometimes joined This game too was prohibited on Sundays. Recourse was also had to marbles. Marbles would be hardly expected to offer an opportunity for creating a noise, and yet the students were able, for that reason, to make it objectionable on many occasions; a party playing before the door of a member of the Faculty in 1837 used so much profanity that they were reported to the chairman. "The disorder consequent on marble playing," said he impatiently, "is becoming so serious that it must be checked"; but the only result of the effort to do so was to drive the students to the yards behind the dormitories, where they not only played on Sunday, but raised such a hullabaloo at all hours that additional measures of repression had to be adopted.

The young men were not permitted to keep either a dog or a horse within the precincts. Riding on horseback seems to have been disapproved even when the animal was stabled in Charlottesville,— on the ground that

336 HISTORY OF THE UNIVERSITY OF VIRGINIA

the diversion was very expensive, and that it wasted valuable time. The consent of the chairman had to be obtained if the rider was to relieve himself of the charge of violating the law; and it was granted on the sole excuse of bad health. It was only when the ordinary student was compelled to use a horse to carry him from his home in the country to the University, that this act passed without censure. Races were held near Charlottesville, during this early period, and the collegians were not prohibited from being present, although it was known that they usually went armed with pistols, and that, not infrequently they became mixed up there in serious affrays. In 1830, when certain students were pointedly questioned by the chairman as to why they carried pistols on their persons to the race-track, they replied that they were afraid of being attacked by " citizens of Charlottesville "; but this was probably a reason which had little foundation beyond their own imaginary apprehensions.

XXXVII. *Athletics*

Jefferson, in his famous Rockfish Gap Report, failed to recommend that provision should be made for instruction in gymnastics as one of the departments to be set up in the projected University, and yet, in that report, he candidly acknowledged that it was a " proper object of attention " for every institution devoted to the education of youth. The explanation of his omitting to advise a course in physical culture was apparently the fact that the prevailing system of athletics bore no direct relation to the character of modern weapons, or to the modern methods of warfare In ancient times, the weapon and the method alike called for athletic skill of the highest order. Wellington, it will be remembered, expressed the conviction that the Battle of Waterloo was really won on the cricket field of Eton, by which he meant that the soldierly qualities of his officers at least had received their earliest training on that ground of physical and moral endurance and competition.   It was the indirect, and not the direct, influence that he was thinking of most. Jefferson declared himself in favor of lessons in manual exercises, military manoeuvres, and tactics, in preference to lessons in athletics, simply because the former, and not the latter, would equip the students for the duty of national defense; he seemed to take it for granted that athletics were of no particular importance so far as they afforded only an increase in the individual's power of self-protection; and yet, as we know, two gymnasia formed a conspicuous feature of his general scheme of buildings   Why did he add them to his architectural scheme?   Because he thought that they would be useful in strengthening the health of the students; and above all, because he considered that they would be indispensable when instruction came to be given in the military courses of study.

In October, 1824, five months before the lecture-halls were first used, these two apartments, which were situated next to the basement of the Rotunda, on its south front, and were known as the Eastern and Western gymnasiums, were, at Jefferson's instance, dedicated to the " gymnastic exercises and games " of the students.   They were long low structures covered with flat roofs that were converted into a public walk.   The flooring of both, at first, consisted altogether of an uneven mass of red clay, which even during the collegiate career of Professor John B. Minor, were, as he said, " sometimes wet and always filthy."   The roofs had begun to leak after heavy rains in the spring of 1827.   In April of the previous year, before this condition arose, the military tutor, Mr. Matthews, had been permitted to use these apartments in giving instruction in military science. The only other purpose which they seemed to have served at this time was of banqueting halls, for, here on July 4, 1826, the students celebrated the anniversary of the Declaration of Independence with a public dinner. It was plainly not known at the time when this dinner was in progress, or during the delivery of the ensuing oration, that Jefferson was then dying, or even lay dead in his chamber at Monticello. So empty did the gymnasia remain, so unserviceable were they for at least the athletic exercises which were expected to be held in them, that, in July, 1830, the Visitors decided to turn them into public halls; and the Faculty was asked to submit a plan for their alteration at the Board's annual meeting twelve months afterwards. That body apparently reported then in favor of converting one of the apartments into a large lecture-room, and the other into two small rooms of the same character; but as the cost of the proposed change was found to be fifteen hundred dollars, the project was abandoned. How useless for gymnastic exercises the two were considered to be in 1835, was shown by the action of one of the teachers of athletics at that time in petitioning the Board to build an entirely new and independent hall for his pupils' convenience; and this request was not complied with only because there were no funds in the University treasury which could be expended upon such a structure.

As late as 1839, Cocke, in a letter to Cabell, refers, with unrepressed impatience, to "the present worthless gymnasia." As there was still an acute need for more lecture-rooms, he urged that the two should be converted into several apartments for this purpose. "The want that has always existed," said he, " cannot be supplied by any other plan that will not involve double, if not treble, the expense. Last year (1838), this measure was postponed for want of funds. The improvement, according to Mr. Spooner's estimates, will cost five thousand dollars."

There were two reasons why the alteration suggested by Cocke had been so long deferred,— one, the lack of money, to which we have already alluded; the other, the fear that the symmetrical beauty of the Rotunda, and its immediate environment, would be seriously marred by the proposed elevation of the roofs. When the money was ultimately found, however, this apprehension was put aside. In 1840, the executive committee was instructed to report, at the next meeting of the Board, upon the proper assignment of the lecture-rooms into which they had decided to divide the gymnasia. A plan of alteration had already been submitted by Cocke, which was adopted in the form recommended by him. The work began at once, and by the beginning of the session of 1841–2, the changes seem to have been completed. They apparently embraced the addition of new roofs as well as the reconstruction of the interior partitions. Thus was permanently altered the original purpose for which these two front wings of the Rotunda had been built, but which, even while they remained in their first condition, they had never subserved, except so far as to afford an area for military exercises,— which too, in time, were discontinued.

Three branches of athletics,— boxing, fencing and single stick,— were taught at the University almost from the very start. In 1828, Ferron was granted a room in Hotel D on East Range, which had been vacated by Spotswood; and here he was soon employed in giving lessons in the several arts in which he was so great an expert. This room was named by him somewhat pretentiously " salle d'armes." At one time, as we have mentioned, he excited the Faculty's displeasure by drawing away pupils from Blaettermann's classes to his own private French school; but when this was stopped, they offered no objection to his giving elementary courses in the French and Latin tongues to the small boys of the University community. He was required, however, to vacate the room in Hotel D, as the entire building was now assigned to Colonel .Colonna, the tutor in modern languages. Ferron rented instead a school-house situated near East Range and on the Lynchburg Road; but he continued to teach the arts of self-defense within the precincts. A dormitory on West Range was reserved for him and his pupils, and the noise made by them in practising raised many complaints. His charges seem to have been moderate,— the fees were eight dollars for a course of boxing, fifteen for a course of fencing, and twenty-five for a course of quarter-staff. His profits were increased by the sale of gloves, swords, and masks; the price of a pair of boxing gloves ranged from two dollars and a half to three dollars, and a sword and mask from five to six. In 1833, the Faculty, under provocation, decided again to deprive him of the room in which he had resumed his lessons; but they do not seem to have revoked his license.

A rival to Ferron appeared, this year, in the person of Alexander A. Penci, a Corsican by birth and a major in rank. Penci was authorized to give lessons in boxing, fencing and quarter-staff; and in addition, he conducted a gymnasium, the subscription fee of which was six dollars. This establishment, as the proctor's accounts reveal, had a large number of patrons among the students.   The first apartment which he occupied for this purpose was unsuitable, and, in 1834, he asked for more ample accommodations.   He told the Faculty that, during the warm season, he could not teach gymnastics properly unless he resided within the precincts,— perhaps, because, during this part of the session, he gave his lessons at night.   A large room in the upper story of Hotel F was assigned him as a domicile.   He was now known as the Instructor in Gymnastics and Fencing. He seems to have given satisfaction professionally and personally, for, in September, 1835, the whole of the upper apartments of the southeast hotel were reserved for the use of his family.   He finally withdrew from the University, in the hope of recovering his health, which had been shattered by consumption.   The esteem in which he was held was clearly manifested by the contributions of the professors and students in defrayment of the expense of his journey to Havana, where he remained until his death.   His wife, who was afflicted with the same disease, died soon after in the house which they had occupied within the University precincts; their little daughter, Beatrice, was adopted by Mrs. Fitch, the wife of the proprietor of the hotel of that name in Charlottesville; but at the age of seven returned to her kinsfolk in Italy; and in time so entirely forgot the language of her birthplace, that she was unable to converse with a citizen of Albemarle, Mr. S. W. Ficklin, who visited her in 1849.

Penci was succeeded by Christopher Grimme, whose series of lessons embraced quarter-staff, fencing, broadsword sparring, and gymnastics.   His terms for instruction in the last were three dollars for an entire session. Like Penci, he was granted the use of an apartment, which was known as the Gymnasium.   This room, no doubt, was fully equipped with the more simple athletic appliances

There is no evidence that athletics, in any form, aroused, during the first seventeen sessions, any interest except among a few students, embracing (1) those who looked upon fencing and boxing as gentlemanly accomplishments; and (2) those who turned to gymnastics as a method of preserving health while following a sedentary life within the college precincts.

XXXVIII. *Publications*

In the remote situation of the University, accessible to the world at large, in these early times, only by a sluggish and muddy stage, the arrival of the post must have caused pleasurable excitement in the lives of the students   There was then no daily mail to make the letter pouch a familiar and commonplace object. From some quarters of the compass, the mail coach came in only twice a week, and while there must have been more frequent deliveries from Richmond and the eastern region, this was certainly not so until the railway had been extended to Louisa county.   Previous to the spring of 1826, the student had to call at the post-office in Charlottesville to obtain his letters; but after this date, through the influence of William C. Rives, the representative of the district in Congress, a branch of that office was established at the University.   A dormitory was reserved as the place for the distribution of letters,[1] and

[1] "Our post-office when I first recall," says Colonel Charles C Wertenbaker, a son of William Wertenbaker, "was the dormitory in the same block with Washington Hall, the old proctor's office, next to the alley going up to the Lawn. Next, it was at the southern end of East Range in the room next to the alley leading to the Lawn at the end of East Range; next it was in a dormitory at the north end of the central pavilion on East Range   Finally, it was moved to the building near the new gate (at the main entrance to the grounds)."

apparently the librarian, for the time being, served as *ex officio* postmaster. William Wertenbaker, who played several parts simultaneously, or in succession, in the University community, —librarian, assistant proctor, secretary of the Faculty, and hotel-keeper,— was also, during many years, the postmaster of the institution. In 1832, William Brockenbrough was the librarian, and automatically upon him, during that year, also fell the duties of the postmastership.

The stamp had not come into use. The charge for posting letters was fixed by their weight. The ordinary fee seems to have been twelve and a half cents for a moderate distance; but to a point as far as New York, twenty-seven and a half   The postage on a pamphlet of small size ranged all the way from seven and a half cents to fifteen. With prices for forwarding mail so excessive, it is not probable that the students were much in the habit of writing letters, however pleased to receive them. There were numerous orders on the proctor, however, in payment of bills for postage sent in by the postmaster The fact that there was a system of credit would seem to indicate that this official was not too much burthened by his duties.

Only a few of the students subscribed to newspapers This, no doubt, had the approval of the Faculty, who deprecated, as we shall see, all heated political feeling within the precincts of the University. The ledgers of the shopkeepers show that there were many of the young men who purchased books for their private reading. These volumes faithfully reflected the predominant tastes of the times. Byron was the most popular author of the age, and not the less so with young men than with old The scornful spirit of revolt which inflamed that great poet throughout life, the romantic incidents of his career, his cynical citizenship of the world, his virility, audacity, solitariness,— each so fresh in the public mind, because he was still, or had been so recently, an actor upon the stage,— cast a glamour over the susceptibilities of all those who turned to his verses for recreation. Five copies of this moody and fiery writer were bought at the University for every one purchased of other authors of equal or higher merit. Even Shakespeare and Milton paled their ineffectual fires in the rays of his refulgent sun. In comparison with him, Pope was in a state almost of eclipse, although the *Essay on Man* and the *Rape of the Lock* were sometimes obtained from the local shopkeeper.

Second only to Byron in the eyes of these youthful purchasers stood Thomas Campbell, and for the same reason in part: his manly, vigorous, and martial poems appealed with singular force to the young Southerner's unbounded admiration for splendid deeds of bravery. Then came Thomas Moore, whose love songs, in spite of their artificial and fashionable glitter,— or, perhaps, for that very reason,— were known to many of the students by heart. *Don Quixote, Gil Blas,* and *Tom Jones,* — renowned masterpieces of manners and sentiment,— were the favorite novels. It is astonishing to discover that none of the stories of Scott are to be found in the sales accounts; but Sterne had his group of worshippers: many copies of *Tristram, Shandy* and the *Sentimental Journey,* but not of the *Sermons,* were bought; so were Thomson's *Seasons, Rasselas,* and the tales of Miss Edgeworth. Such imposing works as Gibbon's *Decline and Fall* and Plutarch's *Lives* are included in the lists of sales; so was the *Spectator,* which retained in Virginia down to the middle of the nineteenth century the popularity which it had enjoyed in the Colonial Age [1]

Two small purchases of books by students in 1833, throw light on individual tastes at that time. The list of J. J. Hill embraced *Peregrine Pickle, Vivian Gray,* Robertson's *Histories of Scotland and America,* the *Essays* of Locke, the *Tatler* and the *Guardian;* the list of John W Eppes, *Roderick Random,* the *Poems* of Garth, Collins, and Gray, the works of Voltaire, and Cuvier's *Animal Kingdom.* These volumes were bought, not for study, but for transient entertainment only.

By 1840, several new literary planets had swum into the collegiate ken. Bulwer, the man of the world, had now become the popular novelist and playwright, and copies of *Night and Morning* and *The Lady of Lyons* are noted among the students' purchases; Marryat's sea-tales too were favorites with the same youthful buyers; and even attenuated Mrs Hemans was not neglected by them   Not infrequently, they are found turning away from books like these,— which were valuable for amusement's sake alone,— and taking up those possessing only the merit of utility; such was the formidable collection known as the *Family Library* published in twenty volumes; and such too the ponderous *Library of Useful Knowledge.* The purchase of a complete set of *British Poets* disclosed less alienation from genuine literature. As a rhyming dictionary was sometimes bought, it is to be

---

[1] In 1846, there was a student in the University who bore the name of Dean Swift Boston   The works of Swift were then as much read by the Virginians as the works of Addison   One of the homes of the Carrington family in Halifax county was named " Mildendo" after the capital of Lilliput   The present home of the Bruce family in that county is known as "Berry Hill," a name adopted from Miss Burney's *Evelina*   These names were given to these residences early in the nineteenth century, or late in the eighteenth, at a time when Swift and Burney were more in vogue in Virginia than they are to-day

inferred that some of the young men diverted themselves with experiments in versification.

The first periodical associated with the history of the University was suggested by Dunglison, and was issued under the patronage of the Faculty. It bore the pedantically ambitious name of *Virginia Literary Museum and Journal of Belles-Lettres, Arts, Sciences, Etc.* The Etc. was perhaps intended to cover the remaining provinces of knowledge, which were too numerous to be specifically mentioned in a title. The periodical was usually spoken of as the *Museum;* and this was a very pertinent designation in the light of the extraordinary variety of its contents. Its purpose was stated to be to " communicate the truth of science to the miscellaneous reader, and encourage a taste for polite literature "; but it had also a subordinate and a more practical object: " It will keep," wrote Dunglison to Madison in February, 1829, " the University of Virginia perpetually before the public, and it will diminish the expenses of the institution by printing in its pages matter that is now issued in an independent form."

Dunglison, who seems to have been of a utilitarian turn of mind, with little esteem for the quality of imagination, favored the admission only of articles full of solid information " We had better discontinue the *Museum,*" he solemnly said, " than suffer its pages to contain anything which will detract from the reputation of the University or its professors " When Tucker, a man of humor and imagination as well as of facts, suggested that a story would be occasionally needed to lighten those pages up, Dunglison replied rather loftily that there was, in the composition of tales, as a rule, none of the requisites that equip a man to serve as a teacher in a literary institution; but he modified this oracular expression so far as to add that, " if the tale carried a useful lesson, its objectionableness would be removed." Fortunately for the literary character of the periodical, his ponderous literary judgment was not the only one relied upon. All the professors were looked to for contributions, and the wide field which they were expected to cover indicates the just confidence felt in their ability and learning alike. All the branches of science were to be traversed, but in such a skillful way as to make the articles of interest to the popular mind Local history was not to be neglected: information about every State of the South,— its origin, progress, laws, manners, and dialect,— was to be gathered up for the enlightenment of the *Museum's* readers. A separate department was to be reserved for the University of Virginia, the transactions of its Visitors, its ordinances, its courses of instruction, the distinctions won by its young men in the examinations, its list of professors and students. The *Museum* was to receive and transmit hints on the subject of collegiate discipline and government; but all discussions of partizan politics, theological dogmas, or sectarian controversies, were to be avoided with unfailing circumspection.

It was anticipated that the University's association with Jefferson's principles would give the new periodical a high standing from the earliest number It had not been issued so soon as the institution opened for several reasons. (1) the instructors had been laboriously occupied, during several years, in collecting and assorting information for additional courses of lectures; and (2) coming as they did from a distance, they were unable to judge at first as to what would be acceptable to the public taste in their new theatre of action, or be best adapted to the public needs It was expected that the *Museum* would materially diminish the professors' sense of seclusion from the world at large springing from their remote situation; and that it would also create an engine for successfully combating the vindictive hostility which was so constantly assailing the University.

There was a combination of facts which led the Faculty to decide finally in favor of a weekly rather than a quarterly journal: (1) there were already three reviews issued quarterly in the United States, and from the pages of these all literary intelligence and all short articles were excluded, because this type of periodical, it was said, was established to appeal " to reflective persons, and not to the young, the thoughtless, and the gay." In a weekly publication, on the other hand, all sorts of contributions could be consistently printed; miscellaneous facts, briefly related; poetry, sketches, creàtions of the imagination,— no matter what the character of the article, it could be inserted without impropriety. Reason, Fancy, Feeling, — there was room for them all in such a periodical. In short, its pages were to be as open to the " sportive effusions of fancy and wit as to the most erudite disquisitions of scholarship, or the profoundest researches of philosophy." Hammered into shape upon this anvil the *Museum* was expected to partake at once of the character of a magazine, of a newspaper, and of a review, and all this compacted between the same two covers. " Whether we fail or succeed in our main purpose," concluded the editors, " we will at least add to the stock of harmless pleasure."

Did the numbers of the *Museum,* so far as they were issued, accomplish the primary object of the magazine; namely, the interpretation of the University? The periodical undoubtedly succeeded in its literary purpose; its pages were filled with an extraordinary variety of matter,— reviews, fiction, poetry, accounts of travel, scientific articles, notes of philology, and miscellaneous odds and ends, all presented in such polished literary form as to entertain the reader, whether the information was solid or not. The tales by Bonnycastle, like the *Story of the Blue Ridge,* the poems by Dabney Carr Terrell, the friend of Gilmer and Ticknor, and the former student of Geneva, and the translations from the German,— these have a distinct literary excellence of their own The articles on scientific subjects are thoughtful and learned; and there is a quaint flavor and a pungent humor in very many of the less ambitious contributions.

A magazine edited by men who had come from other parts of the world was not likely to possess much local raciness, or reflect the natural bent of local genius. The *Museum,* in spirit and contents, was as much a child of Boston or London as of Virginia, but from a literary point of view, it was all the more cosmopolitan for this very detachment. The very universality of its appeal was probably the main cause of its early death There was no elbow-room at this time for another purely literary magazine like itself. As its course was confined to the old channels, it lacked the saliency and the originality necessary to win a large *clientele* of its own from the ranks of its already flourishing rivals in Old England, New York, and New England With the issue of June 9, 1830, it was discontinued The reasons given by the editors for this abrupt ending, were: (1) that the professors' articles were not supplemented by contributions from independent pens, and that they were too overburdened already to give up more of their hours to supply this fatal deficiency; and (2) that no journal could expect a wide circulation that refused to use the highly flavoured sauce of politics in its pages.

The magazine had obtained subscribers enough to remove all danger of personal loss, but not a sufficient number to ensure a substantial margin of profit.   There being no duty on the importation of English periodicals,
the *Museum*, like all other American periodicals, found
it very arduous to compete successfully with them; and
moreover, the remoteness of the University was so great
that material which might have been copied into its pages
from new books had already been anticipated by Northern magazines for the benefit of their readers.   The editors further asserted that they had to contend with a·
grave difficulty in the fact that they resided a mile and
a half from their press, for this, they said, obliged them
to submit to the mortification of seeing every number, and
almost every page, deformed by false syntax and faulty
orthography, or by those far more annoying blunders
which alter the sense in a way not detected by the reader.
It is to be inferred from this complaint that the editors
thought themselves too busy to examine their proofs in
person, and that, in consequence, they relied upon their
printers for that indispensable but irksome labor.   This
unhappy state of mind was aggravated by the frequency
with which the *Museum* was issued; had that periodical
been a monthly, the distance to Charlottesville would
hardly have justified their failure to correct the mistakes
in the printing; but even as a weekly, there was no reason why the dispatch of the proofs to them could not
have been effected through a messenger with perfect
ease and regularity.   This slim excuse for discontinuance
would seem to argue that the editors had begun to grow
tired of their rather complicated enterprise.

It was but natural that the young men should have
balked at accepting the *Museum* as the mouthpiece of
their own literary tastes and aspirations.   As early as

1831, they issued the prospectus of a college magazine, on which they had bestowed the poetical name of the *Chameleon*.   The mere suggestion of such a project had excited nervous apprehension among members of the Board, even before they had seen a copy of this preliminary notice.   Cabell wrote to his nephew, James L. Cabell, now a student at the University, to inquire as to the ulterior object of this proposed excursion into the province of literature, and he seemed to look upon it as at heart a new kind of rebellion.   The boys had made a rush in a novel quarter, and he was evidently timorous as to its real significance.   Dr Patterson, on the other hand, outspokenly favored the venture, on the ground that it would encourage those trials in English composition which had always been so much neglected in the University.   The editors, who were among the most successful and exemplary students in attendance, solemnly promised that they would walk with such wariness between the pitfalls of Religion and Politics as to tumble into neither; and they also removed all fear of their burning too much oil over the preparation of original articles by announcing that they would obtain most of the contents of the *Chameleon* from the pages of other magazines,— presumably from those published in cultured Boston and London.[1]

The first number appeared on April 22.   " As it is established," Patterson wrote in a soothing spirit to Cabell the same month, " we must try to make the most

[1] Frank Carr, who succeeded Brockenbrough as proctor, wrote to Cocke in March, 1831, as follows   "The students have a project of publishing a literary paper called the *Chameleon*, and have issued the prospectus of their plan   If a sufficient number are engaged in it to enable them to conduct it without abstracting them too much from their academic pursuits, it might have a good effect on their habits by creating an additional demand on their diligence and increasing their self-respect " Cocke Correspondence.

of it." He was of the opinion that this initial issue was, from a literary point of view, very creditable to the good taste of the students. Unfortunately, the editors, in their prospectus, had stated that a restrained discussion of the propriety of all new ordinances was one of the purposes contemplated in its publication. This compelled Patterson, even after the printing of the first number,— which seems to have been free from criticism,— to allay Cabell's apprehensions again by assuring him that the committee of young men in charge could be relied upon to shut out all papers that exhibited or even hinted at insubordination.

The *Collegian*, a magazine projected by the students, was issued for the first time in October, 1838. Its editors, like those of the *Chameleon*, seemed to have been confronted at the start by the opposition of the Faculty, who thought that the periodical would "impede the performance of duty and the purposes of a liberal education" The editors, on the other hand, were convinced that it "would chasten the taste of the students; increase their knowledge; develope the resources of their minds; divert them from the excesses of dissipation; foster a vigorous literary spirit; promote skill in literary composition; and enlist the dormant talent of the University." It is debatable whether the *Collegian* rose to so high a platform as this, however loyally and assiduously the ideal may have been kept in view. The contents range from the trivial moralizing essay to the ambitious disquisition on science or literature; from light amatory verses, in rather halting measures, to elaborate tales of affrighting incidents,— the whole interspersed with sensible, informing articles, in excellent literary shape. This magazine survived to 1842. It terminated with its fourth volume, thus adding a third suspension to the two that had preceded it.   There was less justification for its failure to survive than there was for the *Museum's*, for it did not pretend to appeal to any readers beyond the University precincts, and, therefore, had more claim on local support.   As we shall see, it was soon succeeded by a periodical of the same character.

xxxix. *Debating Societies*

Among the intellectual diversions of a large section of the students were the debates in the literary societies. These societies reflected a side of their lives more congenial to their tastes than the successive periodicals that had languished and died within the same precincts   Oratory has been an art that has always aroused an extraordinary degree of enthusiasm among the Southern people, and this feeling was never stronger than during these times, which were still lighted up with the after-glow of the Revolutionary Era.   Traditions of the eloquence of the Fathers were kept in full flame by the survival down to 1826 of one of the greatest of them all,— John Adams.   Twenty-five years after Henry's death, the story of his triumphs was told with as much fervor as if he were yet alive to repeat them, and his name was still as much the synonym of the orator as the name of Demosthenes, and far more so than that of Chatham or Mirabeau.

When the first debating society was canvassed at the University of Virginia, it is probable that no other designation was suggested for it except the " Patrick Henry Society," the one that was adopted; but there was no side of the institution, beyond an abstract love of freedom and loyalty to the Commowealth, that was identified with the principles of this great Revolutionary leader or remindful of his fame as a statesman   Indeed, there were no principles which Jefferson more heartily detested than those which had guided Henry towards the end of his life, for he was then a friend of Adams and the supporter and advocate of the Federalist Administration in some of its supposed iniquities. It seemed to be almost an offense to Jefferson to associate Henry's name with any branch of activity in the University which he had founded; but if he harbored any disposition to protest,— of which there is no evidence,— he sank it in recollection of the popular reverence for the memory of the supreme orator of the Revolution. The action of the projectors of the Society was a tacit acknowledgment that, however high the distinction which Jefferson possessed, it was not won, even partially, by achievements as a speaker. It was Henry, not himself, who was first thought of by the youthful aspirants for forensic fame.

In the beginning, the Society perhaps met in a dormitory, for the main floor of pavilion VII, where it convened at a later date, was, for some time, used as a library. Wherever it may have assembled, the apartment was known as the " debating room," which had been fitted up for its purpose by important alterations, for, in December, 1825, the builder, Crawford, was paid for lumber which he had provided for these changes. As he also received a separate amount for the bench, thirty feet in length, which he supplied on the same occasion, the members of the Patrick Henry Society must have been in the habit of listening to the debate on very hard seats. The Society, during the rest of its brief period of life, possessed no regular place of meeting. It seems to have come together at one time in those rooms of pavilion VII which had previously sheltered the library; at another, in an apartment in Dr. Johnson's pavilion; and at still another, in one belonging to the pavilion afterwards occupied by Dr. Emmet.   Later yet, it obtained permission to hold its sessions in a vacant hotel.   It is probable that the bench which had been purchased for it in the beginning followed it in these different wanderings.

During the first months of its existence, the Patrick Henry Society was free from the disturbing presence of a rival, but this, so far from increasing its prosperity, seems to have diminished it   It is said that its "universality" caused its popularity to dwindle.   A spirit of discontent arose in its ranks, and in July, 1825, sixteen members withdrew with the intention of organizing another body.   The leaders in this secession,— which was to be lasting in it consequences, unlike the other similar movements of that day,— were Robert Saunders, J W. Brockenbrough, Thomas Barclay, Edgar Mason, R. A. Thompson, W. S Minor, J H. Lee and M. A Page. It is recorded that the birthplace of the new organization was No 7 West Lawn; the "Jefferson Society" was adopted as its name, and a constitution drafted for its government.   Contrary to the example set by the Patrick Henry, all strangers were denied admission to the room when the Jefferson was in session   There was always a scene of tumult at the meetings of the former, owing to the presence of curious outsiders, and the rival body, to escape from this unhappy condition, closed its doors to all but its own members.   It assembled at first once a week, but afterwards altered this rule to once a fortnight.

Jefferson was soon elected an honorary member.   The reply accompanying his refusal to accept this invitation reveals a nice sense of public duty possibly carried so far as to appear too refined.   "I could decline no distinction conferred by them (the Society)," he wrote on August 12, "no service I could render them, but on reasons of still higher importance to themselves. On maturely weighing the general relation in which the law of the University and the appointment of the Visitors have placed me as to every member of the institution, I believe that it is my duty to make no change in those relations by entering into additional or different ties with different associations of its members. The duties with which I 'am charged require that, in all cases which may arise, I should stand in an equal position as to every person concerned, not only that I may preserve the inestimable consciousness of impartiality to all, but the equally inestimable exemption from all suspicion of partialities."

This letter gives us a very clear impression of the solemn view which Jefferson took of the importance of his university, from the most conspicuous department down to the smallest and most obscure. There was not one, in his opinion, so inconsiderable in itself,— not one so exalted over the rest,— as to call for any real difference in his relations with it. So far as his fostering supervision was concerned, each one, big or little, great or insignificant, was entitled to it, on a footing of perfect equality. On the other hand, neither Madison nor Monroe strained at the honor. When' elected to complimentary membership in the same society, they allowed their names to be enrolled without one conscientious protest. In such enthusiastic respect, indeed, was Monroe held by the Jefferson Society that it declined to bestow the same distinction on John Randolph, because he had been an opponent of that statesman, and had even dared to speak of the sacred Jefferson himself with a sneer as St. Thomas of Cantingbury.

As avid a taste for constitutional discussions was shown by the members of the Jefferson as their fathers had exhibited in the Revolutionary conventions; but they do not seem to have been quite so conservative, for such a thirst for change in their organic law did they display, that it was found necessary at last to impose a fine of a dollar upon every one who offered an amendment to it. In seeking a dwelling-place, the Jefferson was as much knocked about as the Patrick Henry. It too found a temporary domicile in pavilion VII,— which enjoys the distinction of having sheltered more wandering houseless associations, from libraries and societies to clubs, than any of the buildings on the ground.

During the first years of its existence, the Jefferson Society apparently elected no public orator, although the recurrence of April 13, must have offered an itching temptation to do so. In 1832, however, it asked the Faculty's permission to choose among its members one to make an address on this anniversary. Their consent having been obtained, Merritt Robinson was selected, and he was instructed to send a copy of his speech to the chairman before its delivery Promptly submitted, it was read and approved by that official. At this time, there had sprung up in Virginia a very persistent demand for the abolition of slavery, but this demand was encountering a stubborn opposition. The controversy had already grown to be an embittered one. Mr. Robinson strongly favored emancipation, and quoted very pertinently in support of his own convictions, opinions which had been expressed by Washington and Jefferson and other founders of the Republic. To the chairman, the sentiments of the youthful orator,— who, it turned out, had more foresight than most of his elders,— appeared to be incontestable moral truths; but the Faculty, after listening to the address, considered it to be highly indiscreet, because it brought up a public question about which the minds of men were then hotly at variance The University, they said, was supported with equal fidelity by all parties, and it was unwise to introduce there any topic that was causing dangerous antagonisms among the influential people of the Commonwealth. They issued a general notice that thereafter no oration was to be delivered on any distracting question of state or national policy; and although no point in sectarian controversy had been broached by Mr. Robinson, they went further and reiterated their determination that no theological dispute should, in the future, be touched upon in any address,— a fulmination that, so far as the Jefferson Society was concerned, must have seemed rather wide of the mark, unless the youths of those times were more interested than the youths of our own are in the dogmas of the Church. Possibly, the raw sensitiveness of the Faculty on this subject may, on some recorded occasion, have tempted a mischievous young orator to express his green convictions on the doctrines of Athanasius or of Dr. Pusey, when he should have been confining his remarks to abstract principles, too axiomatic to allow of any room for a difference of opinion.

Not at all daunted by the Faculty's dissatisfaction with Mr. Robinson's speech, the Society requested that body to assent to the appointment of an orator for the ensuing Fourth of July; and this was complied with on condition that his address should receive the approval of the entire Faculty before it was spoken. Confidence in the chairman's judgment alone seems to have been, at least temporarily, shaken by his endorsement of the oration which had caused so much agitation on the previous thirteenth of April. When this latter date rolled around in 1833, the Society was not permitted to celebrate the event with a speech in the imposing circular apartment of the library; but no objection was offered to its delivery in Charlottesville, provided that a tavern was not chosen as the scene.

In 1837, the Jefferson Society was granted the possession of the large room in Hotel C; an adjacent room in addition was soon thrown open to its use; and four years later, it was authorized to make important alterations in the shape of these apartments.

In March, 1833, there was an Academic Society in existence. Convening in the basement story of the Rotunda, its object seems to have been limited to general intellectual improvement But its membership was large enough, in the following July, to justify it in asking the Board of Visitors for the use of a room in a vacant hotel According to Leiper Patterson, who left the University in 1835, with his father, the Washington Society had been organized by this time, and held its sessions in the middle hotel of West Range; but in November of this year, it applied for the use of the former library-room in pavilion VII. This must have been unsuccessful, for a second application was submitted in 1837, two years afterwards. By this time, the members of this Society had begun to celebrate the twenty-second of February, the anniversary of the birth of its patronymic. The increase in the number of imprudent young orators, brought about by the organization of another debating society, seems to have been so irksome to the patience of the Visitors that, in 1838, they positively refused to consent to the delivery of public speeches. The reason given for action so summary was that the elections were accompanied by such turbulence as to degrade the reputation of the University; and that, in addition, they created dangerous personal feuds and diverted the members' attention from their normal studies. A committee of the Washington Society denied with emphasis the correctness of these charges.

" We meet together," they said, " not as a body of students, not as persons desirous of elevating a personal or political friend, but as a band of brothers, all having the good of the Society at heart, and anxious to choose him, who, they think, can best advance its interests. The elections are conducted in a friendly manner, there being no electioneering as among the whole body of students. No time is lost. Our minds are not abstracted from our studies, nor our feelings excited. . . . In conclusion, we cannot refrain from saying that we think the societies have heretofore been too much overlooked, and we would most earnestly and affectionately invite your serious attention to them."

The Visitors proved themselves to be deaf to this dignified and feeling statement, but their obduracy did not discourage the two societies from making a determined effort to bring about the restoration of the custom of delivering addresses on the occasion of anniversaries at least. As this also was coldly received by the authorities, the *Collegian* expressed the indignant sentiment of the students when it said with pardonable bombast: "We are forbidden to speak; the tongue falters, the lips are closed, and the voice of vivid eloquence must ring through our Corinthian columns no more. It will prostrate our debating societies; taste for classical literature will be diminished . . . and a meagre sheepskin will be held up as the sole incentive to intellectual exertion." A year later, the *Collegian* reiterated this complaint, but it acknowledged that the students themselves were partially responsible for the languishing condition of the two societies. They were reproached for their failure to support these " nurseries of genius." This lamentable want of interest was due in part, said the *Collegian,* to the fact that the standard of admission to the University was extremely low. There were young men who were discouraged from becoming members, simply because they had entered with such inadequate preparation for their studies, that, in the necessary effort to keep up with their classes, they found that they had no leisure to equip themselves for participation in debate.

There were small associations of a social character in the University from the start, but the first Greek letter fellowship was the Gamma Pi Delta. This brotherhood seems to have been smitten with the prevailing oratorical fever, for, on February 16, 1836, the address which its speaker was to deliver on the following February 22, was submitted to the critical judgment of the Faculty for approval. In the course of the same year, the medical students organized a class society which held its meetings in the Anatomical Hall.

XL. *Religious Exercises*

Before the Great Reformation, the general system of education in England was organized and controlled by the Catholic clergy; and during the first centuries following Protestant ascendancy, all the colleges there persisted,—some to a greater, and some to a lesser degree,—in maintaining the original bond of wedlock with the Church This was discernible even in America, although it was settled to such a large extent by men who had sought its remote forests in order to escape from ecclesiastical restraints and persecutions. Of one hundred and nineteen of the higher seats of learning that were earliest established on the soil lying within the present boundaries of the United States, one hundred and four had their roots mainly in a religious motive. Harvard College was founded to supply a continuous

succession of educated ministers for the pulpits of Massa-
chusetts when the living incumbents, who had been
trained in English schools, should have passed away; and
it was not until 1886 that every formal shackle inherited
from the Puritan past was struck from the religious limbs
of that institution.   The College of William and Mary
obtained its charter for the specific purpose of providing
the Established Church in Virginia with clergymen, and
spreading the Christian faith among the barbarous In-
dians.   One of the central aims which the College of
Yale kept fixedly in view from the hour when its lecture
halls were first thrown open, was to qualify young men
of a religious bent for a career in the ministry.   As late
as 1784, prayers were held at the College of Hampden-
Sidney at six o'clock every morning, and five o'clock
every afternoon; and each student was subject to a severe
penalty should he fail to attend, or attending, forget to
deport himself with " gravity and decency."

When the University of Virginia was incorporated in
1819, the opinion was still general that the dignity of
every important seat of learning required that either a
bishop or a doctor of divinity should preside over its
temporal and religious affairs.   Neither the French nor
the American Revolution, destructive as both were of
ecclesiastical and political inheritances of all sorts, had
been able to undermine this scholastic tradition.   But
there was an ever growing number of persons who had
no sympathy with it whatever; and the most conspicuous
among these iconoclastic spirits was Jefferson.   We have
seen that it was principally through his determined ini-
tiative that the bonds between Church and State in Virginia were disrupted.   While he made no pretension to
being an orthodox Christian,—indeed, he was a deist or
unitarian in faith,— he never failed to exhibit reverence

for religion; but, with equal consistency, he never omitted to show his detestation of sectarianism; for sectarianism, in his opinion, was the deformed foster-mother of intolerance, bigotry, hatred, and selfishness even when every denomination was compelled by law to stand on a footing of equality with its fellows

Had he, like some of the modern philanthropists, been able to found a great seat of learning by his own gifts and endowments, he would still have seen to it that every branch of this malignity was barred from its threshold.   As the institution which he did establish was a State institution, dependent upon all classes and all denominations for support, it would have been the climax of presumption as well as of folly in him to propose that the authority of any single Church should predominate in its government.   Had he been an Episcopal bishop himself, with the longest and whitest of lawn sleeves, he still would not have ventured to make such a suggestion as this to the General Assembly, or slyly, and on his own responsibility alone, have plotted to encourage the growth of but one ecclesiastical influence in the University after it had been founded.   "Education and sectarianism must be divorced," was an iteration as characteristic of him as "Carthage must be destroyed" was of Cato He did not mean a divorce between education and religion; certainly not religion so far as it denoted a great system of morals   There could be no religious freedom, he thought, in any seat of learning in which an atmosphere of pestilential sectarianism existed, for religious freedom consisted of the absolute possession by every one of the unbounded right to follow the dictates of his own spiritual cravings whithersoever they might lead.   How could this be made practicable within the precincts of a university with a doctor of divinity pulling its scholastic strings? Put such a dignitary over the University of Virginia,— nay, more, fill the chairs with professors of the same denominations, whether it were the Episcopal, Baptist, Methodist or Presbyterian, and in Jefferson's opinion, it would be the first step towards the re-establishment of a State Church. And even should those chairs be divided among ministers of the gospel of different tenets, that policy would still have a tendency to introduce ecclesiastical influence into the heart of the environing civic life, with all its demoralizing train of consequences to the political and religious welfare of the people. To persons in our own times, accustomed as they are to tolerance and liberality of view in the relations of the sects, these apprehensions seem exaggerated, if not groundless, but it must be recalled that Jefferson had grown up under the colonial system, which was indisputably accompanied by many serious abuses.

It would have been presumed that the exclusion of all forms of sectarianism from the University of Virginia would have been satisfactory to every denomination because preference was given to none. All of them must have acknowledged that such preference, had it been shown, would have been out of harmony with the character of a State institution; and yet no citizens of the community were more active than some of the apostles of the several churches in spreading abroad the report that the new seat of learning had been really founded to disseminate the principles of infidelity. It was to be the seed-plant in America of Parisian atheism and Genevan rationalism, while the European professors had been imported to fill its chairs, not because they had been cultivated at Oxford and Cambridge to the ripest scholarship, but because they were deeply tainted with the impiety of Hume and Voltaire. As a matter of fact,

Tucker, Long, Key, Dunglison, and Bonnycastle had been reared strictly in the tenets of the Anglican Church; Emmet of the Catholic; and Blaettermann of the Lutheran; and there is no reason to suppose that there was a single scoffer among them.

Even if Jefferson had been an ardent disciple of Tom Paine rather than of Doctor Priestley, he was still too shrewd to imagine that the foundations of his infant University could rest safely upon a corner-stone that discarded all moral teachings in the larger sense. "The relations which existed between man and his Maker, and the duties resulting from these relations," said he, "are the most interesting and important to every human being, and the most incumbent on his study and imitation." Policy and principle alike dictated to him irresistibly that religion, in some form or other, direct or indirect, should be recognized in his new institution. How could this be done without countenancing this or that branch of sectarianism? The methods which he adopted at first to accomplish his purpose, could only have been satisfactory to a moralist interested in the purely historical aspects of the subject. These methods were, (1) instruction in the Greek, Latin and Hebrew languages, which would enable the students to read the "earliest and most respected" authorities of the Christian Faith; and (2),— which was more pertinent in a general way,— instruction, through the professor of moral philosophy, in those abstract principles of virtue, in which all sects believe and which all endeavor to practise   "The proof of the being of a God," said he, "the Creator, Preserver, and Supreme Ruler of the Universe, the author of all the relations of morality, and the laws and obligations which these infer, will be in the province of the professor of ethics." And to supplement these purely scholarly lessons in natural piety, a large number of volumes, embracing the most learned commentaries on the Evidences of Christianity, were purchased for the library to assist the inquiring student in his search after religious truth.

Rationally enough, Virginians of a very fervent religious temperament found little satisfaction in these very vague provisions, for they seemed to place the University of Virginia on the platform of an institution that did equal honor to Christ, Confucius, and Buddha, and the other great exemplars of general morality. " Why was no chair of Divinity created? " they asked. In reality, Jefferson did not object to the establishment of a purely historical chair. But apart from the expense of this additional professorship, who could probably fill it but a clergyman, and how could a clergyman be obtained without going to one of the denominations, and thus upsetting the equilibrium which he considered to be so indispensable? He candidly acknowledged that " the want of instruction in the various creeds of religious faith among our citizens was a chasm " in his new seat of learning; and in admitting this, he confessed that his critics were correct in asserting that the teachings of Professor Harrison and Professor Tucker, in their respective courses, were a very impoverished substitute for the teaching of a professor of Historical Divinity. Such a chair, under a different name, has been erected in recent years, and has been found perfectly consistent with that religious toleration which he guarded with such jealous fidelity.

Jefferson was determined that the University should be neutral; and in its original shape, he made no real concession to religious feeling beyond providing a room in the Rotunda, as we shall see, for religious worship. The religious sentiment of Virginia, however, demanded more, and this demand he met by putting forward a proposal that was, on its face at least, as practical as it was ingenious   This proposal,— which is stated in one of his reports to have been suggested to him by " some pious individual,"— provided that each of the principal denominations should establish its own theological school just without the confines of the institution.   By this means, its pupils would obtain prompt and convenient access to the lectures delivered by the different professors and enjoy all the benefits of the library.   In their turn, the students of the University would be able to attend religious services, each under the clergyman of his own particular sect, and their exercises might be held, either in the Rotunda,— in the room set apart there for religious worship,— or in the neighboring chapels of the different seminaries [1]   Jefferson, as the spokesman of the Visitors, expressed their readiness to assure to the

[1] The advantages of the scheme to the University were said at the time to be as follows (1) the students would have an opportunity to learn the tenets of their respective denominations from the most competent teachers belonging to those denominations, (2) the reproach of indifference to religion would by it be lifted from the institution, without the authorities taking a single step that would alarm the popular suspicion of sectarian interference, (3) the great religious denominations would be disposed to feel a warmer interest in the prosperity of the University, and be more active in widening its sphere of usefulness, (4) it would foster influences that would promote a spirit of order and sobriety among the University students, and (5) it would complete the circle of sciences brought into the institution

The advantages to the theological schools were hardly less obvious (1) one University professor could fill the place, which, if the theological schools were separated, would require four instructors to fill, (2) it would enlarge the scholarship of the theological pupils, (3) it would bring each sect more prominently before the collected youth of that sect at the most impressionable period of their lives, and finally, (4) by assembling the most learned representatives of each denomination in easy access to each other, it would create mutual tolerance, sympathy, and helpfulness See Professor Minor's *Sketch of the University of Virginia* young men who would enter these theological schools every facility for improvement which the University could extend.   The only reservation would be that each school of theology should be independent of the University and of the other denominational schools in its vicinity.   In this way, the constitutional freedom of religion, "the most invaluable and sacred of all human rights," he said, " would be preserved inviolate."

The apparent cordiality with which Jefferson assented to this memorable proposal is a further proof that his attitude towards religious exercises at the University was not one of fixed hostility, provided that there was an equality in the relation to it of all the sects.   No one, after the publication of this report, could justly accuse him of a desire to place the institution in permanent antagonism to the Christian Faith; nor was it his fault that the several denominations declined to accept an offer that would have conferred the highest scientific advantages on their students.   Indeed, there would have been an element of grandeur in the situation of these great schools, had they been, not dispersed, as they are at present, at different spots in the State, but planted in the form of a splendid girdle around Jefferson's central institution, receiving scientific light from it, and in their turn, radiating religious light back to it,— a light reflected, not from the doctrines of one sect, but from the combined doctrines of all the principal sects.

The Presbyterian Church alone exhibited a disposition to transfer its seminary to the vicinity of the University, but not until Jefferson had been dead for a generation. A committee was appointed in 1859 to ascertain the terms on which its students would be admitted to the lectures and the library; but temporary obstructions to the progress of negotiations soon arose, and as the shadow of war was already falling over the land, all further steps were, in 1860, postponed.[1]

Jefferson has been criticized for not foreseeing and adopting the system which was afterwards introduced; namely, the annual appointment of chaplains belonging to the four great Protestant denominations in succession, and their support by the voluntary contributions of the students, professors, and Visitors. Such a system was entirely in harmony with that principle of religious freedom which he had always advocated, and which was so essential to the character of a State institution; and at the same time, it directly subserved the spiritual needs of each set of young men, by supplying them in turn with a minister of the gospel of their own religious doctrines. It was the only practical solution of a very embarrassing problem, and it was one that has proved eminently happy and satisfactory in its operation. As a matter of fact, Jefferson had, by his action, at least suggested this solution when he accepted, with so much cordiality, the proposal that the University should surround itself with an *enciente* of independent theological schools whose clergymen would be called upon, one after the other, to preach within the precincts. Whether he anticipated it or not, he had, independently of these schools, provided for this very solution by furnishing an apartment for religious worship in the projected Rotunda, for, in that apartment, religious exercises could, in the future, be held by ministers of the different sects invited in turn from Sunday to Sunday to conduct them

If Jefferson failed to give more distinct form than this to the plan that was afterwards adopted, Madison, his

[1] When the question of removing the Union Theological Seminary from Hampden-Sidney was under debate in 1894, the University Faculty and Board of Visitors favored its reestablishment near the University of Virginia

successor in the rectorship, could not justly be accused of the like neglect. "I have indulged the hope," he wrote Chapman Johnson, in 1828, "that provision for religious instruction and observance among the students would be made by themselves or their parents and guardians, each contributing to a fund to be applied in remunerating the services of clergymen of denominations corresponding with the preference of the contributors. Being altogether voluntary, it would interfere neither with the characteristic peculiarity of the University, the consecrated principle of the law, nor the spirit of the country."

The proposal to encompass the University with theological seminaries having failed to obtain an affirmative response from the several denominations, and the room reserved for religious worship remaining too often silent and empty on Sunday, the only course left open was to adopt the plan suggested by Madison. This, however, was not done at once. In the meanwhile, the want of some steady rule for holding religious exercises within the precincts continued to be taken by many as a confirmation of the charge of infidelity which was still so loudly raised against the institution. When the epidemic of typhoid fever broke out there in 1829, fanatical persons looked upon it as a punitive visitation from God; and this idea found reflection, as already pointed out, in the sermon delivered at this time before the students and Faculty by Rev. William Meade, of the Episcopal Church, afterwards a very distinguished Bishop of Virginia. He eloquently and forcibly maintained the doctrine of a conscious and overruling Providence in all the multitudinous affairs of men, as opposed to the unpiloted action of unconscious chance. Institutions as well as men, he said in substance, should be governed by Christian influences and principles,— otherwise they must fall under the ban of reproach for atheism, and sink into temporal decay and collegiate futility.

This discourse was heard with undisguised indignation by the congregation, for it was considered to be a covert attack on the University, the Visitors, the Faculty, and the memory of Jefferson. The furtive injustice of it was probably most deeply felt by the Faculty because they had, but the year before, turned to the only means at their disposal then to establish a permanent course of religious services, for, in their private capacity, they had invited the Rev. F. W. Hatch, the Episcopal clergyman of Charlottesville, and the Rev. Mr. Bowman, the Presbyterian minister of the same town, to preach on alternate Sunday afternoons in the apartment in the Rotunda reserved for religious worship. No additional salary was guaranteed them for this pastoral task. The arrangement was voluntary on both sides, and might be discontinued on seven days' notice. Previous to the delivery of these sermons, the young men of a devout temper had no recourse but to attend the morning services in Charlottesville. "I have been three or four times," wrote Robert Hubard, of Buckingham county, to his sister, "and would go more often, but it is so long a walk, and the dust all the way has become so disagreeable, that I could not undertake the journey." The same element, quite probably, was an equal impediment to many of his companions.

XLI. *The Chaplains*

Rev. Mr. Hatch, who inaugurated the religious services at the University, rises first to view in association with two scenes of an antipodal nature. He was the clergyman who visited Francis Walker Gilmer during the last days which that young Virginian passed on earth,

and it must have been a melancholy sight for him to witness the rapid wasting of a spirit gifted with so much
talent and learning.   In the second scene in which Mr.
Hatch is earliest discovered, he was engaged in marrying
a couple in a cabin on the mountain-side.[1]   When the ceremony ended, the bridegroom, with great embarrassment,
told him that he was too poor to pay the expected fee.
It happened that the clergyman, as he entered the room,
had noticed hanging against the wall a bunch of large
gourds, then in common use as light and fragrant water-
dippers.   Pointing to them, he said, "I will be satisfied
with some of those gourds."   The bridegroom, very
much relieved, not only, with alacrity, took them all down
from the wall, but assisted the clergyman in festooning
his horse's neck with them as his only available means of
carrying them off to town.   And so Mr. Hatch cheerfully departed, the gourds dangling and clattering in
front of him, while his own thoughts probably wandered
so far away as to be oblivious of the ludicrous spectacle
which he presented as he rode forward along the public
road.   As he began to descend Vinegar Hill, in Charlottesville, his horse suddenly took fright, and dashed
down the street at the top of his speed, with the clergyman clinging desperately to his neck, and the gourds
bouncing and clashing in the rush of air.   Not since John
Gilpin ran his "famous rig," had there been a more fran-
tic horse or a more helpless rider.   A great commotion
was aroused among the astonished bystanders as he flew
by, and not until the horse stopped at the door of the
rectory stable did the wild race come to an end.
Whether the gourds survived the pounding is not mentioned in the record of the event, but the clergyman for-

[1] I am indebted to Woods's *History of Albemarle County* for the details of this amusing incident.

tunately escaped without personal injury, to continue his
faithful services among his widely dispersed parishioners.

The arrangement with Mr. Hatch and Mr. Bowman
was not protracted beyond twelve months. It could
never have been convenient to these clergymen, since it
required them to traverse a considerable distance before
they could reach the precincts; and it also interrupted the
performance of the full duty which they owed to their
respective flocks in town; nor could afternoon services
alone at the University itself have brought contentment
to those professors and students who were, by nature and
training, interested in religious exercises.

The first regular chaplain, the Rev Mr. Smith, of
Philadelphia, was appointed in 1829. He was a Presbyterian in doctrine. The term was now limited to a
single session. During the sessions of 1830–1831 and
1831–1832, the chaplaincy was in abeyance. This was,
perhaps, to be laid at the door of the smallness of the
voluntary contributions made for its support, a condition
all the more to be deprecated because the chaplain, at
this time, was constrained to secure a living-room at his
own expense beyond the precincts. During the brief
period of suspension, there was no recurrence to the clergymen in Charlottesville, but, in their stead, the chairman invited pastors of the different Protestant sects to
preach at the University in turn. These accepted without any expectation of a fee. Rev. Mr. Armstrong, of
Richmond, Rev. Calvin Catlin, of New York, Rev. Ben-
jamin Rice and other men of distinction in their calling,
delivered, in succession, moving and edifying sermons in
the apartment in the Rotunda reserved for religious
services.

It was the students, and not the Faculty, who took the
initiatory step for the restoration of the chaplaincy

At the beginning of the session of 1832, a committee, composed of McClurg Wickham and three other prominent collegians, informed the chairman that a large number of the young men had entered into a mutual pledge to contribute such a sum as would make certain the celebration of divine services within the precincts on every Sunday Thirty-three signatures were appended to this honorable list, and among them were to be found the names of several men who won distinction in after life, — John W. Stevenson, John A. Meredith, John B. Young, Frank S Ruffin, and David H. Tucker. The professors as well as the visitors swelled the fund by their relatively large subscriptions of twenty dollars respectively.

During the winter of 1833, Rev. Mr. Ragland, who had been attending a course of lectures, preached with regularity in the Rotunda; but before the close of the following spring, Rev. Mr. Hammet was formally appointed chaplain, at a salary of three hundred dollars per annum, which was guaranteed to him by an agreement between the students, on the one hand, and the professors and Visitors, in their private capacity, on the other. The salary was retroactive from the first day of the previous January Hammet possessed an uncommon gift as a pulpit orator, and soon secured a firm hold on the attention, respect, and affection of the students Indeed, his influence with them was so strong, that, when, during his chaplaincy, they resented the closing of their assembly hall by the Faculty, they sent him, as their sympathetic ambassador, to warn that body of the bad consequence of showing an unconciliatory spirit in the settlement of the dispute. The chaplaincy was still limited to a term of one year When Rev. Mr. Hammet retired in accord with this rule, the Episcopal Convention,— which met in May, 1834, and which was granted the privilege of nominating his successor,— designated Rev. N. H. Cobbs for the post. Cobbs was a youthful clergyman of remarkable talents, who was then the rector of a rural parish in Virginia. The formal invitation to become the chaplain at the University was received by him in June, and it was with reluctance that his vestry released him from his charge, because, they said, the salary of six hundred dollars offered was insufficient for his support. Cobbs was justly of the same opinion " This sum," he wrote, " would not cover my expenses; but by extending my labors of an evening to the church in Charlottesville, I may be enabled, with rigid economy, to avoid the painful evils of debt "

No clergyman with a known itching for disputation was permitted to preach within the precincts even after the presence of regular chaplains, representing, in succession, the several Protestant denominations, had ensured the institution's reputation for religious equality When one of the pastors of the Charlottesville churches, in 1835, requested that Dr. Thomas, of Richmond, should be invited to deliver a sermon in the Rotunda, the reply was a refusal, on the ground that he was a Campbellite Baptist, said to be ambitious of making converts to his creed, which would be attempted at the University only by a series of controversial arguments certain to arouse a spirit of antagonism in the hearts of his auditors The chairman, in announcing the refusal, restated the rule which he had been instructed to follow; namely, that no one but the chaplain and himself should have the right to ask foreign clergymen to fill the University pulpit on occasion; and that only sermons free from controversial taint were to be tolerated. The reply that was made to Dr. Thomas, the disciple, was repeated when the like application was received from Dr. Campbell, the founder of this new branch of Baptists. Campbell promised to avoid the subject of sectarianism in his discourse, and to restrict his remarks to the evidences of Christianity. When this conservative pledge on his part became known, the chairman was made a target of censure; a large body of students expressed their disapproval of his extreme·position; but an equally large body sustained it. This incident reveals the jealousy with which the religious services at the University were guarded,— a jealousy that sometimes, as, in this instance, verged on intolerance.

Rev. Robert Ryland, a Baptist, succeeded Mr. Cobbs. Diffident by temperament, he made no pretension to oratory. Col. Pendleton described him .as a plain, sensible, and pious man, of decided force of character, but mild in his deportment and pleasant in his manners. A Presbyterian, the Rev. Mr. Tustin, followed Ryland. During the session of 1827–8, Rev. J. P. B. Wilmer was the incumbent; and at intervals of one year, down to the end of the session of 1841–2, the duties of the chaplaincy fell in turn upon Rev. D. L. Doggett, a Methodist, Jas. B. Taylor, a Baptist, W. S. White, a Presbyterian, and W. M. Jackson, an Episcopalian. The delicate balance of the ecclesiastic scales was never shaken. All these men were young, full of energy, and full of talent, and with hardly an exception, rose to eminence in their calling in after-life. Hammet,— apparently without abandoning his sacred profession,— was elected to a seat in the National House of Representatives. Cobbs was advanced to the Episcopal prelacy of Alabama, and Wilmer to that of Louisiana. Doggett was long the eloquent Bishop of the Methodist diocese of Virginia, and Ryland, the respected President of Richmond College. Taylor, during many years, occupied a position of unique influence among the Protestants who resided in the shadow of the Vatican.   Jackson was chosen to a pulpit in Norfolk, and enjoyed a wide reputation for his saintly life in that community, while White was called to a pastorate in Staunton, and until his death, was a beloved minister of his denomination

We have, in the course of our previous narrative, mentioned that a room in the Rotunda was explicitly reserved by Jefferson himself for religious exercises   This apartment having become too small, by 1835, to accommodate with comfort the group of students and professors who appeared at the door on Sunday morning, the members of the Faculty formed themselves into a committee for the purpose of collecting funds enough for the erection of a spacious church edifice within the precincts of the University.   They chose, as the tentative site, the ground that lay south of the Lawn and opposite the Rotunda; and from an architect of high reputation, they procured the plan of a structure in the Gothic style, which would hold not less than eight hundred persons   It was calculated that the cost of this building would amount to twenty thousand dollars.   An address to the public was drawn up, and Mr Cobbs, the chaplain, was the first to be appointed to solicit and receive subscriptions.   The members of the Board, at that time, approved of this scheme in every detail but one: they ordered the postponement of the choice of a site.

Four years passed, and it would appear that the efforts to raise the required fund had either proved fruitless, or some objection to the plans was offered by the new set of Visitors, for the chapel remained unconstructed.   When they assembled in August, 1839, the only one among them who urged its erection, was William C. Rives; but as there were several absentees, including Cocke and Cabell, who shared his favorable attitude, he induced the members of the Board to put off their decision. It seems that two of those present were hostile to the project because they were apprehensive lest the Unitarians should claim the privilege of being represented in the chaplaincy, in their turn,— which these two Visitors asserted, with acute solicitude, would be " a gross abuse of the principles of religious freedom and toleration." Mr. Cobbs and General Cocke, now his assistant, were still under a pledge to solicit public subscriptions; and both were convinced that there would be no grave difficulty in raising the amount needed just so soon as they should be able to announce that the Board's approval had been got; but this apparently could not be obtained from that body by the votes of the required majority. The eastern gymnasium, having, by 1841, been reconstructed, so as to create room for a larger audience, permission was granted by the Visitors for its use for religious exercises on Sunday.

If the Board shrank from allowing a separate church building to be erected on the grounds, they showed equal timidity in offering a home to the chaplain within the precincts. To do so would, in their opinion, be giving him, as a clergyman, the equivalent of his pecuniary support by the University; and for the institution to aid a man of his cloth, even in this indirect way, was tantamount to the State doing so; and for the State to do it, was to violate the statute for the preservation of religious freedom; and to violate that statute was to bring down on the heads of the officials guilty of it the hot censure of the people. It was by some obscure process of logic resembling this that the Board of Visitors declined to grant Rev. Mr. Hammet the right to shelter his head under the roof of pavilion VII, which had offered an asylum to so many houseless societies and libraries, and even to the wandering and perplexed Board itself, when the doors of Monticello were finally closed. "No room there could be assigned him," said the Visitors, "because he did not come within the scope of a general or special Act."[1] However, he was at liberty to obtain an apartment in the pavilion of some professor, or in a hotel, should one become vacant; but if this was impracticable, then he was to seek for a room in a boarding-house beyond the precincts for the rest of the session; after which, should he continue at the University, it was possible that an apartment might be found for him somewhere within the bounds.

It might be inferred from the account that has been given of the disorder which prevailed among students between 1825 and 1842 that the fires of religious feeling burnt rather low among them during that interval. This would be an erroneous conclusion if it should be presumed to be applicable to the entire body. McClurg Wickham, a student who won great respect for his active part in the religious work of that period, asked permission in February, 1833, to establish a Sunday school within the precincts and to hold its sessions in the Rotunda; but his petition was denied in the latter particular

[1] "The Board received with much pleasure the address of a committee of students, communicating the measures which they have adopted, in concert with the professors, to procure a minister of the gospel The Board approved the measures adopted by the students and professors, and while they do not feel warranted in appropriating the public money to his support, the Visitors individually will cheerfully contribute to that object" Minutes of Board of Visitors July 17, 1833 The first chaplains to reside within the precincts, beginning with Cobbs and ending with Jackson, occupied pavilion I, which had been the home of Emmet until his removal to Morea The later chaplains had two rooms in pavilion VII. See Patton's *Jefferson, Cabell, and the University of Virginia*, p. 291

at least, on the ground that the apartment desired in
that building was reserved for the delivery of lectures
and sermons.   It is possible that the spectre of the
statute for the preservation of religious freedom, which
so often shook the professorial soul in those times, had
again flitted across the chairman's path, for he seemed
to think that sermons had been legalized at the University by the clause in the Act of Incorporation allowing
religious worship, but not Sunday schools.   The Board of
Visitors exhibited a more liberal spirit of interpretation:
in July, 1833, they instructed him to assign a room to the
projected Sunday school in whichever building he should
consider the best adapted to its meetings.

When this school was reorganized at the beginning of
the session of 1834, as many as sixty students joined it.
Mr. Cobbs was now the chaplain, and his personal popularity to some degree explains this large attendance.   A
Bible class was also in existence at the University in 1841.
There was, however, observed a recession in religious
feeling among the students after 1835; and this palpable
fact was boldly commented upon by a prominent religious
journal,— which even went so far as to reproach the innocent Visitors for impiety, because they had filled one
chair by the appointment of Kraitser, a Roman Catholic,
and another, by the appointment of Sylvester, a Jew.

XLII. *Care of the Buildings*

It required the passage of but a few years to show
that the extraordinary area of flat roofs, created by long
lines of one story dormitories, would add very sensibly
to the expense of keeping the University buildings in repair.   There was at least one advantage which the tall
barracks, so much abhorred by Jefferson, would have pos-

sessed over these low structures; a roof would have been necessary only for the sleeping apartments at the top of the house. The passage of water into the dormitories increased in proportion as their covering steadily rusted or rotted. It began as early as 1827. "There is hardly a room or a house in the University," wrote John Tayloe Lomax, the chairman, to the proctor, "that does not leak." By 1831, this unwholesome inconvenience had reached such a height that the Board was compelled to announce that a permanent fund would be reserved against it so soon as the income at their disposal would permit of such a diversion; and in the meanwhile, the executive committee was instructed to take steps to scotch the evil, — temporarily at least.

The proctor's mind, at this time, must have been very much harassed by the growls which the professors were pouring into his ears. "Will you be so kind as to call in and examine our house," wrote Dunglison, "as we were up nearly all of last night in consequence of the rain soaking through on the floor and bed." And at the beginning of 1831, he again wrote, "Every part of the roof of my pavilion admits water like a sieve"; and the third time he wrote, "I don't know that you can help us, but we are likely to be in a dreadful situation from this thaw. Wherever the boards have been removed from the terraces on the housetops, the water is pouring through" Emmet could not repress his exasperation under the same annoyance "Every member of my family, with the exception of the infant," he wrote in the spring of 1832, "is at present seriously indisposed by violent cold and fever taken immediately after the late rain. The room occupied by Mrs. Emmet dripped incessantly. I slept in the chamber with the children and felt the drops falling steadily on my pillow.

I positively state to you my conviction that the complete prostration of my family is dependent on the leaking condition of the roof." "The roofs of all the dormitories and some of the pavilions," reported Colonel Pendleton, the proctor, in December, 1833, " either from imperfect construction originally, or the lapse of time, require now thorough repair. All are now exposed to rapid decay." He thought that not less than twenty thousand dollars would be required for the complete restoration of the University buildings; nor was this figure really wide of the mark if the Faculty's statement in November of the following year, can be taken as strictly correct: they asserted then that the pavilions, dormitories, and hotels were literally " inundated by the rains."

A large quantity of tin sheeting was purchased in December; but Cocke, who had become an expert more or less in every branch of building, counseled that it should not be put on at that season, owing to its liability to crack when under the influence of an icy spell of weather. "A few more mistakes in the management of our buildings," he said, " and the expense of wear and tear will become insupportable." "From this cause alone," he added, " we are obliged to keep the price of a University education so high as to exclude the sons of one half of the independent farmers of the State. The cause will be seen sooner or later, and if we do not provide against it, our raree shŏw of architecture will be abandoned, and the public funds bestowed where students can live in more comfort, and obtain equal instruction at less expense."[1] It was quite probably due to Cocke's practical advice that the covering for the roofs, after a certain area had

---

[1] At present the roofs of the pavilions on East Lawn are covered with tin (1920). It is possible that the slate was placed, in 1837-8, only on the pavilions on West Lawn and on the dormitories in general.

been laid in this unsatisfactory material, was restricted to slate. By August, 1835, the contractor for supplying the raw slate, E W. Sims, had transported to the University a sufficient quantity to overspread the roofs of numerous dormitories. " I shall be glad to hear," wrote Cocke, in September, " how the slaters and carpenters are getting on." Spooner,— who was regularly employed in carpentry for the different buildings,— had charge of the wood-work necessary for the slating; and Colonel Pendleton reported, in reply to Cocke's letter, that the recovering of the roofs of all the dormitories on the Lawn would be finished by the advent of the first day of December. But the substitution of slate for tin throughout the precincts was still in progress in November, 1837, two years later; but this is probably explainable by the occurrence of intermissions in the work.

Colonel Woodley followed Colonel Pendleton in the proctorship, and it was to him that Sims, the contractor, sent word, in November of that year, that he had one hundred squares of slate piled up on the banks of the James near Columbia, which he intended to bring up to Milton by batteau so soon as the water in the Rivanna should rise. This cargo had reached Columbia in August, and, during the interval, had remained there waiting for a break in the drought. The charge for wagonage was too heavy to permit of its transportation overland. This slate was probably designed for the roofs of East and West Ranges. It would seem that it was not until June, 1838,— two years after the use of slate had begun,— that the protracted task of recovering all the dormitories was finished In September of the same year, the substitution of slate for tin on the roofs of the pavilions was in progress. How necessary this improvement had become is revealed in a letter of the

proctor to Cocke: " I fear that some of the professors," he wrote, " will be forced to abandon their homes
if we do not succeed in securing their roofs before the
winter." [1]

With the buildings constructed for the most part
of starkly inflammable materials, there was always a
lurking apprehension of an outburst of fire, which, from
the defective preventives, might soon grow into an
all-consuming conflagration.   There were more than two
hundred hearths within the precincts in constant use in
the winter.   As Lawn and Range formed practically a
single structure, either by actual contact or by proximity,
a fire starting at any point was likely to sweep over the
entire area, unless arrested before much headway had
been won.   Such a fire might spring up at any moment,
either through accident or through incendiarism.   A student who would not scruple to shoot down a professor
would probably not balk at the sly application of a candle's flame.   This fear was persistently in the minds of
the Faculty when an insurrectionary spirit flared up
among the young men: and it is creditable to the latter's
sense of discretion, that, in the midst of their most im-
petuous mutinies, recourse was never had to such an act
of desperation,— all the more alluring because its per-
petrator could easily cloak his identity.

As early as 1826, the Faculty began to perceive the
need of a fire-engine, and of a more copious supply of
water for its effective use.   Sellers and Pennock, of Phil-

[1] The following letter shows that Cocke anticipated either an alteration in the buildings then standing, or the adoption of another style whenever an addition to them had to be made   Mr. Thos. S Clay wrote him
on November 4, 1834, " Mr Quincy of Boston, son of the President of
Harvard College, has politely procured for me plans for several of the
buildings at Cambridge, which are herewith transmitted. . . . They may
prove useful should any change be attempted in the mode of accommodating the students at Charlottesville."   Cocke Papers.

adelphia, were now advertising an engine of sixteen man-power, that carried eight hundred to one thousand feet of hose. One of these, known as a hydraulion, was bought, and successfully tested; but there was no occasion to demonstrate its real value before 1831, when a fire broke out in the terrace situated between Dr. Patterson's pavilion and pavilion VII. A blustering wind was blow-ing, but fortunately it was in the early afternoon when persons were walking about in all parts of the precincts. Professor Tucker said publicly afterwards, that, had the fire started at a late hour at night, the whole row of buildings on West Lawn would have been consumed, and that, not improbably, the conflagration, in the end, would have leaped across the first gymnasium to the Rotunda and thence by the second gymnasium to East Lawn. As it was, the flame,— which, it seems, had been caused by ignition of rotten wood on the roof by a spark from a chimney,— was quickly extinguished. There were two threatening fires during 1831. In one of these cases, a glowing log on the andirons of a dormitory rolled on the floor in the absence of the occupant, and set the planks ablaze; and in the other, a log, in the like state, set fire to the timbers below the hearth. The very natural nervousness felt by the entire community when an alarm of this kind was sounded was shown by the excitement caused by the burning of soot in one of the chimneys of Dr. Emmet's pavilion during the same winter. There was a very high wind abroad at the time, and the flames from the chimney top leaped up in lofty tongues, and were tossed about so angrily from side to side, that the roof itself appeared to be in flames.

Very strict and clearly defined rules were adopted, in 1834, to guide the persons who should be called upon to put out a fire within the precincts: (1) the chairman was to be in supreme command; (2) the proctor, assisted by the janitor was to have control of the engine; (3) a committee of two members was to have charge of the lines that should be made up to pass backwards and forwards the full and empty buckets of water; (4) a second committee of the same number was to indicate the precise spots to be flooded, and give the word when the time had arrived to inundate the adjacent dormitories or to tear off their roofs; (5) a third committee was to be responsible for the removal of the furniture and the other portable contents of a burning apartment. The students not in authority were instructed to obey silently and promptly all the orders that should be called out to them in the struggle to quench the flames.

The success of this prearranged plan, when the actual test came up, would depend principally upon an abundant supply of water. This was perceived from the beginning. The pipes that had been laid down had soon begun to rot, and for a time, the wells within the precincts had been the sole reliance even for drinking water.   In the summer of 1826, many of these, owing to the drought, went entirely dry. Brockenbrough, the proctor, reporting the fact, suggested the boring of Artesian wells. The Board, in the course of August, 1827, were disposed to erect a large cistern in the centre of the Lawn, but so constructed that it would not be visible above the surface. A second cistern, to be excavated near the proctor's house, presumably on Monroe Hill, was also contemplated. From these reservoirs, the water, in case of a fire, might, it was expected, be propelled, by means of a hose, to any part of the precincts; but this supposition was disputed by the proctor, who pointed out that the distance of the hotels, A, B, E, and F,—which stood on the corners of the East and West Ranges,— was at least six hundred feet from the cistern on the Lawn, the nearest of the two, whilst the available hose was not longer than four hundred feet. He suggested that several cisterns should be built, — one near his own house, a second in the vicinity of the Rotunda, in order to catch the water from its roof; and others in different areas of the precincts.

In July, 1833, the Board instructed the proctor to repair the wooden pipes that tapped the main reservoir, and also to complete the cistern which had been begun in the vicinity of Professor Tucker's pavilion, while all the cisterns nearest to the lawn were to be linked up with the roofs by means of iron pipes, that would carry off the rainwater. Apparently, the regular flow from the reservoir entered the cistern not far from the proctor's house, and from that receptacle was distributed to the other cisterns. By 1835, the repaired wooden pipes had again rotted so much that it was necessary to find some substitute for them if there was to be a supply of water, which, in case of fire, could be relied upon with confidence. During several years, it would seem, most of the water in use was hoarded from the roofs, and this fact led to an increase in the number, and an enlargement in the size, of the cisterns. But this was a precarious dependence, for, in the course of droughts, the contents of these cisterns always subsided to a very low level. In 1839, the Board appointed Professors Rogers, Davis, and Bonnycastle, as a committee, to report upon the feasibility of obtaining, by iron pipes, an abundance of water from additional springs that bubbled up on the University lands.

We have seen that Jefferson's skill in landscape gardening was as excellent in its refinement as his skill in architecture. It was due to the surviving inspiration of his taste, that, after his death, the adornment of the University precincts with graceful and stately trees was undertaken; the proctor, as early as 1826, was instructed to plant numerous specimens of several varieties about the different buildings; and in July, 1827, an elaborate scheme was also adopted for laying off a park on soil lying south and southwest of the Lawn and West Range. The purpose in view was stated to be to create a broad plat of pleasure ground where the sauntering professors and students would be able to obtain the exercise necessary to their health. The stone-wall already enclosing a section of this area, was to be repaired; a new fence was to be raised along the line of the public road which formed the southern boundary; while the residue of the space was to be shut in by means of a post-fence. The surface was to be laid off in walks, and diversified with trees in clumps and avenues. Provision was made, by an annual appropriation, for the maintenance of this park. It was directly for the purpose of ornamenting it, that, in the following October, Cocke advised the proctor to procure from Monticello a large number of Lombard poplars and Otaheite mulberries, the original stock of which had been brought in by Jefferson.

In 1830, a plan was matured for the laying off of gardens on the eastern and western sides of the University grounds; and between these gardens and the Ranges, rows of shade trees were to be planted. The trees were, no doubt, planted at once; but it was announced that the erection of the gardens would depend upon the amount of funds on hand; and, perhaps, this part of the scheme proved to be too expensive to be carried out. The small area of sloping ground lying between the Anatomical Hall and the Dead House was changed into a lawn, and planted in rare trees, with a view to its becoming a beautiful section of the Botanical Garden, which was then again in contemplation.

The original plan was to light the precincts after dark with the murky primitive lantern, which had been in use in American and English towns at night for so long a period; but Jefferson postponed the adoption of this unsatisfactory method until he could decide upon the practicability of employing gas.   The constant presence of five servants was now necessary for the preservation of the library, lecture-rooms, and grounds even in a moderate condition of order and cleanliness; and a patrol, too, was kept up to warn off the straggling negroes who infested the precincts at night and on Sundays   Hogs and cows, belonging to the professors and hotel-keepers, were in the habit of rooting and browsing about in unblocked freedom, until the damage which they caused became so extensive that a fence was put up at the foot of the southern terrace to shut them off, at least from the greensward of the Lawn; but an indignant petition of the students in 1833 brings out the fact that these criminals frequently broke through this barrier.   Our earliest view of Professor John B. Minor, who was to be associated with the institution with so much distinction in the future, was when he protested to the authorities against the squealing of the numerous pigs that gathered under his dormitory window, and thus interrupted the philosophic tranquility of his studies.

XLIII. *Martin Dawson*

The year 1835 will always be marked with a white stone in the history of the University of Virginia as the date of the first gift of importance [1] which was made to it by one of that class of noble-minded and public-spirited benefactors, who were rarer in those times of small for-

---

[1] The previous gifts had been confined to books.

tunes than they are in our own of stupendous ones.[1]   The
fourteenth paragraph in the will of Martin Dawson,—
who died very much lamented in the course of that year,
after a long life of private and public virtue,— was expressed as follows: " I give my tract of land, called College Estate, lying within three miles of the University of
Virginia on Biscuit Run, containing upwards of five hundred acres, to the Rector and Visitors of the University
of Virginia, and their successors in office, for the use of
fuel for the University forever."

In this brief provision, the temper of the man is disclosed in a broad light, for it unveils, not only his venera-
tion for learning, and his desire to advance it, but also
that quality of character which was one of his most conspicuous traits,— his homely modesty.   Now, it was
completely within his power to order the sale of his
valuable farm and the conversion of the money accruing
from that sale into an endowment fund, to be designated
by his name, and to be perpetually associated with the
purely intellectual activities of the institution.   But he
did not do this.   He was aware that the authorities were
irked by the annual inconvenience and expense of buying
its fuel of surrounding landowners.   It was a recurring
annoyance, not the less irritating because an obscure one.
There was no real distinction to himself in removing that
annoyance by his will, but it would be practically useful in
him to do so, and that was sufficient to decide him.   .It
was this unassuming and retiring spirit of beneficence
which made Dawson a true disciple of Abou Ben Adhem.
Indeed, within the narrow compass of his provincial fortune, he showed that he was as genuine a lover of his fel-

---

[1] The principal authority for the life of Martin Dawson is the admirable monograph from the pen of Professor Charles A Graves, a great-
great-nephew, on the maternal side, of the philanthropist.

low-men as the greatest of the princely philanthropists of our own age; and perhaps he was more genuine than most of them, for he must have known that his gift was necessarily too small to raise up a cloud of incense to his memory.

He had the good fortune to be born in a great age, the age of great measures and equally great men. The American Revolution had vigorously touched every civic and patriotic chord; it had created a new spirit of democratic helpfulness and of humanitarian sympathy. The chief figures of Virginia, Washington, Henry, Jefferson, Marshall, and Madison, stood for public service,— for the use of individual virtues, talents and acquirements, not for purposes of self-advancement, but for the benefit of the whole community. In 1783, Dawson was only eleven years old, and he grew up under the influence of this noble principle, which had been so splendidly illustrated in the war then recently terminated, and which continued to live, in another form, long after that epochal series of military and political events had come to an end Across his own doorway, as it were, during his youth and early manhood, fell the shadow of the last, and from some points of view, the most inspiring, exemplar of this unselfish public spirit which had descended from the Revolution,— Thomas Jefferson   Dawson was born in Nelson county within a short horse-back ride of Monticello, the career of the proprietor of that famous mansion had been known to him from childhood; and after his removal to Albemarle, he must have been brought into intercourse with the statesman on many occasions   Although the association was perhaps only casual, owing to the difference in age, he may have learned something from Jefferson in person about schemes of public education.   In a practical, benevolent, and disinterested mind like Dawson's, those schemes must have aroused a quiet enthusiasm as the wisest that could be devised for the improvement of the community; and they undoubtedly left a controlling impression on his own plans for the disposition of his modest fortune.

The first view that we obtain of Dawson discloses the confidence reposed by the University in his integrity and business competency. From 1822 to 1834, the year that preceded his death, he was annually called upon to examine the books of the proctor and the bursar; and in this responsible labor he had, throughout that time, neither assistant nor competitor. He was, towards the end of his term of service, always spoken of as commissioner of accounts. On at least one occasion, he was employed in posting ledgers and striking off balances, during a period of three months. When, in 1834, a discrepancy of $134.09 was discovered in the University books, and the cause of the error could not be traced, it was he who was asked to unravel the perplexing tangle. In 1823, he was appointed, at Jefferson's request, to examine the accounts; and at other times, he was sent for for the same task by either Cocke or Cabell, two men fully capable of correctly judging his trustworthiness and ability.

Dawson, when barely more than seventeen years of age, had settled in the little adjoining town of Milton, which was situated at the foot of the wooded Monticello slopes, on the banks of the Rivanna, at the shallows that blocked up the further navigation of the stream northward. As we have noted in the history of the University's building, this town formed the nearest port of entry for all freight carried up to this region by water; and it was also the port of shipment for a large share of the miscellaneous loads which the canvas-covered wagons brought

across the Blue Ridge by the numerous gaps that de-
bouched from the Valley. Grain, tobacco, and flour,
transported by this laborious means to its wharves, were
thence sent down to Richmond by batteaux; and here were
landed the building materials, the hogsheads of bacon,
the sacks of salt, and the like ponderous articles, which
could only be conveyed from the distant lower country
by boat. The business transacted was that of forwarding agents and commission merchants, and in the course
of it, many very respectable fortunes were slowly piled up

Dawson was the owner of lots in the town itself, and
of a considerable area of land close to it; and he had
also purchased a fertile farm known as Bel Air, which
lay in the southern part of the county; and to this
tranquil spot he withdrew, near his end, in the possession of a moderate fortune, every dollar of which had
been earned by the clean-handed strokes of his own un-
tiring industry. But he had not allowed his mercantile
calling to impoverish his civil services to his own community. In that quiet way that characterized all his conduct, he had a useful share in the public affairs of the
county. It is quite possible that, being of a modest and
unobtrusive disposition, he was first drawn into this new
channel by the solicitations of his neighbors, who had the
firmest confidence in the inflexibility of his probity and
the soundness of his judgment. In 1806, he was chosen
a magistrate, and very often filled a seat on the county
court bench, which was made up of judges appointed from
the circle of the county justices   "The magistrates who
compose these courts," said the great Chief-Justice Marshall, in the Convention of 1829–30, " consist in general
of the best men in their respective counties "

With the exception of the short interval of 1811–15,
Dawson occupied this honorable office from 1806 down

to 1835, a period of twenty-four years altogether,— an indication of the high esteem in which he continued to be held until the close of his life.   The earliest proof which we have of his practical interest in public education was his willingness to serve as a commissioner under the State law that assigned a definite fund to each county for the rudimentary instruction of children whose parents were unable to stand up under the expense of sending them to a private school.   The duties of this office were obscure yet arduous; but this only made him the more conscientious in their performance.   It was, perhaps, the insight into the imperative demand for public education which this office gave, in fortification of his independent conclusions, that led him to provide by will for three seminaries of learning to be located in the counties of Nelson and Albemarle.   This testamentary clause was not upheld by the courts, as it was decided to be too vague in its terms; but an alternative which he inserted in the same document, was favorably passed upon, and the fund reserved for it has, during many years, contributed to the usefulness of the public schools of the two counties, the objects of his philanthropy.

The farm which Dawson devised to the University fell into its possession without dispute.   It was at first rented, and in 1846, the tenant was William Dunkum, probably the partner in the firm of Farish and Dunkum, who sold the students annually a large quantity of their clothing.   The income from the land in time began to wane; two hundred and forty dollars in 1840, it had dwindled to one hundred and five in 1846; and it continued to shrink, until, finally, the Board of Visitors concluded to sell the estate.   An act to authorize this was obtained from the General Assembly in 1858, and the

farm was then disposed of in two shares.   The total
amount accruing from the sale was $19,433 50

A characteristic which Dawson shared with most of
the enlightened men of his day who were interested in
public education, was his sympathy with the policy of
gradually emancipating the slaves,— the failure to carry
out which was to precipitate the terrific calamities of War.
He directed in his will that his bondsmen should be sent
to Liberia; but should the law block this benevolent provision, they were to be assisted to live in comfort, in
the altered circumstances, which, he knew, would follow
his death.

END OF VOLUME II

PRINTED IN THE UNITED STATES OF AMERICA